"Essential reading for anyone working in safeguarding within international aid. Honest, insightful, and deeply grounded in the realities of our sector."
Lucy Stoner, *Director of Safeguarding, CARE*

"This is not just a book, it's a mirror held up to a sector that must do better. *When Vulnerability Meets Power* speaks to those of us who know the complexity involved in getting safeguarding right and the painful experience of what happens when safeguarding fails."
Dame Jasvinder Sanghera, *Survivor Advocate and Founder, Karma Nirvana*

"The safeguarding and wellbeing of the communities we work with is at the heart of everything we do. This book brings together the experience and expertise of some of the best practitioners offering practical advice based on lived experiences."
Tim Wainright, *Chief Executive, WaterAid UK*

When Vulnerability Meets Power

Recent crises relating to non-governmental aid organisations have brought into sharp focus the need for a greater understanding of the safeguarding challenges which the international aid and development sector faces, and how to respond to them in a consistent, systematic and effective way. This essential safeguarding guide provides insight to operational, organisational and cultural challenges within the international aid and development sector.

The book brings together carefully chosen key professionals who have extensive operational experience of addressing and responding to these issues. In a highly challenging environment, with multiple competing demands, this book is a clearly focused and accessible resource. It sets out what leaders in the field need to be aware of, what responses they need to make and how to maintain necessary change in the long term. In relation to each key issue, through its range of chapters, the book explores what the challenge is, what is current or suggested best practice and what future developments are needed.

It provides the sector with an accessible, authoritative and ultimately essential handbook for all those working in the international aid and development sector, whether they are practitioners, safeguarding specialists, senior leaders in governance roles or regulators. The emphasis is on facilitating sector-wide change, embedding best practice and encouraging work that effectively ensures the safety and wellbeing of the world's most vulnerable people.

Steve Reeves, MA, MBE, is an internationally recognised specialist in combating abuse and sexual exploitation. As Executive Director of Global Safeguarding, he advises governments, NGOs and law enforcement on approaches to eliminate abuse and promote change.

Marcus Erooga, MA (Econ.), has spent his career in safeguarding roles and is now an independent Safeguarding and Sexual Abuse Consultant, consulting to organisations about the adequacy and effectiveness of their safeguarding processes and procedures, researching, publishing and providing training and presentations.

When Vulnerability Meets Power

Safeguarding in the International Aid and Development Sector

Edited by
Steve Reeves and
Marcus Erooga

LONDON AND NEW YORK

Designed cover image: Getty (Dusan Stankovic)

First published 2026
by Routledge
4 Park Square, Milton Park, Abingdon, Oxon OX14 4RN

and by Routledge
605 Third Avenue, New York, NY 10158

Routledge is an imprint of the Taylor & Francis Group, an informa business

© 2026 selection and editorial matter, Steve Reeves and Marcus Erooga; individual chapters, the contributors

The right of Steve Reeves and Marcus Erooga to be identified as the authors of the editorial material, and of the authors for their individual chapters, has been asserted in accordance with sections 77 and 78 of the Copyright, Designs and Patents Act 1988.

All rights reserved. No part of this book may be reprinted or reproduced or utilised in any form or by any electronic, mechanical, or other means, now known or hereafter invented, including photocopying and recording, or in any information storage or retrieval system, without permission in writing from the publishers.

For Product Safety Concerns and Information please contact our EU representative GPSR@taylorandfrancis.com. Taylor & Francis Verlag GmbH, Kaufingerstraße 24, 80331 München, Germany.

Trademark notice: Product or corporate names may be trademarks or registered trademarks, and are used only for identification and explanation without intent to infringe.

British Library Cataloguing-in-Publication Data
A catalogue record for this book is available from the British Library

ISBN: 9781041136842 (hbk)
ISBN: 9781916925625 (pbk)
ISBN: 9781041057925 (ebk)

DOI: 10.4324/9781041057925

Typeset in Galliard
by Newgen Publishing UK

To Mum, whose ever present pride has always guided me, and to Carlo, whose unwavering support keeps me going

To Caroline – *this may be the last time…*

Contents

List of Figures xi
List of Tables xii
List of Contributors xiii
Foreword by Peter Taylor xxiii
Preface xxix

PART ONE

1   A Safeguarding Crisis in the UK International Aid Sector: A Review of Recent Inquiries and Investigations 3
       MARCUS EROOGA AND STEVE REEVES

2   Leadership and Culture: How to build Safer Cultures Through Leadership – and Why it's Essential We Do 21
       FRANCES LONGLEY

3   Aid Workers: Personal Risks, Responses and Recovery 36
       NOREEN TEHRANI

4   Donor Power and Safeguarding: Enforcing Compliance or Enabling Organisational Safety? 56
       STEINA BJORGVINSDOTTIR, SHERMIN MOLEDINA, AND KAREN WALKER-SIMPSON

5   The Challenge of a Standards-Based Approach To Safeguarding 72
       KAREN WALKER-SIMPSON

6   The HR Professionals' Dilemmas – and How to Resolve Them 90
       KATHRYN GORDON

7   Gender As A Lens Into Safeguarding 104
     MAYUMI FUCHI

PART TWO

8   Sexual Violence As A Weapon of War 125
     CÉLINE BARDET AND LÉA DARVES-BORNOZ

9   Sexual Violence among Humanitarian Aid Workers:
     No Wind of Change 134
     MELANIE SAUTER

10   The Global Policing Challenge: Protecting Vulnerable
     Populations in Humanitarian Crises 145
     PAUL STANFIELD

11   When Vulnerability Meets Power: Rethinking Mandatory
     Reporting in Safeguarding 152
     MAYUMI FUCHI

12   Whistleblowing: The Personal Cost of Speaking Out and
     the Human Benefit of Whistleblowers' Courage 160
     LEIGH HEALE

13   Strengthening Safeguarding and Accountability Through
     an International Aid Ombuds for Children 167
     MA-LUSCHKA JEAN-LOUIS AND KIRSTEN PONTALTI

14   Shaping the Future of Safeguarding in the International
     Aid and Development Sector 179
     STEVE REEVES AND MARCUS EROOGA

Appendices

Appendix 1 A Brief Timeline of Events from
2011 to 2018 (based on BBC, 2018) 193
MARCUS EROOGA

Appendix 2 Understanding Effective Safeguarding
Culture 198
BOND

Index 209

Figures

3.1 Simple, Complex and Chaotic Spaces Model 40
3.2 Roles within the Trauma Drama 42
6.1 The HR Decision-Making Approach (Academy to Innovate HR, Decision-Making in HR: How To Take the Right Approach – AIHR) 92
6.2 Writing a Code of Conduct: 10 Simple Steps (Academy to Innovate HR, Decision-Making in HR: How To Take the Right Approach – AIHR) 102
7.1 Vulnerabilities to Sexual Exploitation and Abuse in Sudanese Refugee Camps 108
13.1 Ombuds' Principles 169
13.2 Ombuds Model 170

Tables

3.1 Trauma Symptoms and Behaviours Found in Traumatised Organisations 41
3.2 Levels of Mental Health Conditions Found in Six Professional Groups Compared with the General Public 44
9.1 Facilitative Conditions of Misconduct 136

Contributors

Céline Bardet
Céline Bardet is a recognised independent expert on justice and security issues. She works regularly as a consultant on projects funded by the European Commission and the United Nations, in particular on complex criminal issues such as war crimes, corruption, terrorism, drug trafficking and organised crime, post-conflict justice, and sexual violence in conflicts. She is also an associate judge at the Cour Nationale du Droit d'Asile – the national court of asylum, in Paris.

In 2014, Céline Bardet founded the NGO "We Are NOT Weapons OF War" (WWoW) dedicated to fighting sexual violence in conflicts by proposing a new way of working on the ground with victims.

Steina Bjorgvinsdottir
Steina Bjorgvinsdottir is the Executive Director of the Funder Safeguarding Collaborative, a network of over 100 philanthropic funders aimed at transforming the role of funders in safeguarding by driving action that creates safer organisational cultures and practices.

With two decades of experience spanning child protection, organisational development, and humanitarian action, Steina is deeply committed to safeguarding vulnerable populations worldwide. She holds a postgraduate diploma in international human rights law, a master's degree in international development, and a bachelor's degree in international social work. Steina brings a versatile skill set honed through two decades of experience and previous roles with organisations like Oak Foundation, UNHCR, and UNICEF.

Léa Darves-Bornoz

Léa Darves-Bornoz is Operations Manager at "We Are NOT Weapons OF War" (WWoW). Léa is a lawyer and international criminal investigator specialising in sexual violence and justice issues. She spent two years in Iraq working on crimes committed by the Islamic State before joining WWoW in 2024, where she oversees operations and the development of the justice department.

Marcus Erooga

Marcus Erooga is an independent Safeguarding Consultant and past Editor-in-Chief and Associate Editor of the Journal of Sexual Aggression (Taylor and Francis) as well as a past Chair of NOTA (the National Organisation for the Treatment of Abuse).

He spent the majority of his employed career in various roles at the NSPCC as a practitioner, team manager and operational Assistant Director as well as service, practice and policy development relating to child sexual abuse and sexual offending. Since 2012 he has been an independent Safeguarding Consultant working with a range of organisations including Save the Children International (SCI); Save the Children UK (SCUK) and Oxfam. He is an experienced trainer and presenter having worked across the UK as well as Canada, Italy, Norway, Singapore, Spain and the USA.

Marcus is author of a number of some eighty publications on child abuse and sex offender related issues including five previous edited books. His research experience includes as principal investigator on a research study with people convicted of sexual offences against children committed in professional settings (NSPCC, 2012) and as co-principal investigator of a comprehensive literature review of risk and protective factors for institutional child sexual abuse for the Australian *Royal Commission into Institutional Responses to Child Sexual Abuse* (2016). He was the expert witness on grooming for a Royal Commission case study and an expert witness for Phases 1 and 2 of the IICSA (the England and Wales *Independent Inquiry into Child Sexual Abuse*) investigation relating to education.

Mayumi Fuchi

Dr. Mayumi Fuchi is a senior humanitarian professional with over 20 years of experience and a pracademic researcher committed to bridging the gap between NGOs, academia, and policymakers in the humanitarian sector. With her expertise grounded in extensive field experience managing large-scale humanitarian response and development programmes across Asia, the Middle East, Africa, and Latin America, she specialises in accountability and safeguarding.

As Head of Quality and Accountability at a faith-based international NGO, Mayumi provides strategic leadership in safeguarding, guiding the implementation of safeguarding policies and overseeing investigations. Her PhD research critically examines safeguarding failures in Sudanese refugee camps, advocating for a shift in power dynamics among key stakeholders.

Mayumi also contributes to global policy in safeguarding and accountability efforts as a member of the Foreign, Commonwealth & Development Office's Safeguarding Independent Reference Committee Ethics and Safeguarding Task Force at the World Organisation of the Scout Movement, as well as the General Assembly at Humanitarian Quality Assurance Initiatives.

Kathryn Gordon

Kathryn Gordon is Co-CEO of VSO. She is a strategic leader with 30 years of experience across private, family-owned, and non-profit organisations, including 15 years with VSO. She is passionate about merging purpose, people, and digital innovation to create large-scale impact. Her introduction to volunteering for development came through the Corrymeela Community in Northern Ireland, where she witnessed the power of collective action for social change.

Kathryn holds an Institute of Directors Diploma in Company Direction and an MIT Data Leadership Certificate. Since joining VSO in 2009, she has served as Director of People and Organisation Development and has been an Executive Director since 2015. She also serves on the global board of Humentum.

Leigh Heale

Leigh is a safeguarding professional with over 16 years' experience within both the national charity and international sectors. Leigh has a background in forensic psychology and previously worked for the HMP Prison Service working with high-risk offenders and led the Global Safeguarding Team at WaterAid as Global Safeguarding Director for 7 years (2018–2025) overseeing safeguarding within its 27 different countries and 7 federation members.

Leigh is an experienced sexual exploitation and harassment investigator and facilitator, who enjoys designing and delivering training as well as strategic safeguarding work, helping organisations build their safeguarding cultures beyond that of a culture of compliance.

Leigh currently is the UK Head of Safeguarding at The Scouts where she works to oversee the national safeguarding and vetting functions, working to ensure high standards are met to maintain a safe space for 250,000 young people to enjoy Scouting safety across the UK, facilitated by 200,000 adult volunteers.

Leigh has advised Charity Boards on safeguarding matters for several years, and currently is a Board member for Scottish Independent Development Alliance (SIDA), as well as having been a member of the BOND Safeguarding Steering Group. Working to drive up sector safeguarding standards is a key passion and focus for Leigh.

Ma-Luschka Jean-Louis

Ma-Luschka Jean-Louis is the Global Safeguarding Director for SOS Children's Villages International, a distinguished leader and strategic innovator with over a decade of experience in safeguarding, development and humanitarian work, organisational development, and change management. Specialising in education, child rights, child protection, and protection from sexual exploitation and abuse, she is a sought-after trainer and facilitator.

Ma-Luschka holds a Master of Arts in Early Childhood Policies, Education, and Sociology of Development, along with certifications in project management, conflict resolution, coaching, and process improvement. Her interdisciplinary background combines analytical rigor with a deep understanding of human behaviour, enabling her to foster environments where teams thrive and organisations excel.

An educator at heart, Ma-Luschka reached 13 years of teaching experience before transitioning to the development and humanitarian sector. With over a decade of field experience working across multiple continents with Save the Children, as well as collaborating with other child rights organisations and UN agencies, she has led transformative safeguarding initiatives in multicultural settings. Ma-Luschka is deeply committed to advocating for children's rights to education, ensuring that every child has access to education and is safeguarded from harm. She consistently promotes the mainstreaming of safeguarding, and best safeguarding practices in all her leadership roles.

A sought-after speaker, coach, and mentor, Ma-Luschka's dedication to social impact extends beyond the workplace, supporting initiatives that empower underrepresented communities. Her vision, integrity, and relentless pursuit of excellence continue to inspire those around her, making her a transformative force in leadership, humanitarian and development work, and safeguarding.

Frances Longley

Frances Longley is a respected not-for-profit leader with a career spanning social justice, global health and women's rights. As a practitioner, speaker and writer she is a compelling champion of the importance of healthy and respectful cultures, and courage and integrity in leadership.

In 2023 Frances became Chief Executive of FIGO, the International Federation of Gynaecology and Obstetrics – a leading global voice for women's health and rights with members in 140 countries. Prior to that she was the first woman to lead ActionAid UK in its 50-year history. As Chief Executive of Amref Health Africa UK she led the organisation through a period of recovery and new growth, underpinned by a programme of cultural transformation. She has also held senior leadership roles in CARE International UK and Unicef UK, and has worked in the UK, Eswatini and Afghanistan.

Frances was a lead spokesperson for the UK international development sector from 2018 as it responded to failures in safeguarding practice. She co-chaired the national Leadership and Culture for Safeguarding working group and co-authored an innovative culture development tool to improve safeguarding in the sector.

Frances is a member of the BBC Appeals Advisory Committee and a board member at the grant-making Allen Overy Shearman Foundation. She sits on the University of Oxford Social Sciences and Humanities

Research Ethics Committee. Frances has a Masters in Development Studies from SOAS.

Shermin Moledina

Shermin Moledina is an independent practitioner working as Regional Advisor – Africa for the Funder Safeguarding Collaborative (FSC). Previously, she was the Regional Safeguarding Lead for FSC's work with communities of practice in Asia and Africa. She is also a Safeguarding Advisor with Segal Family Foundation (SFF), providing support to developing a strong safeguarding cultures and practice for SFF and its partners.

Shermin is passionate about social justice and challenging cultural norms that prevent women and children from living as equal citizens. She has a master's degree in social work and 30 years' experience working on child protection, safeguarding, homelessness, and mental health programming with children, youth, and families. She has worked with nongovernmental organisations, primarily in East Africa and the US, leading, developing, and managing evidence-based programming on child welfare, protection, homelessness, and trauma-informed care.

During the last twelve years, Shermin has worked as a consultant supporting organisations and governments in developing interventions and methodologies in working with children, youth, and their families, with a particular focus on child protection, systems strengthening, family reintegration, alternative care, and safeguarding.

Kirsten Pontalti

Dr Kirsten Pontalti is an experienced researcher, innovator, and writer specialising in child and youth development, protection, and systems change in conflict-affected and low-income settings. She was awarded her doctorate from the University of Oxford, where her research explains how children influence continuity and change across generations in Rwanda.

Over her 20-year career, Dr Pontalti has led or co-led research and innovation projects for several prominent organisations, including UNICEF, Oxfam International, Grand Challenges Canada, and SOS Children's Villages. She serves as Co-Executive Director and Senior Associate for Proteknôn Foundation for Innovation and Learning. As a Senior Associate, she was project lead for the design, piloting, and global rollout of the first organisational Ombuds system for children in SOS Children's Villages, spanning 70 countries.

Dr Pontalti's expertise lies in bridging research and practice, using innovative mixed methods approaches to drive systems change and scale for social impact. Her recent research includes studies on the drivers of child neglect in humanitarian contexts and on the impact of COVID-19 school closures on child protection and education. Her contributions have informed safeguarding practice and accountability frameworks as well as health, education, and child protection and well-being policies and initiatives in development and humanitarian settings.

A passionate advocate for children's agency and accountability to children, Kirsten has authored academic and policy publications for peer-reviewed books and journals, government policy, UN agencies and international NGOs, ensuring children's voices are at the centre of the conversation and decision-making processes.

Steve Reeves

Steve is an internationally recognised speaker and specialist in combatting sexual exploitation and abuse in organisational settings.

Steve sits on various advisory boards, including the FCDO's Safeguarding & PSEA Independent Reference Group, and is a Strategic Advisor to the British Transport Police. Steve was one of three members of the Independent Safeguarding Board for the Church of England, providing independent scrutiny and oversight.

Steve was previously the Safeguarding Director of Save the Children, responsible for the organisation's safeguarding arrangements, acting as principal advisor to the Trustees. In this role Steve was instrumental in shaping the sector's response to safeguarding challenges, including acting as the catalyst for the creation of Project Soteria, INTERPOL's operation to tackle exploitation and abuse in the aid and development sector, and Steve remains an advisor to the project.

Steve provided input to the UK Department for Health's review of the offending of Jimmy Savile and wrote the foreword to the seminal volume on organisational safeguarding which followed Savile's exposure, *Protecting Children and Adults from Abuse after Savile: What institutions and Organisations Need to Do* (Erooga, 2018, Jessica Kingsley Publishers).

Prior to Save the Children, Steve was the Head of Safeguarding for The Scout Association, the UK's largest co-educational youth organisation. This role involved the establishment of Scouting's first specialised central safeguarding team, allowing a significant increase in safeguards for young people and a reduction in organisational risk.

Steve was also the Training Manager for an overseas development NGO delivering education and health projects in rural East Africa – work which resulted in the organisation winning a National Training Award. Previous roles have involved working with young people at risk of offending and children subject to neglect.

Steve has a first degree in International Politics and a master's degree in criminology, coupled with extensive professional training and experience in the field of safeguarding and the prevention of child sexual abuse.

Steve was appointed a Member of the Order of the British Empire (MBE) in the Birthday Honours List of 2010.

Melanie Sauter

Melanie Sauter is an assistant professor of analytical international politics at the University of Mannheim and holds a PhD from the European University Institute in Florence. Her research focuses on the micro-dynamics of political violence and the role of humanitarian organisations and peacekeepers in armed conflicts. She has previously worked as a Protection of Civilians Officer for the United Nations Multidimensional Integrated Stabilisation Mission in Mali (MINUSMA).

Paul Stanfield

Paul Stanfield is the Chief Executive Officer of Childlight, a global child safety institute hosted by the University of Edinburgh, United Kingdom, and the University of New South Wales, Australia. He leads the organisation's mission to safeguard children from sexual exploitation and abuse (CSEA), driving strategies that unite governments, law enforcement, industry, academia, and civil society to deliver transformational, evidence-based change.

Before founding Childlight, Paul spent over 30 years as a senior international law enforcement officer in the UK and overseas. As Regional Director for the UK's National Crime Agency in Africa, and later as INTERPOL's Director of Global Organised and Emerging Crime, he worked with heads of state, governments, and global agencies to combat serious and organised crime, human trafficking, and cyber-enabled threats across more than 190 countries.

Paul brings this experience into Childlight, harnessing the power of data to reveal the true scale and nature of CSEA and calling for it to be treated as a global public health emergency. He has provided evidence and strategic advice to the United Nations, US Congress, and the UK Government, and has been recognised with numerous awards and commendations, including two from the UK Home Secretary.

Qualified in Strategic Management and Leadership, with a degree in Applied (Criminal) Investigations, a Distinction in covert policing methods, and completion of the International Senior Police Leadership Programme, Paul combines operational expertise with strategic vision.

He serves on INTERPOL's Crimes Against Children Advisory Board and previously on the WeProtect Global Alliance Board (2017–2020) and INTERPOL's Board for Tackling Exploitation and Abuse in the Humanitarian Sector (2017–2025). With a global network of partners, Paul works to accelerate change with a simple mantra: children can't wait.

Noreen Tehrani

Noreen Tehrani is a Chartered Occupational, Health, and Counselling Psychologist with a passion for supporting individuals facing challenging and distressing circumstances. With a focus on assisting those in high-risk professions, she has provided tailored support programs for emergency services, humanitarian organisations, legal professionals, and journalists.

Noreen has played an integral role in managing the aftermath of major incidents such as the 9/11 and 7/7 terrorist attacks, the Shoreham air crash, and the Grenfell fire. Her support extends to first responders and victims coping with the psychological impact of such disasters.

Additionally, she has provided psychological support to journalists in conflict zones such as Ukraine, Iran, and the UK. Together with her associates, she offers psychological surveillance, training, resilience-building, and trauma-focused therapy, emphasising the importance of cultural sensitivity in adequate support provision.

Karen Walker-Simpson
Karen Walker-Simpson is the founder and Technical Director of the Funder Safeguarding Collaborative (FSC), a global network of grant making organisations committed to strengthening organisational cultures and practices that keep people safe. Karen launched FSC after conducting research into the effectiveness of international safeguarding standards and donor requirements as part of her professional doctorate with the University of Bedfordshire.

Before launching FSC, Karen was the Head of Safeguarding at Comic Relief and had previously spent eight years as a Safeguarding Specialist for international NGOs working across Africa, Asia, and Latin America.

In her early career, Karen led a number of services working with children and young people, including a helpline and specialist residential home for children in the UK and an Ecuadorian NGO providing therapeutic support for street-working children and their families.

Foreword

Peter Taylor
Head of the Safeguarding Unit in the UK Government's Foreign Commonwealth and Development Office (FCDO).

Who is this book for?

This book is for anybody involved or interested in international humanitarian, development or related work: I use the term "aid" for short. Aid is fundamentally about relieving suffering, reducing poverty and creating opportunities for people. You might be directly involved in aid delivery as a leader, a front-line worker, a funder, or somebody who aid is trying to help. You might be an aid supporter, a sceptic or just inquisitive. The book is also for people interested in how power dynamics can play out and lead to sexual harm to vulnerable individuals.

What do we mean by safeguarding?

Transparency and openness, when used sensitively, help prevention and response from sexual harms. Sexual urges exist. Sexual activity happens. None of us would be here without it. But the word sex makes some people uncomfortable. So, in some situations, a less explicit term, such as safeguarding, may generate more effective discussions.

Sex can and should be a positive experience. But far too often people – usually men – use force, coercion and power differentials for their own sexual gratification and against the will of another, most often a woman or a child. Sexual harms occur in all walks of life (see Chapter 6). But there are specific power differentials and risks linked to aid work (see, e.g., Chapters 7 and 9).

In recent years, many aid actors have converged around the descriptor "Protection from Sexual Exploitation, Abuse and Harassment," or

PSEAH, to describe the safeguarding work that this book focuses on. "Protection" covers prevention and response. Exploitation, abuse and harassment all mean different things and to different people.[1] Debates will continue about terminology in specific settings, but what we are talking about is people connected to aid work exploiting power imbalances and vulnerabilities for sexual gain.

How widespread an issue is it and why does it matter?

We don't know how many aid-related SEAH cases occur each year (see, e.g., Chapter 10). The available data, combined with known high levels of non-reporting, suggests it is many thousands.[2] Whatever the number, it is too many. And as various authors (e.g. Chapters 2 and 9) note, it feels more egregious when the perpetrators are individuals whose role is to help people and whose organisations and workers are seen by some as ethical role models.

There are multiple angles to the harms caused. They include to the victim-survivor; to the achievement of aid programme and policy objectives; to support, confidence and trust among those who provide the resources that allow for the aid investment; and to the culture of organisations SEAH happens because of a combination of the actions – or sometimes inactions – of individuals, organisations and governments.[3]

What value does this book add?

As I write in May 2025, this book is timely for two main reasons. First, we need to step back and take stock about whether choices made during the heat of the 2018 safeguarding-related "crisis" still feel like the right ones. The publication of the 9 February 2018 stories in The Times changed everything for the UK and many others as Steve and Marcus describe in the Introduction and in Appendix 1.

Since April 2018, PSEAH has been the focus of my working life in the UK Government's Department for International Development (DFID) and then the UK's Foreign Commonwealth and Development Office (FCDO) following the merger of DFID and the Foreign Commonwealth Office (FCO) in 2020. My work has been guided by the 2020 UK Strategy for Safeguarding Against SEAH in the Aid Sector (HM Government, 2020). That strategy focuses on improving safeguarding in three areas: within UK departments that spend aid; in programmes the UK funds; and right across the international aid sector. FCDO has been working hard to get its own house in order and been transparent about progress made and challenges faced.[4]

But no organisation can keep its staff or others it works with safe without coordination. The commitments made at the October 2018 London Safeguarding Summit mentioned in the Introduction shaped coordination efforts across the international system until 2024.[5] Every quarter since 2018, I have chaired or participated in multiple internal and external coordination groups to drive delivery against those and related commitments. The most visible and wide-reaching has been the Cross-Sector Safeguarding Steering Group (CSSG) which brought together those who made commitments at the 2018 London Summit and who until 2024 reported annually on progress against those commitments.[6]

Some of the projects we started in 2018, or soon after, are still work in progress. Others have taken root. Others have been paused as they don't add enough value for key stakeholders. The progress reports referenced above give a sense of all that.

The second reason this book is timely is that the whole international cooperation system is having to adapt to a series of seismic political and economic events and shifts in the past decade, including aid cuts. We need to review and as needed adapt PSEAH approaches in and between organisations, while ensuring it is adequately funded and that we don't compromise on the fundamentals such as ensuring aid does no harm and that we have a zero tolerance to inaction when it comes to SEAH.

We need to work across groupings such as: "humanitarian," "development" and "peace-keeping"; public and private; government and non-government; "for-profit" and "not-for-profit"; donor and recipient. Many aid projects and programmes include stakeholders from all of those groups. And when it comes to PSEAH, many perpetrators may move between organisations and "sectors" or conversely never leave the community where they live.

Finding broad principles that allow for joined up thinking and action across multiple settings and actors is hard, but essential. It is what the 2024 Common Approach to Protection from SEAH (CAPSEAH) does: providing a shared vision to help guide and mutually support decisions taken at local level in all those different and context-specific settings and which are connected and impact on each other to varying degrees.

I wasn't involved in writing the rest of this book or the roundtable described in Chapter 14 and was asked to write this foreword after the book had been completed. I'm delighted to do so and have been fortunate to work with some of the contributing authors since early 2018 and to learn from their and colleagues' many years of experience. I hope this Introduction also provides a perspective from a major bilateral donor which isn't always considered in books of this kind.

Grounds for optimism?

Since 2018, and well before, debates have raged among stakeholders about how best to make a difference. In areas such as mandatory reporting there are no easy answers that feel "right" for everyone (see Chapter 11). But we've always tried to identify what will be effective for as many individuals and groups as possible while protecting some key principles.

Working on safeguarding is tough even if you're not a survivor-victim. SEAH in the aid sector can't be eradicated. SEAH happens in all sectors due to structural societal and cultural issues which aid work can help address, but can't change by itself. But we must do all we reasonably can to deter and prevent, actively manage the risk and also improve the response.

Aid work has never been perfect. But done well and safely, aid has made and continues to make an invaluable contribution to improving the lives of hundreds of millions of people worldwide. It builds cooperation and bridges between communities across the world.

Just like fraud, SEAH is a clear and present risk and reality in aid and all other types of work. Many funders encourage reporting and are likely to be more worried about large organisations or programmes that report few or no cases. There is no easy "solution" to SEAH. This is messy, sensitive work involving unpredictable human beings. It requires bravery, professionalism and emotional intelligence (see Chapter 6). PSEAH must not be seen as an optional extra which can be dropped to save money or time. PSEAH work requires sustained focus and resourcing and is an essential part of aid work to ensure its effectiveness and value for money.

There are many grounds for optimism when it comes to PSEAH and the progress made to improve things and rebuild confidence since early 2018. I've mentioned CAPSEAH and the CSSG. Project Soteria is covered in Chapter 10. Other examples include the Safeguarding Resource and Support Hub[7] focusing on building grassroots organisations' capability and confidence; the Misconduct Disclosure Scheme[8] to improve sharing of information about known misconduct; the Investigator Qualification Training Scheme;[9] the Community Outreach and Communication Fund;[10] coordinated funding of country-level PSEA Coordinators;[11] and efforts to apply aligned[12] and pragmatic[13] approaches to due diligence through the Core Humanitarian Standard and the Humanitarian Quality Assurance Initiative. Each of these has helped to build dialogue and practical, aligned but also contextualised coordinated action on PSEAH involving stakeholders who before 2018 rarely spoke to each other about SEAH. This is a great platform to build on.

Please keep reading. PSEAH deserves and needs more attention. This book is a valuable contribution to efforts to share knowledge, learning and ideas to help safeguard more vulnerable people from harm, continue to rebuild stakeholder confidence and help aid have more impact.

Notes

1. The Common Approach to Protection from SEAH (CAPSEAH) which was launched in June 2024 after 18 months of global consultation has a brief section on definitions and how frequently used terms in this space can be used and interpreted.
2. Two publicly available sources are: that provided by the United Nations related to its work; and the newer Harmonised Reporting Scheme hosted by the Core Humanitarian Standard Alliance. At the time of writing, the two had agreed in principle to align their data sets to improve data comparison and transparency.
3. This is why CAPSEAH sets out possible actions at multiple levels (e.g. individual; organisational; project) to aim for alignment and consistency, while emphasising that implementation will vary in different contexts.
4. See annual progress reports on gov.uk for example one published in April 2025.
5. For the commitments, see Safeguarding Summit: commitments – GOV.UK
6. See annual reports on gov.uk the final one of which was published in 2024 at which point the group felt it no longer made sense to report against the 2018 commitments, not least given the launch that year of CAPSEAH.
7. Safeguarding Resource and Support Hub, https://safeguardingsupporthub.org/
8. The Misconduct Disclosure Scheme, https://misconduct-disclosure-scheme.org/
9. Investigator Qualification Training Scheme | CHS Alliance, www.chsalliance.org/get-support/training/investigator-qualification-training-scheme/
10. PSEA Outreach Fund, www.icvanetwork.org/pseafund/
11. Protection from Sexual Exploitation and Abuse Capacity Project (PSEACap) | IASC, https://interagencystandingcommittee.org/protection-sexual-exploitation-and-abuse-capacity-project-pseacap
12. HQAI CHS Certification passported by FCDO – HQAI, www.hqai.org/en/news/CHS-certification-passport/
13. Bond.org, www.bond.org.uk/news/2023/09/how-bond-is-supporting-organisations-with-safeguarding-due-diligence-for-implementing-and-local-partners/

Reference

HM Government (2020) UK Strategy: Safeguarding Against Sexual Exploitation and Abuse and Sexual Harassment within the Aid Sector https://assets.publishing.service.gov.uk/government/uploads/system/uploads/attachment_data/file/916516/Safeguarding-Strategy-10092020.pdf, accessed 18 May 2025

Preface

"May you live in interesting times"

It has entered into folklore that this quote is a Chinese curse, with "interesting" a euphemism for challenging or chaotic, although no reliable source can be found for its' origin. It was, however, the phrase that came to mind when considering the context in which this book has evolved.

The initial impetus for the book was the crisis around safeguarding in the international aid sector following the revelations about Oxfam and other NGO's in 2018, a timeline of which is outlined in Appendix 1. However, during the time the chapters were being written two major developments had a huge impact on the international aid sector. In the UK, an incoming government decided one measure it would take to address the economic challenges it faced was to reduce the UK's aid spending from 0.5% of gross national income (GNI) to 0.3% of GNI in 2027. The International Development Minister resigned following the announcement, saying the fall in aid spending will *"likely lead to a UK [aid] pull out from numerous African, Caribbean and Western Balkan nations"* and a reduced UK role internationally (UK Parliament, 2025). Shortly afterwards, following an initial 90-day pause in spending, the incoming US administration reviewed the budget of the United States Agency for International Development (USAID). USAID administers humanitarian aid programmes on behalf of the US government and at the time of the review employed around 10,000 people, two-thirds of whom worked overseas, with bases in more than 60 countries and working in dozens of others. Most of the work on the ground was carried out by other organisations contracted and funded by USAID. As a result of the budget review, more than 80% of USAID programmes were terminated, with effects on programmes around the globe (Debusman, 2025).

Interesting times indeed – the combination of a major safeguarding crisis and of unprecedented budget cuts such that the viability of multiple programmes affecting millions of lives are in real jeopardy or have simply been ended. We would like to be able to say that this book has the answers to those existential challenges. Sadly not, but what it does do is address what we identified as key issues for the sector and draw together authoritative authors with considerable expertise in their topic to define the problems and offer possible ways forward. The authors range from senior managers writing from experience, academics who have researched their topics and other key figures with a career of involvement in the issues they discuss. We have tried to respect the diversity of their experience by not trying to impose a single "style" of writing, and thus, some of these chapters are written in more academic style, while others provide more of a first person perspective. All though have been committed ensuring there is an evidence base to their writing, and all chapters are fully referenced.

To maximise the space available in a book like this, we have divided the content into three sections. In the first are Chapters 1–7, chapters of a conventional length, the second section comprises Chapters 8–13 which are shorter briefings on key topics. Each chapter outlines a current issue but crucially also suggests a constructive response. The final section has a full length chapter offering some conclusions.

Part One opens with a chapter outlining the context of the safeguarding challenges in recent times and is supplemented with Appendix 1 which gives a timeline of key events. Our intention is that this both sets the scene and means that authors don't need to repeat the detail. It continues with Chapter 2 from an experienced CEO exploring issues of organisational culture and good leadership, concepts often referred to but rarely addressed in straightforward and practical language as they are here. This chapter is supplemented by Appendix 2, a valuable tool hosted by bond, the UK network for organisations working in international development, on their website. The book continues in Chapter 3 by addressing issues at the other end of the organisational structure, with a trauma psychologist addressing how humanitarian work can affect humanitarian organisations, their workers and their functioning.

The following two chapters, Chapters 4 and 5, address the unintended consequences of two well-meant phenomena, the power of donors when they try to ensure appropriate standards and the challenge of such a standards-based approach to safeguarding.

In Chapter 6, a current CEO with an HR background then gives a very personal and valuable perspective on addressing HR challenges. The section concludes with Chapter 7 on how safeguarding challenges in the international aid and development sector are influenced by the gendered power imbalance deeply embedded both within the structure of the sector and the communities in which they operate. It goes on to provide a tool for analysis of the issue, explaining how to use it to evaluate how gender power imbalance manifests itself within the fragile context of refugee camps.

Part Two starts with two chapters on the issue of sexual violence. The first, Chapter 8, provides the current understanding of the use of sexual violence by state actors as a weapon of war. Chapter 9 addresses sexual violence against humanitarian aid workers and suggests that organisations tend to focus on sexual violence perpetrated by staff *against* affected populations, neglecting internal dynamics of violence among staff.

The section continues in Chapter 10 by addressing the challenges of global policing in the context of international aid, with its highly mobile workforce. It provides insights into global initiatives, such as Project Soteria and the Childlight Global Child Safety Institute, and how they aim to address exploitation while also outlining practical strategies for improving global responses to exploitation within aid organisations. Finally, Chapters 11–13 are on different aspects of policies intended to maintain appropriate standards and integrity: mandatory reporting, whistleblowing, and developing an effective ombuds system.

The book concludes in Chapter 14 by addressing the way forward. It is based on a round table discussion with a number of the authors, so that it could benefit from the perspectives they had shared in their chapters and the responses they had suggested, as well as new insights created by bringing a group of experienced professionals together.

We hope this book offers front line workers the opportunity to reflect on their experience and consider what changes they would like to see in their own practice and their organisation that will sustain them in being able to continue in their roles and provide effective services. Equally, we hope that senior managers will have the opportunity to reflect on their organisation and how it meets the challenges addressed here and whether some of the positive responses advocated here are applicable for use by them.

It is a truism that no organisation expects to experience a major scandal, and yet, if that can happen to organisations as established and well respected as Oxfam GB and Save the Children UK, it surely demonstrates that no organisation is immune from that possibility, not least in these "interesting times" when there is ever more pressure to do more with less.

We are immensely grateful to all our authors, a book like this is a long-term undertaking, and our thanks to them for persevering with this joint project. Our gratitude is also to Franziska Schwarz at bond. Franziska was a "friend to the project" in its early, uncertain, stages and facilitated us participating in bond's annual questionnaire to members, which confirmed our view that there was no other single resource that addressed the safeguarding related issues faced by international aid organisations and the appetite for having such a book available.

Finally, we sincerely hope that this book will be a valuable resource to all in the sector and support them in the invaluable work they do.

Marcus Erooga and Steve Reeves, May 2025

References

Debusman, B., 2025, More than 80% of USAID programmes 'officially ending', BBC News www.bbc.co.uk/news/articles/cdx2401vn5ro

UK Parliament, 2025, UK aid: Reducing spending to 0.3% of GNI by 2027/28 https://commonslibrary.parliament.uk/research-briefings/cbp-10243/

Part One

Chapter 1

A safeguarding crisis in the UK international aid sector

A review of recent inquiries and investigations

Marcus Erooga and Steve Reeves

Chapter objectives

By the end of this chapter, you will:

1 understand the nature and scale of the safeguarding challenges facing organisations delivering aid and development;
2 be aware of the historic context of the safeguarding challenges for the aid and development sector, including periods of heightened public, political and media attention;
3 understand the authors' analysis of a range of the findings of a range of inquiries and investigations into issues which have been identified in a range of relevant organisations;
4 be aware of the authors' analysis of inquiry findings and how they affect organisational culture, efforts to reinvent the system, and the impact on survivors of abuse and exploitation.

Introduction

Recent challenges facing safeguarding in the international aid and development sector were triggered by a significant chain of events which led to a number of review processes being instigated.

On Friday 9 February 2018, the (London) Times newspaper published a front-page article under the headline: '*Top Oxfam GB staff paid Haiti survivors for sex*'. The article alleged that major UK-based international aid NGO (non-governmental organisation), Oxfam GB, covered up claims that senior staff working in Haiti in the wake of the 2010 earthquake exploited local sex workers, some of whom may have been children. What followed was an unprecedented level of concern and scrutiny by both the UK government and the public of the conduct of NGO staff overseas and the diligence and transparency of NGOs in investigating and addressing such concerns. The timeline of events is outlined in Appendix 1. As well as an existential crisis for Oxfam GB, which also lost public confidence and considerable financial support, these events presented a major challenge for the entire sector.

The reason for drawing attention to the events of a few weeks in early February 2018 is that they were both the trigger and the backdrop to much of the scrutiny and self-reflection addressed in the inquiries considered below.

While some of the reports referred to here predate the 2018 Oxfam GB revelation, and the majority do not relate specifically to abuse or exploitation of beneficiaries, the themes arising from them are strikingly similar across inquiries and form the context within which such behaviour became possible. These themes and the actions recommended to address them are explored further in this chapter.

We are aware that there are multiple reports (e.g. Feather et al., 2021) of other 'actors' – peacekeepers, local community leaders and individuals – who also sexually exploit local communities. The focus of this book is NGOs delivering humanitarian aid and international development and, because we need some boundary for our limited wordage, these other issues are outside the remit of this book, although our reflections may also be relevant for addressing those.

Saviour mentality

The media coverage associated with the revelations of misconduct by Oxfam GB staff in Haiti highlighted the significant role which staff of international origin (often described as 'expatriates') played in the exploitation of women and children. This issue of aid workers, usually male, often white, and largely from the industrialised Global North, deploying to the latest international crisis is increasingly recognised as problematic, with an understanding of the 'white saviour' concept increasingly acknowledged as a problematic issue in aid work.

The terminology around what became known initially as the 'white saviour complex' has evolved across time. Originally coined by author Teju Cole in 2012 (Cole, 2012) as the 'White-Saviour Industrial Complex', the concept has evolved and become more widely recognised in a range of fields, not least NGO activity (Jefferess, 2023).

Increasingly referred to as the 'saviour mentality', it has been described as when '*you want to help others but are not open to guidance from those you want to help*' (Cole, 2012).

According to one author (Flaherty, 2016), the adoption of this mentality results in charitable activities at individual and community levels without broader systemic change, leaving unjust power relations unaddressed. He goes on:

> The prototypical saviour is a person who has been raised in privilege and taught implicitly or explicitly (or both) that they possess the answers and skills needed to rescue others, no matter the situation. The saviour mentality means that you want to help others but are not open to guidance from those you want to help. The saviour always wants to lead, never to follow. When the people they have chosen to rescue tell them they are not helping, they think those people are mistaken. It is almost taken as evidence that they need more help.
>
> (Flaherty, 2016, pp 17–18)

Alongside not recognising the issues related to the saviour phenomenon, international organisations have, historically, operated in ways that have failed to take sufficient account of a range of other issues, not least the inherent power imbalances, cultural insensitivity and the perpetuation of harmful stereotypes involved in their work. These approaches extend to most areas of NGO operations, being seen overtly in fundraising campaigns which portray children from Africa as existing in never-ending and abject poverty, but also in more covert ways, such as employment hiring practices.

The aid sector is also affected by wider social changes, such as the impact of *#AidToo* (Midden and Deshmikh, 2017) a sector variant of the *#MeToo* movement. Where appropriate the inherent paternalism, dependency, and cultural appropriation often associated with aid work are reflected on in the chapters which follow, and emphasis is given to the importance of listening to and empowering local communities. For those readers interested in exploring *#AidToo* more thoroughly, we recommend reviewing the website of Devex.com, a global development journalism website who have written extensively on the issue.

Organisational culture

A strikingly common theme from the majority of the reviews considered here is the central importance of the organisation's culture, a term ubiquitous in management and leadership texts. In the context of considering its role in the context of safeguarding context, culture can helpfully be described as representing '*...the collective values, beliefs and principles of organisational members. (It) includes the organisation's vision, values, norms, systems, symbols, language, assumptions, beliefs, and habits*' (Needle, 2010) – in short it is '*the way we do things around here*' (HSE, undated). Consciously or otherwise, organisational behaviour defines the organisation's culture, and that culture forms the context within which the organisation's people judge the appropriateness of their behaviour, whether or not those behaviours are what leadership intends, or are even aware of.

The role of leadership

As leaders are in positions of power, they have a fundamental responsibility to demonstrate leadership and commitment, for establishing and maintaining an organisational culture that is conducive to safeguarding best practice. Leaders play a key role in communicating the assumptions, values, beliefs and norms they expect organisational participants to exhibit (Schein, 1985): discussed further in Chapter 2.

Clearly stated values and commitments

A key element of a child safe organisation is that '*...the institution publicly commits to child safety and leaders champion a child safe culture*' (Valentine et al., 2016). Self-evident though it may seem, if it is to be achieved, then it is crucial that an organisation clearly expresses its values and commitment to safeguarding. So, for example, something as simple as a commitment that '*...anyone working on (our) behalf, and anyone benefitting from the work (we) are doing, does not come to any harm, either intended or unintended, as a result of this work taking place*' (UNICEF, 2018) clearly and unequivocally sets out the organisations' position and intention. It also communicates to all potential members of the organisation, existing members and beneficiaries where the organisation stands in relation to safeguarding.

Operationalising those cultural commitments

In its research paper on Key Elements of Child Safe Organisations, the Australian Royal Commission describes the need for '*governance arrangements (that) facilitate the implementation of the child safe elements and accountabilities (that) are set by institutional leaders, at all levels of the institution's governance structures*' (Valentine et al., 2016). Those commitments need to be expressed as a clear code of conduct. This is more than simply a list of rules but rather is a set of guiding principles which helps staff and children understand acceptable behaviours and sets clear boundaries. That needs to be supported by '*…clear policies and procedures so staff know what is expected of them and facilitate raising of concerns*' (Wonnacott and Carmi, 2016).

Leadership modelling desired culture

If it is to consistently achieve its safeguarding aspirations the organisation's clearly stated values and commitments need to be seen to apply to the whole organisation, seen to be applicable and acted out by senior managers and experienced as 'lived' by the whole organisation from the newest intern to the Chair of the Trustees. That process is eloquently described in the *Independent Review of Workplace Culture at Save the Children UK* (Shale, 2018) following the concerns about the behaviour of senior managers:

> Trustees, along with senior leaders, set and convey normative expectations about a charity's culture and how people associated with it should behave. Charity leaders do this in part by what they are seen to represent, and also in part by the standards of behaviour they model through their own behaviour towards others.
>
> But perhaps the most important way in which leaders set normative expectations is through the value choices they make in difficult situations. This is when leadership has its most potent effect on the culture of an organisation, signalling to staff the fundamental principles the charity will uphold.
>
> (p 8)

If not consistent and authentic, all too soon disparity between words and deeds will become apparent, will be noted by all. The message received will be that '*we say one thing but do another*' or '*the rules only apply to some*' and the organisational culture adjusts accordingly, with ensuing negative effects.

Transparency of systems and processes

If that positive modelling is to be achieved, then a key element will be transparency, both of organisational systems and processes and at an operational level. When safeguarding is concerned that is frequently likely to be challenging, involving sensitive issues which may also be confidential and inappropriate for detail to be shared. This can, however, be ameliorated to some extent by an explicit commitment to being *as transparent as possible*, with an accompanying rationale for that commitment being a qualified one. If information is shared when possible, and when it is not possible for the message that it can't be shared is worded in such a way that indicates a respect for the rights and needs of those concerned, it is more likely that it will be perceived as appropriate, rather than the toxic message that the organisation is being opaque in order to mask inconsistent or expedient actions.

At a corporate level, *The Oxfam GB Independent Commission on Sexual Misconduct, Accountability and Culture Change Final Report* (Oxfam International's Commission) (Bangura et al., 2019) recommends a number of measures which, while specific to its review of Oxfam GB, can be generalised to be good practice more widely in the sector. These include:

- Regular public release of reports of anonymised safeguarding cases, with an annual report that includes an end-of-year tally on cases by type and status of investigation, briefly describes each proven case of sexual exploitation and abuse in a way that maintains confidentiality but allows the reader to understand the role and level of the perpetrator in the organisation's hierarchy, the substantiated transgression and the resulting disciplinary action. The report should also affirm that feedback has been provided to complainants;
- Establish co-created community reporting mechanisms with regular audits to assess progress towards achieving that or to monitor its functioning;
- Place all safeguarding policies and procedures in an open-access system, both for transparency and to share its learning with partners and the wider sector.

To these might be added:

- Making clear the responsibility of all staff, from beneficiary-facing workers and frontline and volunteers to senior executives to report safeguarding concerns in line with their organisation's policy. An approach which has been increasingly adopted by organisations in the

UK has been a low-level concerns policy. There is not space in this chapter to explore that, but readers are recommended to review a guide to the approach published by a team with considerable experience of its implementation and use (Farrer & Co, 2024);
- Related to this is ensuring that there is a transparent, well-publicised, effective and timely process for notifying a concern and for making and handling a complaint. Any concerns or complaints, whether originated internally or externally, should be addressed, and seen to be addressed, constructively, impartially and effectively;
- There should be clear policies about how confidential information is shared between departments in the same organisation along with comprehensive and proportionate arrangements for collecting, storing and sharing information;
- Finally, a regular review of the organisation's processes for identifying, prioritising, escalating and managing risks, with a review of the effectiveness of the organisation's approach to risk at least annually.

Processes to understand the experience of those involved

It is challenging to analyse and critique a culture that one is a part of, yet crucial for leaders to be able to be informed and reflect on the culture of our own organisation and use information from that ongoing process to inform positive change. To achieve that it will be necessary to have a continuous system of directly seeking meaningful feedback that identifies current perceptions of stakeholders, for example anonymous staff surveys, pulses, user feedback, etc.

Crucial will be how feedback is seen to be responded to – not that all suggestions or views have to be acted on but that they are seen to have been 'heard' and acknowledged. What that should look like is summarised in one of the reviews relating to prolific organisational UK sex offender Sir Jimmy Savile as '*a culture of curiosity, scrutiny and constructive challenge, with processes to underpin these behaviours*' (Proctor et al., 2014).

Reinventing the system

The significant breadth, scale and incoherent approach of actors in the sector became apparent in the intensity of the focus of the media, public, donors and the government following the media revelations in 2018. To ensure action was taken, the UK's Department for International Development (DfID) asked discrete sections of the aid and development landscape to make public commitments in respect of safeguarding. This resulted in commitments being made by eight separate groups (Donors, International Financial Institutions, UK NGOs, UK Private Sector Suppliers, Research Funders, Gavi and Global Fund, United Nations and CDC Group [now British International Investment]) each representing multiple agencies (in some instances hundreds or thousands of organisations and representatives), demonstrating the immense scale of the sector and the varied approaches to the work.

The exercise of gathering safeguarding commitments from these different parts of the aid landscape itself required significant activity; many of the agencies concerned had little contact with their peer organisations and insufficient experience of working together to tackle this kind of challenge. Just as the exercise demonstrated the lack of co-ordination between agencies in similar parts of the sector, it also demonstrated the absence of any meaningful framework to ensure collaboration of any parameters to compel a consistent or co-ordinated approach. As the UK Secretary of State for International Development put it, the necessity was *'...Not just to tinker around the edges. But to fundamentally rewrite the way this sector operates, from root to branch'* (Mordaunt, 2018).

Given the significance of Oxfam GB in the early stages of the 2018 public debate about safeguarding in the aid sector, the UK government took the lead in attempting to drive change. UK Aid was used to fund new initiatives and the exercise of donor power played a significant role in attempts to drive compliance and improvements (see Chapter 6).

A UK Parliamentary Inquiry (International Development Committee, 840, 2018) identified the challenges for domestic regulators attempting to carry out their duties in respect of international aid charities, not least due to the scale of their operations and their international nature.

- In 2018, the Charity Commission's budget was £27m and their remit was to regulate 168,000 charities *'If you contrast the average income for a charity, which I think is about £400,000, UK focused, versus Oxfam GB and Save the Children with £400 million, working across 90-plus countries, they are such different organisations to be regulating'* (para 186);
- In evidence to the Inquiry, a prominent sector whistleblower explained the 'regulatory gap' presented by the sheer scale of the sector's work:

With these aid agencies, you might have an incident happen in country A, the victim is from country B, and the perpetrator is from country C and then moves onto another country. You need to work across multiple legal jurisdictions. That is a really big ask for the Charity Commission.

(para 185)

These concerns resulted in pressure for there to be a dedicated global regulator or ombuds function that would be able to contend with the complexity and scale of the sector's work. Ultimately, this proposal did not gain the support of sufficient global government donors to be implemented and the same regulatory challenges persist today (see Chapter 13).

The UK Government invested heavily in three projects, which it anticipated would help to bring about sustained and consistent change, and provided vocal support to an additional scheme:

- The Aid Worker Registration Scheme, designed to maintain a comprehensive record of aid workers' professional backgrounds, preventing those who had previously committed misconduct from being reemployed in the sector and preventing change of identity in order to evade recruitment checks;
- INTERPOL's Project Soteria, which seeks to improve co-ordination between international law enforcement agencies and the humanitarian and development sectors and increase their respective operational capacities (see Chapter 12);
- The Misconduct Disclosure Scheme (MDS), overseen by the Steering Committee for Humanitarian Response (SCHR), a coalition of major humanitarian agencies, aims to regularise the provision of information sharing regarding instances of sexual misconduct by individual recruits among various aid organisations (SCHR, undated).

While these initiatives are designed to work in tandem, complementing one another in their collective efforts, in practice progress and effectiveness, varies hugely. Objectively, when measured against a benchmark of a challenge to '...*fundamentally rewrite the way this sector operates, from root to branch*', these measures could be described as modest, and each has been the subject of criticism from both inside and outside of the aid sector.

The scale of global government spending (in 2018 the overseas aid spending of 29 countries totalled almost $150bn) provided scope for donors to exercise significant power over the ways in which organisations and agencies used resources, with some imposing new standards and due diligence requirements on grant recipients. At the same time, the UK used its significant (£16bn) funding platform to disallow from accessing funding those NGOs who may have fallen below the standards expected, and in 2018, this was applied to Oxfam GB (DfID, 2018) after it was announced that it was subject to a regulatory investigation. Save the Children UK (Save the Children UK, 2018) voluntarily offered to suspend its participation in bids for new government funding after it was announced that it was also subject to a regulatory investigation.

Common to the findings of many of the reports addressed here is the need for significant systemic change, whether to arrangements in individual organisations or the landscape applicable to all aid actors. The status quo places considerable power in the hands of employers, which UK parliamentarians considered problematic: *'...the international aid sector has been relying on self-regulation. The shortcomings that we have observed during the course of this inquiry demonstrate to us that self-regulation has failed'* (IDC, 2018, HC2017-19, 840).

In addition to the significance of leadership and organisational culture, reviews and reports tend to align on three significant opportunities for systemic change.

Creating effective and accessible complaints/reporting mechanisms

No one to turn to: the under-reporting of child sexual exploitation and abuse by aid workers and peacekeepers (Csáky, 2008) highlights that girls were more likely to be victims than boys, and men more likely to be perpetrators than women, with the most common age of child victims appearing to be between 14 and 15 years. That said, focus groups in Haiti identified several cases of boys being victims of abuse and the report identified at least one example of female perpetrator against a boy (Csáky, 2008). Other reports have emphasised the importance of ensuring that organisations do not respond to solely statistically created pressures to discount the victimisation of boys and that special efforts were required to create an environment conducive to boys reporting sexual abuse are also recognised (UNHCR and SCUK, 2002).

Multiple reports provide insight into the prevalence of exploitation and the vulnerability of many who are directly reliant on aid agencies for basic survival. The dependency on aid was also identified as a significant factor in limiting the reporting of serious misconduct by aid workers:

> Exploiters appear to be able to pay for sex when and with whom they want, and to do so with impunity, since the very people they exploit are not able to complain about their situation for fear of their source of basic survival being removed (UNHCR and SCUK, 2002), exacerbated by the complexity

of the dynamics involved in the context: 'The vulnerability of the victims and survivors of sexual abuse, and the power of the abuser, create multiple interlocking barriers to reporting'.

(IDC, 2018, HC2017-19, 840)

The extent to which the levels of abuse and exploitation were commonly known by communities was consistent in those reports which addressed the issue. Indeed, the exploitation of girls and young women in exchange for essential materials was considered to be so prevalent that one community member reported that *'If you see a young girl walking away with tarpaulin on her head you know how she got it'* and that *'If you do not have a wife or a sister or a daughter to offer the NGO workers, it is hard to have access to aid'* (UNHCR and SCUK, 2002).

The importance of community-level mechanism for reporting exploitation is recommended in multiple reviews, with much emphasis on creating accessible and trusted systems.

The Oxfam International Commission (Bangura et al., 2019) made recommendations for the implementation of multiple channels for community members to use, in their own language and catering for their literacy levels, with a clear expectation that these should be co-created with communities. Additional arrangements for feedback to complainants and survivors at the conclusion of any investigation were recommended. This was echoed in *Improving Child Safeguarding and Preventing Sexual Exploitation and Abuse in the Humanitarian Sector* (Daoust and Dyvik, 2018), in which the authors drew specific attention to the need for reporting mechanisms to be culturally relevant and subject to local negotiation and acceptance:

> This includes attention to the 'enabling' and 'disabling' roles that community structures play in conveying [child safeguarding concerns], as well as alignment or tensions between [Save the Children's] accountability mechanisms and local/traditional justice mechanisms.
>
> (Daoust and Dyvik, 2018)

Development of global systems and services

The absence of a sufficiently effective regulatory framework and few cross-jurisdictional bodies or mechanisms to hold organisations to account has resulted in greater consideration of global measures which may provide some form of redress. The problematic approach to safeguarding was identified by the International Development Select Committee of the UK Parliament, in its 2018 report:

> The aid sector, collectively, has been aware of sexual exploitation and abuse by its own personnel for years, but the attention that it has given to the problem has not matched the challenge. Repeatedly, reports of sexual exploitation and abuse by aid workers and/or peacekeepers have emerged, the sector has reacted, but then the focus has faded... A reactive, cyclical approach, driven by concern for reputational management has not, and will never, bring about meaningful change.
> (IDC, 2018, HC2017-19, 840, p 4)

In addition to recommending the establishment of effective local reporting mechanisms and greater focus on the root causes of abuse, '*No one to turn to*' recommended the creation of a new global watchdog should be established to monitor and evaluate the efforts of international agencies to tackle this abuse and to champion more effective responses (Csáky, 2008). Oxfam International's Commission recognised the desirability of an internal Oxfam GB-wide Ombuds function, while others reported on the necessity of a wider, global approach.

In a report, commissioned by the Netherlands Ministry of Foreign Affairs (Hilhorst et al., 2018), the International Institute of Social Studies highlighted the contrast between the accountability and regulatory environments in jurisdictions which have settled and developed legal processes and those where such systems have never existed or have broken down:

> ...in a country with a functioning rule of law, the abuse of a child by a teacher may lead to various outcomes – the teacher may be prosecuted for a criminal offence and/or be dismissed from the job; he or she may be disciplined by the professional regulator and be barred from teaching for life; or the teacher, school, and education authorities may be sued for damages. In an equivalent example of a child being abused by a teacher working for an international aid programme in a context where the rule of law has broken down, recourse in practice is often limited to the organisation, as the employer, sanctioning the offender.
> (p 11)

Tackling the root causes and drivers of abuse and exploitation

Common to findings of multiple reports is a recognition of the fact that much aid work takes place in settings where poverty is widespread and human rights are yet to be universally obtained. Reviews point to the powerful drivers of abuse and exploitation that exist in many places, with an emphasis on the importance of tackling these underlying causes and drivers of harm.

Sexual violence and exploitation: The experience of refugee children in Liberia, Guinea and Sierra Leone (UNHCR and SCUK, 2002) identified poverty, lack of livelihood options and consequent inability to meet basic survival needs; insufficient food rations/supplies; issues in relation to the management and delivery of humanitarian aid; and pressure from peers and parents as factors contributing to the sexual exploitation of children.

One of the key recommendations of *'No one to turn to'* (Csáky, 2008) is the need for the root causes of abuse to become a greater priority for governments, donors and others in the international community. The report acknowledges the complexity of the challenge but highlights the importance of effective child protection systems to create the environment in which, in this instance, child exploitation and abuse could be prevented and, where this cannot be achieved, children receive appropriate interventions and outcomes. Achieving the scale of systems change required a wide range of actors to act, ensuring that issues such as legal reform, capacity building, research, public education, gender awareness and the active involvement of children are addressed in a concerted manner.

Survivors

The experiences of and insights from members of communities receiving aid and victims and survivors of abuse and exploitation are included in several reports, with some being primarily focussed on this topic.

Oxfam International's Commission gave specific focus to the need to engage effectively with survivors of aid sector abuse, both to ensure that their needs were addressed, and perpetrators are held to account, but also to ensure that future prevention and response to incidents of abuse would be informed by the lived experience of survivors.

In specific recommendations designed to *'support survivors to recover and rebuild their lives'*, the Oxfam International Commission prioritised steps that would lead to the provision of immediate (localised) support, support to survivors to understand and access the options for justice, and appropriate reparations to redress some of the long-term harm inflicted on survivors by their exploitation.

As some of the reviews and reports relate to aid workers themselves being the victims of harassment and abuse by other staff, their experiences were captured too. The reported high levels of prevalence and awareness of abuse by members of local communities are contrasted with the low levels of reporting using existing mechanisms. Reports of sexual misconduct against aid workers, by their colleagues, follow a similar theme:

> Women and LGBT aid professionals who did report were widely dissatisfied with their agencies' responses and experienced more harmful professional and personal consequences than those of their alleged perpetrators, who at times remained in their positions and continued perpetrating.
> (Mazurana and Donnelly, 2018, p 3)

Some of the reports addressing the prevention of future harm include specific recommendations or findings about the role gender plays in the context of preventing and reporting abuse. There was a recognition that, given the general acceptance that girls and young women are the most identified victims of exploitation and abuse, the absence of senior female leaders in the aid sector is problematic. There is an acceptance that visible and senior women in aid organisations are an important step towards creating an environment in which abuse might be prevented.

There are findings from the very earliest reports focussed on these issues that the gender of aid workers in specific roles can provide a protective factor. *Sexual violence and exploitation: The experience of refugee children in Liberia, Guinea and Sierra Leone* (UNHRC and SCUK, 2002) made recommendations that agencies should *'Deploy more female staff, especially at the level of direct contact with the refugees. Services concerning girls and sexual health especially should be operated by women'* and that prevention in education programmes should include work which

> Build in safeguards into education structures to ensure that sexual exploitation does not take place within the school system e.g. close attention to recruitment and monitoring of teachers, more female staff.
> (p 17)

There was a strong sentiment, particularly on the part of policymakers, that positive progress to improve safeguarding in the sector would only be achieved by understanding the power imbalances, often focussed on gender disparity, and effective engagement with survivors of abuse. The International Development Committee made it clear, in their 2018 report, that:

Victims and survivors should demonstrably be front and centre of all efforts to tackle sexual exploitation and abuse and this means the inclusion of victim and survivor voices in policy-making processes on an ongoing basis. A failure to listen to and consider the needs of victims and survivors of sexual exploitation and abuse will engender a response that is not only ineffective, but potentially harmful.

(IDC, 2018, HC2017-19, 840, p 5)

Conclusion

In recent years, the entire international humanitarian aid sector 'ecosystem' has faced what it would be no exaggeration to describe as an existential crisis – that its continued existence was at times in question due to the response of government and the public to the revelations discussed above. The major UK agencies involved have taken action to address those issues and have made commitments to improve and prevent any recurrence of past events. In this, the sector is supported by various standards, for example those contained in the Sphere handbook, which comprises Humanitarian Charter, Protection Principles, Core Humanitarian Standards and minimum humanitarian standards in four areas of response (Sphere, 2018) and a range of standards and guidance developed by Bond, the UK network for organisations working in international development (bond.org.uk).

Key messages and learning

- Change occurs in organisations with leadership which is clearly committed to developing a positive organisational culture, where safeguarding is explicitly embedded;
- Abuse and exploitation have always existed in aid and development contexts, resulting in periodic (occasionally intense) public, political and media attention. This public discussion of abuse and exploitation has driven the sector, along with governments and donors, to make changes to the operation of individual agencies and the sector as a whole;
- By definition, aid and development often take place where there is intense and profound need, making those receiving aid and development assistance particularly vulnerable to the exploitation of a disparity in individual and societal wealth and resources;

- While prevalence and scale of harm are sometimes difficult to accurately quantify, there is extensive evidence that exploitation is widespread with women and children most likely to be victims.
- There are systemic changes that could assist in the reduction of harm to victims/potential victims and increase the accountability of perpetrators and their employers.
- The testimony of whistleblowers and movements targeting broader social change, such as #MeToo, can have a powerful impact on both awareness and response to exploitation in the aid and development sector.

Further reading

1 Bond hosts an online tool for leaders to review, develop and monitor their organisational safeguarding culture (Bond, 2021). We commend this to anyone either in a leadership role, or in a position to influence leadership, as an accessible and practical tool to engage with those issues.
2 Teju Cole's the *White-Saviour Industrial Complex* (2012) provides the basis for the ongoing consideration of these issues in aid and development.
3 *Violating Peace: Sex, Aid, and Peacekeeping* by Jasmine-Kim Westendorf provides a valuable insight into many of the issues addressed in this book, but with a focus on Peacekeeping operations.

References

Bangura, Z, Sierra, K, Cottrell, J, Mouillesseaux, S, Heald, O, Ohlsson, B, Kanyoro, M, Samara- Wickrama, K and Lassegue, M (2019) *The Oxfam GB Independent Commission on Sexual Misconduct, Accountability and Culture Change Final report*. Oxfam GB, www.OxfamGB.org/en/what-we-do/about/safeguarding/independent-commission, accessed 27 September 2023.

Bond (2021) *Developing and Modelling a Positive Safeguarding Culture: A Tool for Leaders*, https://safeguarding-tool.bond.org.uk/

Cole, T (21 March 2012) The White-Saviour Industrial Complex. *The Atlantic*, www.theatlantic.com/international/archive/2012/03/the-white-savior-industrial-complex/254843/, accessed 14 October 2023.

Csáky, C (2008) *No One to Turn to: The Under-Reporting of Child Sexual Exploitation and Abuse by Aid Workers and Peacekeepers*. London: Save the Children UK.

Daoust, G and Dyvik, S (2018) *Improving Child Safeguarding and Preventing Sexual Exploitation and Abuse in the Humanitarian Sector*. London: Save the Children/University of Sussex.

Department for International Development (2018) *Statement from the International Development Secretary on Oxfam GB*, www.gov.uk/government/news/statement-from-the-international-development-secretary-on-oxfam, accessed 21 August 2025.

Farrer & Co (2024) *Developing and Implementing a Low-level Concerns Policy: A Guide for Organisations Which Work with Children*, www.farrer.co.uk/globalassets/clients-and-sectors/safeguarding/developing-and-implementing-a-low-level-concerns-policy.pdf, accessed 21 August 2025.

Feather, J, Martin, R and Neville, S (2021) *Global Evidence Review on SEAH in the Aid Sector*. London: Safeguarding Resource and Support Hub.

Flaherty, J (2016) *No More Heroes: Grassroots Challenges to the Saviour Mentality*. Edinburgh, UK: AK Press.

Hilhorst, D Naik, A and Cunningham A (2018) *International Ombuds for Humanitarian and Development Aid Scoping Study*. International Institute of Social Studies. Erasmus University Rotterdam

HSE (undated) *Organisational Culture*, www.hse.gov.uk/humanfactors/topics/culture.htm, accessed 29 October 2023.

International Development Committee (2018) *Sexual Exploitation and Abuse in the Aid Sector HC2017-2019, HC840*. London: House of Commons.

Jefferess, D (2023) Humanitarianism and White Saviours in Ravulo, J, Olcoń, K, Dune, T, Workman, A and Liamputtong, P (eds) *Handbook of Critical Whiteness*. Singapore: Springer. https://doi.org/10.1007/978-981-19-1612-0_61-1

Mazurana, D and Donnelly, P (2018) *STOP The Sexual Abuse Against Aid Workers*. Fletcher School of Law and Diplomacy, https://data.parliament.uk/writtenevidence/committeeevidence.svc/evidencedocument/international-development-committee/sexual-exploitation-and-abuse-in-the-aid-sector/written/80767.pdf, accessed 19 October 2023.

Midden, K and Deshmukh, S (2017) #AidToo: *How Development Organizations Can Respond to Sexual Violence*, www.devex.com/news/authors/1341745, accessed 14 October 2023.

Mordaunt, P (2018) *Keynote Speech at Safeguarding Summit. 18th October 2018*. London: Queen Elizabeth II Centre.

Needle, D (2010) *Business in Context: An Introduction to Business and Its Environment*. Memphis: Southwestern Publishing.

Proctor, S, Galloway, R, Challoner, R, Jones, C and Thompson, D (2014) *The Report of the Investigation into Matters Relating to Savile at Leeds Teaching Hospitals NHS Trust*. Leeds: Leeds Teaching Hospitals NHS Trust.

Save the Children UK (2018) *Save the Children Offers to Suspend Bidding for New DfID Funding*, www.savethechildren.org.uk/news/media-centre/press-releases/save-the-children-offers-to-suspend-bidding-for-new-dfid-funding, accessed 7 November 2023.

Schein, E (1985) *Organizational Culture and Leadership*. San Francisco, CA: Jossey-Bass Publishers.

Shale, S (2018) *The Independent Review of Workplace Culture at Save the Children UK Final Report*. London: Save the Children.

Sphere (2018) *The Sphere Handbook: Humanitarian Charter and Minimum Standards in Humanitarian Response*, https://spherestandards.org/handbook/editions/, accessed 6 November 2023.

Steering Committee for Humanitarian Response (SCHR) (undated) *Inter-Agency Misconduct Disclosure Scheme*, https://interagencystandingcommittee.org/system/files/inter-agency_misconduct_disclosure_scheme_final_draft_002.pdf, accessed 6 November 2023.

UNHCR & Save the Children UK (2002) *Sexual Violence and Exploitation: The Experience of Refugee Children in Liberia, Guinea and Sierra Leone*. Geneva: UNHCR.

UNICEF (2018) *Child Safeguarding Toolkit for Business*, www.unicef.ca/sites/default/files/2020-12/UNICEF_ChildSafeguardingToolkit_FINAL.pdf, accessed 24 September 2023.

Valentine, l, Katz, I, Smyth, C, Bent, C, Rinaldis, S, Wade, C, and Albers, B (2016) *Key Elements of Child Safe Organisations – Research Study*. Sydney, Royal Commission into Institutional Responses to Child Sexual Abuse, www.childabuseroyalcommission.gov.au/sites/default/files/file-list/research_report_-key_elements_of_child_safe_organisations_research_study-_prevention.pdf, accessed September 24, 2023.

Westendorf, J (2020) *Violating Peace: Sex, Aid and Peacekeeping*. Ithaca: Cornell University Press.

Wonnacott, J and Carmi, E (2016) *Southbank International School Serious Case Review*. Hammersmith and Fulham, Kensington and Chelsea and Westminster Local Safeguarding Children Board, www.rbkc.gov.uk/pdf/Southbank%20SCR%20REPORT%2012%201%2016.pdf, accessed 24 September 2023.

Chapter 2

Leadership and culture

How to build safer cultures through leadership – and why it's essential we do

Frances Longley

Chapter objectives

By the end of this chapter, you will:

- have an understanding of the importance of leaders modelling the values and standards that enable an organisation to have a safeguarding culture;
- be aware of the significance of organisational culture.

Introduction

In February 2018, the abusive actions of individuals, and the organisational failings of NGOs where they had worked, were dramatically exposed on the front pages of UK newspapers (O'Neill, 2018) (see Appendix 1). What had been a low rumble of concern across parts of the aid and development sector for years abruptly hit the mainstream, and suddenly safeguarding was all we were talking about.

The most visible change brought about by the revelations about Oxfam GB, Save the Children UK and others was in the approach to preventing sexual exploitation, harassment and abuse. But just beyond that a different reckoning was kick-started inside the UK NGO world. That has influenced our reaction to every challenge since, from COVID-19 to anti-racism and decolonisation to the impact of sweeping cuts in aid funding. It marked a shift from a reliance on process and compliance in operational teams to a re-evaluation of how we lead our organisations, the culture within which we do so and the governance which underpins it. This chapter examines how we got there and what it means for effective safeguarding. It goes on to scrutinise the central lessons about leadership and culture we learned on the way.

This chapter draws in part on the experiences of Oxfam GB and Save the Children UK. They were the two highest-profile cases during 2018, and they have both been subject to an unusual degree of detailed, independent, publicly available scrutiny. It is important to note that the shortcomings in safeguarding highlighted in their organisations were not unique to them. Although they were the most visible in media coverage at the time, much of what is described was also present in other NGOs across the sector. Both organisations have delivered substantial and meaningful programmes of change since 2018. They embraced the necessary and brave path to improvement, and their safeguarding culture and practice are now significantly stronger. The independent inquiries and reports which informed that change provide us all with valuable insights, which is why they are drawn on here.

Impetus for change

When the safeguarding stories broke in 2018 people were horrified. Disgust at the abuses detailed was joined by a strong sense of betrayal by organisations held up as ethical role models. Politicians quickly joined the condemnation, bringing with them threats to government funding for NGOs and their access to policymakers. Two weeks after the Oxfam story broke the Secretary of State for International Development, Penny Mordaunt, made a speech to an annual conference of UK NGOs. She described her view of a sector in which organisations had "maybe" been complicit in exploitation, put income over moral duty and protected their reputations rather than the vulnerable individuals they were there to serve (HM Government, International Aid and Development, 2018).

I was in the hall when she made those remarks, and I've never forgotten their impact. For a sector which many of us had joined driven by a strong ethical purpose, this extraordinary speech, freighted with exaggeration, encapsulated the sudden shift in perception about us, our organisations and our values. In the space of three weeks, NGOs had gone from role models to pariahs. The Chair, Chief Executive and other senior figures at Oxfam GB announced their resignations, and senior leaders elsewhere started to come under closer scrutiny. Perhaps for the first time, the role of CEO or trustee of an NGO had switched from being one of respected public servant to a position of significant professional risk. Careers were being ended and there seemed to be no second chances.

That initial moral outcry was swiftly followed by an emphasis on compliance and box-ticking. Some of the earliest responses from government and donors demonstrated a limited understanding of safeguarding, and, it appeared, a desire to insulate themselves from blame by imposing new processes and checklists. NGOs in receipt of UK government money were instructed to go back through years of files in a matter of days and declare any cases which might now cause concern. The Charity Commission for England and Wales encouraged organisations to file retrospective reports about anything which might now be considered worthy of declaration, even if it wouldn't have met that threshold under the guidelines in place when the event took place. Charities fearing the consequences of misjudging the guidance filed reports for hundreds of incidents, some very low-level, going back many years, 'just in case'. In response, charities faced criticism from authorities for the high number of cases now emerging, with some initially wrongly describing the volume of reports as an indication of a wholesale failure in safeguarding by NGOs. The urgent imperative was to check your paperwork: have you got an up-to-date policy, a reporting protocol, a log of cases? In those frantic early weeks, public and political condemnation fed a response rooted in bureaucracy and the comfort of compliance with regulations. What it failed to tackle was whether any of this was actually preventing harm (see Chapters 6 and 7).

Responses to the sector crisis

Under the heat of this scrutiny the UK international aid and development community quickly came together to formulate a meaningful sector-wide response. Bond, the umbrella body for UK NGOs, set up working groups, initially with participation by the UK government and Charity Commission, to address four areas central to strengthening safeguarding:

- accountability to beneficiaries and to survivors of abuse

- leadership and culture
- the employment cycle
- reporting and complaints mechanisms.

The scope deliberately matched change in operations and systems with a recognition of the vital role of leadership and culture. Together with Clare Conaghan (then at Save the Children UK), and later Sally Proudlove (at the time from Unicef UK), I co-chaired the working group on leadership and culture.

Working group on leadership and culture

Our goal was to devise practical, evidence-based solutions for aid and development organisations of all sizes. Over the course of two years, the working group reviewed research and case studies about the role of culture and leadership in safe, healthy organisations. We put together a specialist task team to crystalise the lessons our leaders and organisations needed to learn if they were to build and maintain healthy, safe cultures.

The diverse task team included survivors of abuse and had expertise in:

- Development and humanitarian work
- Gender-based violence
- Safeguarding
- Safeguarding culture
- Human resources

Two primary lessons went on to inform our work and approach:

- Compliance-based systems aren't enough to deliver effective safeguarding: you need a strong safeguarding culture
- Everything leaders do, or don't do, disproportionately determines organisational culture

The uncomfortable truth is that, without a healthy culture, your safeguarding work is doomed to failure. And you won't get the culture you need without committed leaders.

So what do we mean by leadership and culture? We developed some working definitions:

Leaders: leaders are individuals with the authority and power to make decisions and allocate resources (Proudlove et al., 2021).

Culture: there is a generally accepted understanding of culture, that it is 'how we do things around here' – the values, behaviour and standards we practise and witness around us in a community or organisation. In the working group we took this further and developed a more specific definition of what constitutes a *positive safeguarding culture*:

> an explicit safeguarding culture and ethos with values and behaviours that are articulated and lived at each level of an organisation, focused on keeping people safe from harm.
> (Wonnacott & Carmi, 2016)

On a practical, day-to-day level, this looks and feels like

> a culture of curiosity, scrutiny and constructive challenge, with processes to underpin these behaviours.
> (Proctor et al., 2014)

What we found was that culture and leadership are tightly bound together. The cliché about a fish rotting from the head is true: what is seen to happen at the top has a disproportionately large impact on the culture of the whole organisation.

The UK aid and development sector is large and diverse. It encompasses small charities with no paid staff, and huge INGOs with annual incomes of tens or hundreds of millions of pounds, thousands of staff and offices in countries around the world. But what our work established is that, although the realities of organisation and resources vary widely, the core principles underpinning positive leadership and culture for safeguarding are consistent, regardless of scale.

Informed by this, we developed a detailed tool and a range of resources to enable organisations of any size to assess, and strengthen, their leadership and culture to embed effective safeguarding in all that they do, wherever they do it.

Components of effective safeguarding

Effective safeguarding happens in places where:

- Everyone understands what is expected of them and recognises the warning signs of abuse in others;
- Everyone understands that they must speak up about what they see;
- Where there is a clear and accountable process for raising concerns;

- Where everyone knows that their concerns will be taken seriously and appropriate action will follow.

If we break that down, we can see the core components more clearly:

- Robust recruitment, mandatory training, clear policies and a code of conduct are vital parts of everyone understanding what is expected of them and others, and being able to recognise the warning signs of abuse.
- A range of channels through which concerns can be raised and addressed (e.g. dedicated helplines and email addresses for reporting, whistleblowing policies and mechanisms, named individuals who can be approached in safety). Those concerns are promoted in different ways according to the context and the audience, and create the clear and accountable process for reports to be made.

These elements are vital. They are practical and visible, easily checked in a due diligence assessment. Before 2018, if an NGO had these things firmly in place they were probably ahead of the field on safeguarding.

But there is more in that simple definition.

If every individual is to recognise the conduct expected of them and their duty to speak up, we need clearly articulated values and behaviours that are understood and embedded. And, for everyone to have confidence that their concerns will be taken seriously and acted on appropriately, we need visible, consistent leadership which is also representative of those behaviours and values.

The system elements are essential, but they only really work when they are underpinned by an enabling culture and values-driven leadership.

For a real-world example, we can look at the conclusions of the independent reports into safeguarding at Oxfam GB following the 2018 spotlight on past practice.

The Charity Commission inquiry included the following points in its formal conclusions:

- the importance of responsible behaviours and conduct was not embedded in part of its daily activities across the organisation and its work and people
- this led to a workforce that was not empowered or confident enough to challenge poor behaviours nor did the workforce have the necessary confidence in management and systems for reporting concerns.

(Charity Commission, 2019a, p. 133)

An independent review conducted by INEQE exhorted the organisation to, "move beyond rhetoric and paper action plans. Beneficiaries, volunteers, staff and donors all need to see and feel the difference." (INEQE, 2018, p. 39)

In response to lessons learned inside the charity, Oxfam GB's incoming CEO, Dhananjayan Sriskandarajah, commented:

> The changes we need to make at Oxfam are both systemic and cultural. They include our policies and practices… But they also include our attitudes and behaviours.
> (Charity Commission, 2019a, p. 136)

So we can see that attitudes, behaviour and conduct are central to effective safeguarding, and that individuals need to both see and feel a guiding ethos. 'How we do things around here' – our culture – matters.

For many of us, culture used to be something which sat within the HR team's remit, if it was mentioned at all. It was perhaps covered during inductions and appraisals, but it was often a bolt-on, not taken seriously and not playing a meaningful part in the identity and day-to-day experience of an organisation. It was left to junior and mid-level staff to wrangle – with senior staff perhaps just paying lip-service to it but not actually applying it to themselves. That's been gradually changing as recognition has grown that culture drives performance, profit and impact.

But in many settings, a tension has persisted between the recognition of the importance of culture, and some of the deeply entrenched privileges which have traditionally come with seniority in hierarchical organisations. This tension is at the heart of the need for a commitment to a positive safeguarding culture to be interwoven with committed, accountable leadership.

Hierarchical organisations have historically been built on the seductive premise that the rules become less restrictive as you rise through the ranks. You have more leeway in your day-to-day job, and exceptions will be made for you because you are so valuable and important. These were the visible rewards for hard work, for excellence, or for staying in the favour of people who had the power to lift you up.

This is the system many of us will have experienced at work. It is only in the last few years that it has been routinely challenged. And one of the reasons for that challenge is the recognition that this system is the perfect breeding ground for abuse.

If the reward for seniority is impunity from the rules and norms applied to those further down the hierarchy, and the way to reach the top is to go along with bad behaviour, a culture of fear, disrespect and abuse prospers. It doesn't matter what the rules are, that you've signed a code of conduct and been on a course. If the culture says that those things don't really count for some people, then they will gradually and inevitably erode so that they don't really count for anyone.

What we also know is that failing to model positive values and behaviour in one aspect of conduct signals a lack of commitment to them in every area, and the culture is weakened overall. If the CEO routinely turns up late for work, or fails to step in when differences of opinion in meetings get overheated, or lets favoured colleagues off the hook when it comes to allocating out-of-hours cover, they are clearly signalling that rules and norms don't apply to them or the people in their circle. In that culture, the leader is demonstrating that with power comes impunity, and that it pays to side with them so that some of that impunity gets sprinkled on you too.

None of this behaviour directly involves sexual harassment, exploitation or abuse, but it will inevitably damage the organisation's safeguarding practice. What everyone in the organisation can 'see and feel' is that the CEO doesn't follow or apply the rules consistently, and they aren't committed to making tough ethical choices which might have a detrimental effect on themselves or their inner circle. Crucially, people with power in the organisation do not have to face the consequences of ignoring the rules. In that context, individuals will have come to understand that the deep level of trust needed to report abuse they have experienced or become aware of, which is likely to have been perpetrated by someone with some degree of seniority, simply doesn't exist in that organisation. So they keep quiet, abusers are emboldened, and a culture of covering up misconduct becomes deeply established. Even if this organisation has all the right training, policies and procedures, without the right culture and leadership the system won't work.

The report into the Charity Commission inquiry into allegations of harassment by senior staff at Save the Children UK took a detailed look at organisational culture and leadership. Its conclusions included the observation that:

Inappropriate behaviour could be seen as a cultural issue for the organisation. The Commission agrees with the 2015 culture review that:

> 'This is particularly the case as, with any culture, the behaviour of senior leaders has a powerful impact on the overall culture. Whatever values statements and policies say, people take their biggest behavioural cues from what their leaders are seen to role model and what they are seen to tolerate.'
>
> (Charity Commission, 2019b)

In the UK charity sector, Trustees also have a crucial role to play in defining and upholding a healthy organisational culture. They hire the Chief Executive, who is then accountable to them. Serious complaints about the CEO come to them for investigation and a decision. They have formal oversight of strategy and a legal responsibility to ensure that effective policies are in place and being upheld. They have significant obligations to ensure that systems and processes are in place to deter fraud and ensure that the organisation operates in line with its charitable purpose and the regulatory framework of the Charity Commission. They must ensure that the charity is maintaining high standards in safeguarding, appropriate to the work the organisation undertakes. Trustees are also required to protect the reputation of the charity.

While the expectations placed on charity trustees have grown considerably over the past two decades, the environment within which they volunteer their time has also changed significantly as the charity sector has come under increased media, political and public scrutiny. The reputational and professional peril of the intense spotlight of a critical news cycle has become something many in our sector have come to fear. Over the past decade, damaging initial headlines about UK charities such as the Royal British Legion (Plummer, 2019) and Kids Company (Weakley, 2022), amongst others, led to inaccuracies about charity practice becoming orthodoxies in the public's mind. Misunderstandings gained popular currency alongside facts and the more nuanced truths of both good and poor practice were only revealed months or years later in formal inquiries. By that time, the reputational damage had been done. Trustees had previously been largely invisible, and their voluntary contributions had been viewed as positive, both professionally and personally. Now they suddenly found themselves under scrutiny.

Following the 2018 safeguarding stories, the board Chairs at Oxfam GB, Save the Children International and Save the Children UK stood down. Trustees found themselves named and scrutinised in formal inquiries led by the Charity Commission and Parliament, which were picked up in media coverage. For senior establishment figures, eminent in their fields, this very public accountability risked serious damage to their reputations and careers.

Trustees of other organisations took note. Their regulatory responsibility to protect the charity's reputation was often now magnified by fears for their own individual standing. While this tended to promote support for a strengthening of internal governance and process, it also encouraged much greater consideration of the potential reputational impact of misconduct and complaints. Courageous boards rose to the challenge, while others opted for lower profiles, greater confidentiality, an aversion to risk and playing down of failure. This was at odds with the values-based leadership required for change, and risked undermining the efforts of their senior staff to build a more accountable leadership culture.

The Charity Commission inquiry into Oxfam makes the need for trustee-led openness and visibility very clear in the wider lessons it notes for all charities:

> Effective trustee boards lead by example, setting and owning the charity's values, setting the standard and modelling behaviours that reflect those values, and requiring anyone representing the charity to reflect its values positively. An effective culture of keeping people safe identifies, deters and tackles behaviours which minimise or ignore harm to people and cover up or downplay failures. Failures to protect people from harm should be identified and lessons learned and there should be full and frank disclosure, including to regulators. There should be clear consequences for anyone whose conduct falls short of what is required regardless of how senior they are. (Charity Commission, 2019a, p. 26)

Decision-making driven by a fear of information being leaked and misrepresented is at odds with the need for a leadership culture which role-models consistency, openness and accountability. Yet, it is exactly that combination of robust systems, with the role-modelling of values and conduct from the board of trustees, that is essential for effective safeguarding.

Healthy safeguarding organisational cultures

So how do we build and maintain healthy safeguarding cultures in our own organisations?

Earlier in this chapter, I shared the definition of a positive safeguarding culture which the leadership and culture working group established:

- An explicit safeguarding culture and ethos, with values and behaviours that are both articulated and lived at each level of the organisation
- A culture of curiosity, scrutiny and constructive challenge (with processes to underpin these behaviours)

These characteristics demand visible, consistent role-modelling from leaders. But what does values-driven leadership look like and how can we achieve it?

In 2023, the UK Parliamentary Committee on Standards in Public Life (CSPL) published the findings of a review of leadership practice across the public, private and charitable sectors in the UK (CSPL, *Leading in Practice*, 2023). It provides a wealth of lessons and case studies about ethical leadership, and champions the need for values-based leadership at all levels. In the introduction, the committee chair, Lord Evans of Weardale, states:

> Senior leaders must ensure that values are understood and embedded into all aspects of how their organisations operate – from the way leaders communicate with employees, to the priority given to developing good decision-making, to the approach taken to recruitment and performance management. While the tone from the top is critical, leadership matters throughout an organisation. Leaders at all levels have a fundamental role in exemplifying and helping their teams live up to the Principles in their day-to-day behaviours.
>
> (CSPL, 2023)

If leadership is vital in setting and maintaining the necessary systems and culture for effective safeguarding, how do we judge the impact we're having as leaders ourselves? Building on existing research and insights from practitioners and survivors, the cross-sector culture and leadership working group captured the impact of leaders on culture in seven areas:

1 *The extent to which their words match their deeds and how this is handled when they don't*
2 *The way in which they are seen to handle failure*
3 *The way in which their values are seen to be lived and acted out*
4 *The way in which their interactions and relationships with other senior managers are experienced by the wider organisation*
5 *The decisions they make about who is hired and who is fired, and why*
6 *The decisions they make about who is valued and rewarded, who isn't and why*
7 *The systems and processes that they champion and prioritise*

(Proudlove et al., 2021) (see Appendix 2).

Each point highlights a practical aspect of leadership. As a leader, ask yourself how you live up to each of these elements. Each question is rooted in practical reality: how you do things each day, and how this is seen and experienced by your colleagues. The categories encompass how you show leadership about systems and processes, hiring and managing staff, management culture and personal accountability.

Those seven aspects interrogate the intersection between compliance and culture, because effective safeguarding needs an interweaving of both. We need to ensure we have effective policies and processes, while paying equal attention to how we devise them, how we apply them, how we treat others and, crucially, the standards we apply to ourselves.

Our senior leadership teams must visibly demonstrate accountable conduct which actively champions organisational values. For example, do you attend and actively participate in every mandatory training and feedback session, or do you slip out part-way through because your diary is so busy? Or perhaps you sit at the back of the room checking your phone throughout the session, present but taking no part? If the training is important enough to be mandatory, you need to demonstrate that you take it seriously – not just in words, but in deeds, too. Turn up, join in, ask questions, say when you don't know the answer, encourage others to speak and acknowledge their contributions.

Your team notices your attitude as well as your actions. Everything you do, or don't do, is noticed and interpreted. So it is vital to actively demonstrate your commitment to the values as well as the process. This culturally driven approach supports strong compliance, and lasting behavioural change.

How do we apply these principles consistently across every aspect of our organisations? How do we make sure we have the right systems and processes in place, bolstered by the healthy culture we know we need in order to bring them to life? As part of our accountability, how can we bring our teams together to diagnose our weaknesses and build on our strengths?

Informed by our findings, the culture and leadership working group created a model showing the journey an organisation takes to achieve an effective safeguarding culture. We identified six areas of activity within which an organisation can move from non-compliance, to minimal compliance, and ultimately to achieving an effective safeguarding culture:

1 Policies and processes
2 Reporting
3 Safer programming
4 Survivor-centred approach
5 Safer recruitment
6 Organisational awareness

Under each category, we identified specific examples which act as indicators of where your organisation is on that continuum from non-compliance to minimal compliance and ultimately to achieving an effective safeguarding culture.

An example

Under policies and processes, a non-compliant organisation might not have a safeguarding policy at all, or if it does it is out of date and of a low standard. A minimally compliant organisation may have a policy, but it is rarely used and staff aren't fully aware of it. An organisation with an effective safeguarding culture has a robust policy which is a core part of everyone's induction, and has strong processes in place to back it up which are used and work well.

You can see a summary of all six areas in Appendix 2 at the end of this book.

Using these six categories, the working group developed a practical online tool for leaders to use with their own organisations. It uses supported discussion sessions to work through an assessment of your current position, and to help you to decide what steps you will take together to achieve an effective safeguarding culture. Your notes and decisions combine to create a downloadable action plan, with goals, dates and accountable individuals identified.

The working group developed the tool with Bond, and it is available online as a free resource for any organisation: https://safeguarding-tool.bond.org.uk/. There are two versions: one for small organisations and one for larger ones. The areas covered are the same, with the questions tailored to address the resource differences between different sizes of NGO. Since its launch in 2021, it has been used by hundreds of organisations around the world.

Conclusion

As leaders and NGOs, we have a fundamental obligation to do all we can to ensure the safety of everyone we work with, and for. Although sexual harassment, exploitation and abuse will be committed by one individual against another, organisations and leaders on whose watch they take place are also accountable for them. There is much we can, and must, do to deter perpetrators and protect individuals.

Basic safeguarding requires a strong compliance-based framework of rules, codes of conduct, systems, training, policies and processes. Truly effective safeguarding happens when that framework is combined with values-driven leadership. Organisations which make that shift are able to move from paper compliance into positive and effective safeguarding.

They do so by embedding cultures of curiosity, scrutiny and constructive challenge, championed from the top.

This holistic approach to safeguarding goes beyond policies and processes and takes us to the heart of what kind of leader we are. For many of us, it will require an uncomfortable shift away from a model of seniority which has served us and our careers well until now. It requires openness and vulnerability, a greater emphasis on communication and a willingness to listen – and to share power and decision-making, too. Seniority has traditionally provided insulation from the hurly-burly of organisational life and has muffled the criticisms of more junior staff. The insulation has been stripped away in recent years. Your staff will now make themselves heard, and you will need to listen.

As we saw during the COVID crisis and subsequently in the intensification of debates about anti-racism and decolonisation, your staff and those who support your organisation will demand that you listen to the voices of those who have first-hand experience or authentic expertise to offer. They will require you to explain how and why you are making decisions and that you include them in the process of doing so. Remote, hierarchical and unaccountable leadership, and the cultures which go with it, are no longer viable.

An ethical, accountable, inclusive "culture of curiosity, scrutiny and constructive challenge, with processes to underpin these behaviours" (Proctor et al., 2014) is necessary to achieve effective safeguarding. That this is also now recognised as the hallmark of effective leadership in our increasingly values-driven workplaces is one more incentive to embrace the challenge.

Further reading

1. Bond hosts an online tool for leaders to review, develop and monitor their organisational safeguarding culture (Proudlove et al., 2021). I recommend this to anyone either in a leadership role, or in a position to influence leadership, as an accessible and practical tool to engage with those issues.

References

Charity Commission for England and Wales, 2019a, *Statement of the Results of an Inquiry, Oxfam Registered Charity Number 202918*, 11 June 2019.

Charity Commission for England and Wales, 2019b, *Statement of the Results of an Inquiry, The Save the Children Fund (Save the Children UK) Registered Charity Number 213890*, 5 March 2019.

CSPL, 2023, *Leading in Practice*. Available at: https://assets.publishing.service.gov.uk/media/63cfb022e90e071bad20162d/CSPL_Leading_in_Practice.pdf [Accessed 8 August 2024].

HM Government, International Aid and Development, 2018, *Transcript of Speech by Secretary of State for International Development at Bond Conference 26 February 2018*. Available at: www.gov.uk/government/speeches/international-development-secretarys-speech-at-the-bond-conference [Accessed 6 August 2024].

INEQE Safeguarding Group Ltd (under the Supervision of the Statutory Inquiry into Oxfam by the Charity Commission), 2018, *Oxfam GB Independent Safeguarding Review Executive Summary & Recommendations*, p.39. Available at: https://shop.ineqe.com/blogs/news/ineqe-safeguarding-group-independent-review-into-oxfam-gb.

O'Neill, S, 2018, Top Oxfam staff paid Haiti survivors for sex. *The Times*, 9 February.

Plummer, J, 2019, Olive Cooke case enabled fundraising reform despite charities not being responsible, says former minister. *Third Sector* 20 September. Available at: www.thirdsector.co.uk/olive-cooke-case-enabled-fundraising-reform-despite-charities-not-responsible-says-former-minister/fundraising/article/1660206 [Accessed 7 August 2024].

Proctor, S, Galloway, R, Chaloner, R, Jones, C and Thompson, D, 2014, *The Report of the Investigation into Matters Relating to Savile at Leeds Teaching Hospitals NHS Trust*. Leeds: Leeds Teaching Hospitals NHS Trust.

Proudlove, S, Longley, F, Carter, C and Erooga, M, 2021, *Bond Safeguarding and Leadership Tool*. Available at: https://safeguarding-tool.bond.org.uk/faq [Accessed 6 August 2024].

Weakley, K, 2022, Charity Commission criticises Kids Company over failure to build up reserves. *Civil Society News*, 10 February. Available at: www.civilsociety.co.uk/news/charity-commission-criticises-kids-company-over-failure-to-build-up-reserves.html [Accessed 7 August 2024].

Wonnacott, J and Carmi, E, 2016, *Serious Case Review: Southbank International School* p.12.. Hammersmith & Fulham, Kensington & Chelsea and Westminster LSCB. www.icmec.org/wp-content/uploads/2016/02/Southbank-UK-Serious-Case-Review-and-Report.pdf.

Chapter 3

Aid workers

Personal risks, responses and recovery

Noreen Tehrani

Chapter objectives

By the end of this chapter, you will:

- have an awareness of the history of international aid and development;
- appreciate how humanitarian work affects humanitarian organisations, their workers and their functioning;
- understand the dynamics which can affect organisational and individual functioning.

Introduction

This chapter acknowledges the challenging role of aid workers in delivering emergency and development aid to groups, communities and countries. It would be relatively simple to discuss the symptoms and treatments of the clinical conditions aid workers commonly face. However, doing so would neglect the deeper causal factors, such as civil unrest, ethnic cleansing, disease and economic disadvantage, which contribute to mental health problems for aid workers and raise safeguarding concerns within the aid industry. Examined here is the history of international aid and development and how humanitarian work affects humanitarian organisations, their workers and their functioning.

Background

The role of the aid worker is to provide developmental and humanitarian support to countries and communities needing help to deal with a crisis or disaster or to develop the essential resources and capacities to enable the recipients to become resilient and flourish. In the past, humanitarian aid had been regarded as a short-term response to a specific crisis or disaster, focussed on saving lives and delivered to any country where internal resources are inadequate to cope with the immediate surge in demands. However, over time, the boundary between these aid functions has become blurred with a need for longer-term humanitarian aid, which can last for many years, often without the opportunity to undertake meaningful development activities.

Although many aid organisations are charities raising funds from the public through fundraising, a large proportion of their funding comes from governments. These governments use aid organisations and private sector providers to distribute humanitarian and development aid as an arm of their national and foreign policy. This can strongly influence where and how aid resources are delivered.

Inherent in aid work is the need to respond to the chaos of crises and disasters whenever and wherever they occur. Unsurprisingly, working with stressful and traumatic situations can affect the organisation in terms of its culture, climate and responses; therefore, recognising and responding appropriately to the signs of organisational distress is essential in preventing aid organisations from becoming traumatised and dysfunctional where unresolved trauma is played out between individuals and teams. Aid organisations must be mindful of the needs of their workers by ensuring they have the right policies, resources and support in place to ensure that the organisation and its workers are resilient, whilst remaining sensitive to the needs of their donors, aid recipients and workers.

The History of international aid and development

A recent UN assessment of the number of people affected by long-term crises has shown that over a billion people, or 16% of the world's population, need support (Global Humanitarian Assistance, 2022). The World Health Organization divides humanitarian disasters into four main groups

(Saulnier, Dixit et al., 2020). Natural events include flooding, landslides, forest fires, tsunamis, cyclones and earthquakes (McIntosh, 2019; Greene, 2015; Pasarros et al., 2017). Biological disasters include disease epidemics and pandemics caused by bacteria, viruses, parasites and insects spreading disease to humans, animals and plants (Rogers et al., 2020; Sheek-Hussein et al., 2021). Human-induced disasters include transportation crashes, infrastructure failures and chemical, biological, radiological and nuclear (CRBN) contamination risks (Maes et al., 2000; Sheikhbardsiri et al., 2018), and societal disasters include war, terrorism and ethnic cleansing (Chemtob et al., 2010; Paes and Basabe, 2007).

Many disasters could be avoided or mitigated in communities with robust infrastructures, effective health and emergency services and safe housing (Hartwig and Nguyen, 2023). However, even in communities with a high level of resilience some groups are at greater risk of harm, including those with disabilities, women, children and older people. Marginalised groups, including the homeless, refugees, LGBTQ+ groups and members of minority ethnic or religious groups, can also be vulnerable due to a lack of power to protect themselves (Joseph et al., 2023).

In addition to providing humanitarian assistance, aid workers are also involved in developing interventions to improve communities' health, infrastructure, transport, education, inclusion and security. In the past, the development of resources, skills, technologies and infrastructure often occurred when a stronger or more capable group took over or overwhelmed a less developed community, where self-interest made resources available to create infrastructures, transportation, manufacturing and social structures and so facilitate the gathering, manufacturing and movement of valuable goods and products for sale. An example from history, in Britain, the East India Company, created by Queen Elizabeth I in 1600 developed infrastructures within the colonies to facilitate trade (Miller and Stanczak, 2009). Religious activity has frequently been part of the process of building empires, with religious beliefs giving missionaries and their supporters a sense of purpose and moral authority. However, missionary activity became implicated in empire-building, leading to the loss of indigenous heritage and the imposition of cultural change.

Organisations in crisis

International aid organisations frequently support fragile countries with insufficient capacity, systems and communities to manage or mitigate violence, poverty, inequality, displacement and environmental and political degradation risks. Problems in fragile countries could be reduced or mitigated with greater attention to the nature of that fragility (Carment and Samy, 2019). Carment and Samy reported that when providing aid, consideration should be given to three characteristics critical in determining a move to a more stable state: *authority*, which is the power of the state to make laws, maintain control over its territory, provide public services and ensure the safety and security of its people; *legitimacy*, which is the extent to which the government is respected and trusted by the whole population and not a few interested groups; and *capacity* to increase the ability to mobilise and employ the aid resources to achieve a productive outcome. Carment & Samy reported that building capacity will not reduce fragility if issues of authority and legitimacy are not addressed. Leaving unpopular and unaccountable civilian and military governments to maintain control over the distribution of resources and other benefits can result in the benefits going to a small group of entrenched and unelected elites. Aid workers engaged in capacity building in fragile countries lacking authority, security and legitimacy can find themselves in situations where, to help a population needing support, they have to negotiate and work with illegitimate governments kept in power by an elite group who become the programme's primary beneficiaries. Aid workers can find the lack of progress challenging and may feel conflicted about working with groups whose values are not aligned with their aid organisation's humanitarian goals.

The role of aid organisations is to work in complex and sometimes chaotic environments and situations. To respond to these challenges, aid organisations must recognise that their structures will be affected and have to adapt (Ramalingam, 2013). Ramalingam argues that *"Conventional aid conceives of systems and problems, behaviours, relationships and organisations, and dynamics of change in a highly abstract, idealised and simplified way … these are poorly matched to the realities of the world"* (Ramalingam, 2013, p 360). Ramalingam describes the need to move from simple thinking, where systems and problems are manageable, to an increased understanding of complexity. In simple systems, change can be predicted and explained by a cause and effect assessment. Simple systems are attractive to aid organisations and donors as they are understandable, predictable and easy to audit. However, they are seldom found in practice, where random, uncontrollable events, such as civil conflict, flooding, or pandemics, can disrupt the best laid plans.

In a complex world, aid work involves the interaction of multiple independent factors in a state of constant flux. Complex systems can shift from complexity to chaos, a state where change is difficult to anticipate or predict and impossible to control. Cavanagh and Lane (2012) developed a model to explain the relationship between the three states (simple, complex and chaotic), highlighting the problems organisations face when dealing with increasing complexity (Figure 3.1).

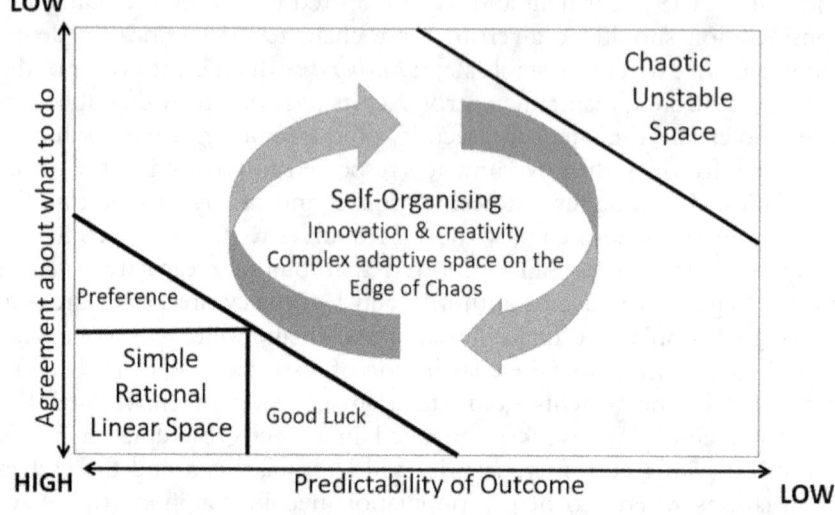

Figure 3.1 Simple, Complex and Chaotic Spaces Model.
Source: (Cavanagh and Lane, 2012).

The model shows where there is a high probability of outcome and agreement about what to do; plans can be made with an increased likelihood of achieving the desired result. As predictability levels fall in this space the outcome begins to rely on good luck, whilst where there is a lack of agreement on actions decisions may be based on the preferences of the aid organisation. In many situations in aid work, these simple linear relationships are rare. A more prevalent state has lower outcome predictability and a lack of agreement on what to do. The command and control systems dominating stable states do not work in complexity. Complexity requires aid workers at the front line to become directly involved in dealing with the on-the-ground situation, taking responsibility and being answerable for making decisions as trusted and self-organising groups. However, these situations are more challenging to manage and can lead to difficulties achieving funders' "simple" goals. Trying to balance the needs of funders with the complexity of the actual aid front-line requirements leads to aid organisations attempting to impose simple solutions on complexity, creating greater complexity, which can throw the front line workers into chaos, making them feel unheard and vulnerable.

This has an effect that goes beyond individual workers. It has been found that organisations that directly or indirectly expose their workers to traumatic events, testimony, or images can, over time, absorb the trauma into the organisational fabric and begin to exhibit behaviours commonly

Table 3.1 Trauma Symptoms and Behaviours Found in Traumatised Organisations

Avoidance:
• The *elephant in the room* syndrome with undiscussable topics. • *Corporate amnesia* with tacit knowledge being lost due to employees leaving or being silenced. • *Learnt helplessness and embitterment* due to a fear of making mistakes. • *Covering up* and hiding unpalatable information or wrongdoing.
Arousal:
• *Hyper-responsiveness* to information or situations, leading to knee-jerk responses. • *Over-reaction and punishment* of those perceived as challenging the status quo. • *Increased authoritarianism* in response to heightened anxiety. • Engagement in *risky personal behaviour*.
Re-experience:
• *A re-enactment* of past failures. • *Hyper-reactive* as if the organisation is constantly under current threat. • *Sensitivity to perceived triggers* related to past failures and a tendency to punish bearers of bad news. • A feeling of *guilt and shame* and a need for reparation or seeking forgiveness.

found in people living with PTSD (Bloom, 2011). Bloom identified several features that characterised traumatised organisations from her work in organisations. These symptoms were similar to the avoidance, arousal and re-experience symptoms experienced in PTSD in individuals. Table 3.1 illustrates the way that trauma symptoms create the behaviours of a traumatised organisation.

Aid organisations are particularly prone to absorbing the trauma, due to the nature of their work. A lack of organisational awareness can cause the organisation to act in a way that is insensitive and persecutory in terms of its processes, procedures and approach. Communication breaks down, there is a loss of trust and authoritarian management styles prevent the organisation from facing and dealing with challenges and change.

Playing out the drama

The Drama Triangle (Karpman, 1968) is useful in examining interpersonal relationships in groups and organisations by helping to visualise the unhelpful pattern that operates in stressed or traumatised groups. Each corner in the drama triangle corresponds to a role that a group

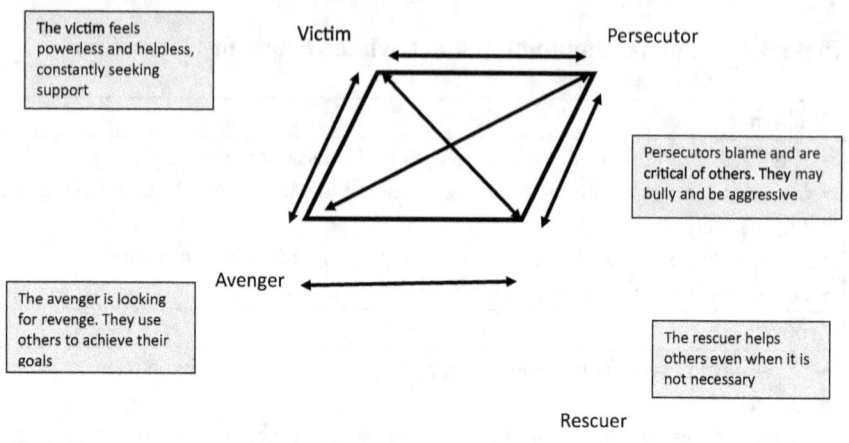

Figure 3.2 Roles within the Trauma Drama.
Source: Tehrani (2012).

member can play. The roles are Persecutor, who is powerful, critical and blaming; Victim, who feels helpless, powerless, pathetic and ashamed; and Rescuer, who wants to fix other people to make themselves feel worthwhile. Karpman described the way individuals may unconsciously prefer one of these roles. However, it is also possible to swap between these roles depending on the group's make-up and circumstances. Tehrani (2012) suggested that there was another role that should be included in a trauma drama, the Avenger. The Avenger is typically someone who has experienced conflict in the past and attempts to deal with their unresolved distress by acting on behalf of others. Tehrani proposes that the four roles interact (Figure 3.2). Each of the roles involves a compulsive maladaptive pattern of behaviour triggered by situations connected to an unresolved trauma from their past.

Players in the trauma drama may move places as illustrated below:

> A manager pressures one of their team to achieve a challenging goal (P). The team member felt unable to be assertive and negotiate additional time (V) and spoke to a colleague who told them they should report the manager to the CEO as the manager was a bully (A). The CEO asks HR to investigate the grievance. The manager is hurt and upset to be in this position (V) and cannot address the situation directly. Another team member feels sorry for the manager (R) and comes to the rescue, criticising the two team members for being underhanded and disloyal (P). The team stops functioning.

Whilst this scenario is fictitious, it is based on many similar stories commonplace in traumatised organisations. In the situation described, the trauma drama will likely be continued unless there is a recognition of the underlying issues which caused the problem in the first place. When an organisation is traumatised, it is hard to escape the trauma drama; solutions will be imposed, and retribution heaped on the perceived persecutor or person seen as threatening the organisational status quo.

What does surveillance data show?

Some humanitarian and other high-risk organisations have introduced psychological surveillance in response to their legal duty of care to their employees (Jachens, 2019). As part of an online psychological surveillance programme (Tehrani and Hesketh, 2018), 649 employees from four humanitarian charities were screened for mental health conditions. There were 479 (74%) women and 170 (26%) men with an average age of 37.3 years (range 23 and 66). Their results were compared with other organisations, including Police Safeguarding, Social Workers, Youth Safeguarding, Lawyers dealing with child abuse and teachers (Table 3.2). All the groups had significantly higher results than the general public. The humanitarian group had the highest levels of post-traumatic stress and secondary trauma and the second highest level of anxiety and depression.

Further analysis of the humanitarian aid worker's data was undertaken using stepwise regression, which identified the percentage of variance that personal and work-related factors could explain. The results for anxiety and depression were similar in that 67% of anxiety and 77% of depression scores could be explained by the aid worker having high levels of emotional sensitivity and exposure to job stress together with poorer attitudes towards their work. 61% of the increased levels of PTSD were explained by greater physiological responsiveness to stressors, a lack of sleep and practical support, and not understanding where their role fits into the organisation. The explanation for 48% of secondary trauma was lower levels of social support, increased exposure to trauma and a high level of sensitivity to others, leading to an increased intention to resign. It is important to note that exposure to trauma did not feature as a significant predictor of PTSD but was significant for secondary trauma. Anxiety and depression were associated with personal factors and job stress.

Table 3.2 Levels of Mental Health Conditions Found in Six Professional Groups Compared with the General Public

Clinical Symptom	Police (n = 855)	Social Work (n = 87)	Humanitarian (n = 649)	Youth Charities (n = 476)	Lawyers (n = 17)	Teachers (n = 23)	General Public
Anxiety	28%	42%	35%	15%	24%	22%	3.5%
Depression	33%	48%	40%	22%	29%	30%	8–12%
PTSD	13%	16%	21%	5%	18%	9%	3%
Burnout	20%	54%	28%	17%	47%	26%	NA
Secondary Trauma	19%	29%	32%	14%	47%	17%	NA

NA = Levels not available.

Case studies: Assessments and interventions

Most research into mental health problems in aid workers has sought solutions at an individual level. However, the evidence presented in this chapter has identified that many problems that lead to aid worker distress result from political or organisational failures and should be addressed at those levels. Bywater (2021) used the term the "Humanitarian Alibi" to describe how humanitarian activities conceal or respond to criticisms of political inaction in response to violent conflict and civilian suffering. Aaronson (2007), a past chief executive of Save the Children, clearly articulated this problem by recognising there was a failure to come to terms with long-running conflicts and human rights violations in many countries and that humanitarian and development aid is not a substitute for effective political action. In the ongoing situation between Palestine and Israel, aid has been used to support the Palestinian population in Gaza and the West Bank; however, the fundamental problems of creating a two-state solution have been neglected for years, allowing the situation to deteriorate. There is a clear issue where aid workers on the ground have been doing their best to meet the immediate and development needs of the civilian population without the commensurate political efforts being made to resolve the problems causing the crisis.

Government level

Aid workers engaged in supporting civilians caught up in conflict situations are exposed to the horror of war and conflict, but equally psychologically disturbing are the symptoms of Moral Injury (Lloyd et al., 2020) created by circumstances where their efforts are continually undermined and destroyed due to a lack of respect and trust in the government, to make laws, maintain control, provide public services and ensure safety for the benefit of the whole community.

> **Case study 1**
>
> A had been working in Kabul as an English teacher for senior school girls. They were enthusiastic and dedicated to learning. A was aware that there were problems with domestic violence and forced marriages. She was very distressed when she had to return to the UK when international forces pulled out of Afghanistan. A found it very difficult to adjust to living with her parents. She felt tremendous guilt for leaving the girls and worried about their future. She feels angry that so much has been done to destroy the Taliban and so little to help develop a fair and functioning civil society and infrastructure.

Assessment

A was found to have high levels of secondary and complex PTSD. She was depressed and experiencing moral injury related to her belief that her government and charity had abandoned the girls, and that she also carried some responsibility.

A's father had left the family when A was ten years old.

Intervention

A needed time to explore her experiences to understand the meaning of what had happened. She also looked at how her experiences in Afghanistan were similar to her feelings of abandonment by her father. She responded well to trauma-focused CBT, which gave her the tools to deal with her symptoms. At the end of the therapy, she decided that she did not want to return to working in fragile situations where there was no certainty of peace.

Organisational level

Aid organisations may find themselves trapped in situations where the major donors (governmental and community) want certainty over the outcomes to be expected from the resources expended, an issue discussed in Chapter 7 on the challenge of a standards-based approach to safeguarding.

This can lead to an increased need to provide evidence to demonstrate that the anticipated results have been achieved. Managers may begin to pressure front-line workers to deliver regardless of the difficulties encountered and the potential opportunities abandoned.

Case study 2

B was an aid worker based in the UK and was sent to undertake a project in her country of birth. She had a good understanding of the culture. She recognised that the approach was unlikely to be successful due to her failure to recognise the difficulties women face in becoming the primary breadwinners in the family. B talked to some of the local village leaders and identified ways around the issues. However, the project lead was not prepared to fund the required work. B returned to the UK and tried to raise her concerns about the project. She heard later that the original project had ended and there would be no follow-up.

Assessment

B had high symptoms of anxiety and depression. She had a low sense of coherence (Antonovsky, 1987) and a strong desire to leave the organisation. She felt she was being discriminated against by what she saw as an inflexible group of managers unwilling to consider any feedback that was not supportive of their ways of working.

> **Intervention**
>
> B was encouraged to examine the organisational dynamics to understand how decisions were made. She came to recognise that the pressures from donors for project feedback created difficulties for managers to make changes, and her direct approach increased their anxiety.
>
> B developed skills in dealing with stress and frustration and began to put her energy into developing influencing skills and identifying how her ideas could be aligned with the project's needs.

Policy and system level

Humanitarian organisations need policies and systems to ensure their workers', donors' and beneficiaries' health, wellbeing and safety. The power differential between the aid worker and the beneficiaries can lead to situations where beneficiaries can be abused (Javad et al., 2021). Organisational probity requires that standards of behaviour with colleagues and beneficiaries are clearly defined and upheld with systems for reporting inappropriate or abusive behaviour. During recruitment, it is appropriate to ensure that recruits do not have a history of abuse or other criminal activity and have the personal and physical resilience to undertake the aid work before deployment.

> **Case study 3**
>
> C had a history of physical, emotional and sexual abuse in her childhood. She had experienced periods of depression and an eating disorder whilst at university. She was recruited to work in a humanitarian organisation, initially in an administrative post, but she constantly sought deployment opportunities. She eventually was allowed to travel to a Middle Eastern country, and the day before she left

decided to walk to a park alone; after she set off, she noticed she was being followed and tried to escape. The man sexually assaulted her, but she did not tell anyone what had happened as she felt she was responsible.

When she returned to the UK, she experienced high levels of trauma symptoms, some related to the abuse she had suffered as a child. She sought help from her GP as she did not want anyone connected to her employer to know what had happened, and she was determined to seek future deployments.

Assessment
Although C had attended training in dealing with kidnapping, C had not considered herself in danger walking alone. She had not had counselling for the early life abuse or mentioned it when she saw a student counsellor for her eating problems. C was aware that other humanitarians had experienced physical and sexual attacks but saw they tended to play these events down. Psychological screening and surveillance for high-risk roles are required under the Health and Safety Legislation (HSE, 2013). The lack of an assessment of the psychological risks and the organisation's culture, which failed to embed and enforce personal security systems, put C in danger. The experience was traumatic, and there was no system for providing a post-trauma intervention.

Intervention
C was assessed by a psychologist who recognised that her early life experiences had predisposed her to failing to identify signals of danger. When she was trapped by the man, she froze and was unable to physically respond; only when she arrived home did she begin to experience the symptoms of trauma, which she tried to hide as she had done as a child. The screening results showed that she had symptoms of complex trauma and was referred for a programme of Eye movement desensitisation and reprocessing (EMDR) therapy (Tehrani, 2019). The advice to the organisation was to ensure that everyone being deployed should undergo psychological screening before and after deployments. There is also a need to have trained supervisors and peers who can deliver post-trauma support (Tehrani, 2023).

Individual level

It has been suggested that aid workers are of three types: missionaries, mercenaries and misfits (Warah, 2008); however, Stirrat (2008) suggests these typologies may be observed at different times in every aid worker depending on circumstances and career stage. Sirrat reflects that these behaviours are today's "white man's burden". The following case studies illustrate how pre-existing vulnerabilities and influences can create dysfunctional behaviours in the aid field.

Case study 4

D worked in communications and had a Master's Degree in International Relations. He was openly gay and active in the gay scene in the UK. He had been on several deployments related to refugees arriving in Greece and migrants trying to cross the channel. He was then deployed to a mainly Muslim country in North Africa. Whilst there, he used the internet to find a sexual partner. He went to meet the person on his own. The location was on a narrow street in the city. As he entered the house, he was grabbed and taken prisoner by two men and a woman. Throughout the night, they taunted him and degraded him by stripping him and forcing him to drink water from a dirty toilet. They continually threatened to kill him. In the morning, they forced him to go back to his hotel to get money before they would release him.

Assessment
The assessment showed that D had been diagnosed with ADHD in childhood and that he had a problem with hyperactivity, recklessness and difficulty with decision making. He knew there was some danger in meeting people outside the hotel but had met people this way before and believed he could handle the situation. He had been having some person-centred therapy focussed on building his self-esteem and coping skills. He resisted recognising that his behaviour was creating danger for himself and his colleagues. Working for a Humanitarian organisation gave him opportunities to live on the edge of danger, which he was unprepared to give up.

Intervention
D was offered an opportunity to talk about his experiences with a trauma counsellor. The safeguarding investigation decided to prevent

> him from being deployed. He continued to engage in risky behaviour, which included behaviour which brought him to the attention of the police. His employment was terminated, but he quickly found another charity role.

In our final case study, we show how good people can be found to have done bad things that have affected recipients, colleagues and their organisations. Some people may join aid organisations with the intention of abusing others; this is a tiny proportion of the abusers (House of Commons, 2020). Most abuse is undertaken by people who joined the organisation with good intentions but fell into carrying out abuse. The potential to commit illegal acts is widely distributed in society, and many adults will commit a crime at some time in their lives, e.g. speeding or failing to pay all due taxes. However, some people are more likely to commit crimes due to the difficulties they experience in managing their drives and desires (Banse et al., 2010). The propensity to abuse is influenced by genetic make-up (Baron-Cohen, 2011), personality (Dudeck et al., 2007), life experiences (Garrett, 2010) and an imbalance of power (Mngoma et al., 2016). The opportunity to abuse is determined by an interaction of individual and situational factors (Wortley, 2018). Offence-related situational factors include having contact with vulnerable people in an environment where there has been a breakdown of social or personal constraints on safeguarding. The stronger the drive to abuse, the more situational barriers will be crossed (Finkelhor, 1984). Offenders will create or seek out circumstances where offending is easier and less risky. Three levels of sexual offenders have been identified (Wortley and Smallbone, 2006): firstly, the predatory or persistent offender who is prepared to expend considerable energy in achieving their goals and who is difficult to deter; secondly, the opportunist offender who has problems in delaying self-gratification and they abuse because they can; and thirdly, the situational offenders where crimes occur in the heat of the moment, due to a failure of self-control (Cornish and Clarke, 2003).

> ### Case study 5
>
> E has been working for an aid organisation for ten years. He had significant experience in delivering developmental programmes. He was deployed to a country that had experienced devastation due to global warming with the aim of introducing more sustainable farming approaches. E was married and had two young children

living in England; he kept in contact via the internet and returned home every few months.

In his senior role, he regularly met with local leaders and would attend events where there was time to relax. At one of the events, one of his colleagues suggested that they invite two of the young women at the event to come back to their hotel for dinner. This event was the start of a series of sexual relationships with a series of young women. The situation became public knowledge when a 14-year-old girl became pregnant and asked the organisation for money to support the child.

Assessment
The situation was investigated by the organisation's HR/safeguarding team, who found that E had abused several young women; there was also an allegation of harassment from a member of staff. The psychological assessment showed that E was experiencing high levels of anxiety and depression; he was worried about losing his family and his job. He was discounting his responsibility for what he had done, suggesting that the women were not aid beneficiaries and the sex was consensual. His wife had left the family home with the children; she was independent and had a successful career. In the assessment, he was found to have been used to being in control and powerful. He had come from a family where no one talked about their emotions.

Intervention
E was supported through the investigation, and the press published details of his activities. His wife and family were affected by journalists outside the family home and many comments on social media. E was taken through a programme of counselling based on the Lucy Faithful Programme (Findlater, 2020), which helped him to recognise how he had been minimising his behaviour and blaming the victims for what had happened to them. The initial counselling was followed by couples therapy, where E and his wife looked at their relationship and the factors that had led to E becoming involved in multiple extramarital relationships with young girls.

Key messages

This chapter does not wish to suggest that aid organisations do not achieve anything; there are many people and communities that have been helped by the delivery of assistance and support at times of need. The main message is that without political engagement in dealing with the underlying problems, the activities of aid workers are often marginal and sometimes counterproductive in their responses to disaster and development needs due to the underlying complex structural issues left unaddressed (Pandi-Perumal et al., 2023). Unrecognised organisational problems cause many of the psychological injuries experienced by aid workers played out in the workplace (Bloom and Farragher, 2013). Although some psychological trauma is due to the primary trauma, where the aid worker is directly exposed to threats to their lives or to the death and suffering of the people they wish to support, much is due to the moral injury caused when they recognise that their efforts are inadequate or ineffective.

Further reading

- For those interested in a step-by-step approach for funders to consider their approach to safeguarding, the *ACF & FSC Safeguarding framework* (2021) offers helpful questions for consideration and discussion.
- Humentum's report *Breaking the starvation cycle: How international funders can stop trapping their grantees in their starvation cycle and start building their resilience* (2022) makes a convincing case that unrestricted funding contributes to keeping people safe.
- Catalyst 2023 brings together funders "walking the talk" in their open letter to shift funding practices. Their ten principles, including building trust and transparency, sharing power and supporting the whole organisation, all contribute to safer ways of working. https://shiftingfundingpractices.catalyst2030.net/
- Ramalingam, B. (2013) Aid on the Edge of Chaos, Oxford, Oxford University Press.
- Saari, S. (2005) A Bolt from the Blue: Coping with Disaster and Acute Trauma, London, Jessica Kingsley.
- Tehrani, N. (2004) Workplace Trauma – Concepts, Assessments and Interventions, London, Taylor Francis.
- Tehrani, N. (2010) Managing Trauma in the Workplace – Supporting Workers and Organisations, London, Routledge.

References

Aaronson, M. (2007) A holistic approach to the war on terror? Opinion 1-13 Nov 2007. Retrieved from www.hdcentre.org/search/node/A+holistic+approach+to+the+war+on+terror%3F

Antonovsky, A. (1987) *Unraveling the Mystery of Health. How people manage stress and stay well*. San Francisco: Jossey-Bass.
Banse, R., Schmidt, A. F., Clarbour, J. (2010) Indirect Measures of Sexual Interest in Child Sex Offenders: A Multimethod, Criminal Justice and Behaviour, 37, 319–335.
Baron-Cohen, S. (2011) Zero Degrees of Empathy: A New Theory of Human Cruelty, London, Allen Lane.
Bloom, S. (2011) Trauma Organised Systems and Parallel Process, In Tehrani (ed), Managing Trauma in the Workplace, Hove, Routledge.
Bloom, S., Farragher, B. (2013) Restoring Sanctuary: A New Operating System for Trauma-informed Systems of Care, Oxford, Oxford University Press.
Bywater, M. (2021) The humanitarian alibi: an overview and a redefinition, Journal of International Humanitarian Action, 6, 22. https://doi.org/10.1186/s41018-021-00106-7
Carment, D., Samy, Y. (2019) Aid Targeting to Fragile and Conflict-affected States and Implications for Aid Effectiveness, Politics and Governance, 7 (2), 93–102.
Cavanagh, M., Lane, D. (2012) Coaching psychology coming of age: The challenges we face in the messy world of complexity. *International Coaching Psychology Review*, 7 (1), 75–90.
Chemtob, C. M., Nomura, Y., Yehuda, R., et al. (2010) Impact of Maternal Posttraumatic Stress Disorder and Depression Following Exposure to September 11 Attacks on Preschool Children's Behaviour, Child Development, 81 (4), 1129–1141.
Cornish, D. B., Clarke, R. V. (2003) Opportunities, Precipitators and Criminal Dispositions: A Reply to Wortley's Critique of Situational Crime Prevention, In M. J. Smith, D. B. Cornish (eds), Theory and Practice of Situational Crime Prevention, MJ Criminal Justice Press. Monsey 111–124.
Dudeck, M., Spitzer, C., Stopsack, M., et al. (2007) Forensic Inpatient Male Sexual Offenders; The Impact of Personality Disorder and Childhood Sexual Abuse, The Journal of Forensic Psychiatry & Psychology, 18 (4), 404–506.
Findlater, D. (2020) Eradicating Child Sexual Abuse – What Does the World Think? Eradicating Child Sexual Abuse – What Does the World Think? Bromsgrove: Lucy Faithfull Foundation.
Finkelhor, D. (1984) Child Sexual Abuse: New Theory and Research, New York: The Free Press.
Garrett, L. H. (2010) Childhood Experiences of Adult Male Child Sexual Abusers, Issues in Mental Health Nursing, 31, 679–685.
Global Humanitarian Assistance (2022) United Nations Report on Humanitarian Affairs and Emergency Relief, Global Humanitarian Overview (unocha.org).
Greene, G. (2015) Resilience and Vulnerability to the Psychological Harm from Flooding: The Role of Social Cohesion, American Journal of Public Health, 105, 1792–1795.
Hartwig, T., Nguyen, T. T. (2023) Local Infrastructure, Rural Households' Resilience Capacity and Poverty: Evidence from a Panel Data from South East Asia, Journal of Economics and Development, 25 (1), 2–21.
House of Commons (2020) Progress on Tackling the Sexual Exploitation and Abuse of Aid Beneficiaries Seventh Report of Session 2019–21. p. 6. https://

committees.parliament.uk/publications/4275/documents/43423/default/
HSE (2013) Managing for Health and Safety, (hse.gov.uk).
Jachens, L. (2019) Humanitarian Aid Workers' Mental Health and Duty of Care, European Journal of Psychology, 15 (4), 650–655.
Javad, S., Chattu, V. K., Allahverdipour, H. (2021) Predictors among Protectors: Overcoming Power Abuse during Humanitarian Crisis through Effective Humanitarian Diplomacy and A Gender-transformative Approach, AIMS Public Health, 8 (2), 196–205.
Joseph, J., Sankar, H., Benny, G., Nambiar, D. (2023) Who Are the Vulnerable, and How Do We Reach Them? Perspectives of Health System Actors and Community Leaders in Kerala, India, BMC Public Health, 23, 748–759.
Karpman, S. (1968) Fairy Tales and Script Drama Analysis, Transactional Bulletin, 7 (26), 39–43.
Lloyd, C. S., Nicholson, A. A., Densmore, M., Théberge, et al. (2020) Shame on the Brain: Neural Correlates of Moral Injury event Recall in Posttraumatic Stress Disorder, Depression Anxiety, 38, 596–605.
Maes, M., Mylle, J., Delmeire, L. et al. (2000) Psychiatric Morbidity and Comorbidity Following Accidental Man-made Traumatic Events: Incidence and Risk Factors, European Archives of Psychiatry & Clinical Neuroscience, 250, 156–162.
McIntosh, T. (2019) Natural Disasters, European Journal of Educational Sciences, http://dx.doi.org/10.19044/ejes.s.v6a5
Miller, J., Stanczak, G. (2009) Redeeming, Ruling and Reaping: British Missionary Societies, the East India Company and India to China Opium Trade, Journal for the Scientific Study of Religion, 48 (2), 332–352.
Mngoma, N., Fergus, S., Jeeves, A., Jolly, R. (2016) Psychosocial Risk and Protective Factors Associated with Perpetration of Gender-based Violence in a Community Sample of Men in Rural KwaZulu-Natal, South Africa, South African Medical Journal, 106 (12), 1211–1215.
Paes, D., Basabe, N. (2007) Social Sharing, Participation in Demonstrations, Emotional Climate and Coping with Collective Violence after March 11th Madrid Bombings, Journal of Social Issues, 63 (2), 323–337.
Pandi-Perumal, S. R., van de Put, W. A. C. M., Maercker, A., Hobfoll, S. E., Kumar, V. M., et al. (2023) Harbingers of Hope: Scientists and the Pursuit of World Peace, Clinical Psychology in Europe, 5 (4), Article e13197, https://doi.org/10.32872/cpe.13197
Pasarros, C., Theleritis, C., Economou, M., et al. (2017) Insomnia and PTSD One Month after Wildfires: Evidence for an Independent Role of the "Fear of Imminent Death", International Journal of Psychiatry in Clinical Practice, 21 (2), 137–141.
Ramalingam, B. (2013) Aid on the Edge of Chaos, Oxford, Oxford University Press.
Rogers, D. P., Anderson-Berry, L., Bogdanova, A.-M. (2020) Covid-19 and Lessons from Multi-hazard Early Warning Systems, Advances in Science Research, 17, 129–141.
Saulnier, D. D., Dixit, A. M. and Nunes, A. R. (2020) Disaster risk factors; hazards, exposure and vulnerability, WHO Guidance on Research Methods for Health and Disaster Risk Management. World Health Organization. https://iris.who.int/handle/10665/345591

Sheek-Hussein, M., Abu-Zidan, F., Stip, E. (2021) Disaster Management of the Psychological Impact of Covid-19 Pandemic, Journal of Emergency Medicine, 14 (19), 1–10. Disaster management of the psychological impact of the COVID-19 pandemic – DOAJ.

Sheikhbardsiri, H., Yarmohammadian, M. H., Khankeh, H. R., et al. (2018) Rehabilitation of Vulnerable Groups in Emergencies and Disasters: A Systematic Review, Journal of Educational Health Promotion, 7, 15. https://doi.org/10.4103/jehp.jehp_159_17

Stirrat, R. L. (2008) Mercenaries, Missionaries and Misfits, Critique of Anthropology, 28, 406–425.

Tehrani, N. (2012) Beyond the Drama of Conflict, In Workplace Bullying: Symptoms and Solutions, Hove, Routledge.

Tehrani, N. (2019) Evaluation of a Trauma Therapy Programme within Emergency Service Organisations, Occupational Medicine, 69, 559–565.

Tehrani, N. (2023) Early Psychosocial Interventions for Individuals and Groups Affected by Disasters, Oxford Research Encyclopaedia, Psychology, https://doi.org/10.1093/acrefore/9780190236557.013.104

Tehrani, N., Hesketh, I. (2018) The Role of Psychological Screening for Emergency Service Responders, International Journal of Emergency Services, 8 (1), 4–19.

Warah, R. (2008) Missionaries, Mercenaries and Misfits an Anthology, Milton Keynes, Authorhouse.

Wortley, R. (2018) Child Sexual Abuse and Opportunity, In B. Gerben, S. D. Johnson (eds) The Oxford Handbook of Environmental Criminology, Oxford, Oxford University Press.

Wortley, R., Smallbone, S. (2006) Applying Situational Principles to Sexual Offences against Children, Crime Prevention Studies, 19, 7–35.

Chapter 4

Donor power and safeguarding

Enforcing compliance or enabling organisational safety?

Steina Bjorgvinsdottir, Shermin Moledina, and Karen Walker-Simpson

Chapter objectives

By the end of this chapter, you will:

1 Understand the important role philanthropic funders play in safeguarding and how this role can either help or hinder the organisations they fund.
2 Be aware of how issues of power in the funder/grantee partner relationship can undermine safeguarding efforts.
3 Understand the authors' analysis of the 2021 FSC study, *Funder Approaches to Safeguarding*, and how existing challenges in the funder/grantee partner relationship can be transformed into positive practices that contribute to good safeguarding.

Introduction

Traditionally, philanthropy has been conceptualised as voluntary giving for charitable causes, rooted in altruism and benevolence (Harvey et al., 2019). While philanthropy may have contributed to promoting social good, there are also inherent tensions around funder accountability and impact (Dark Matter Labs, 2022). The emphasis on scale and quantifiable outcomes can mean that grantseekers must contort their work to fit narrow application criteria and re-word their achievements into resource intensive reporting formats. Funder-driven priorities and funding restrictions can constrain the autonomy of grant recipients, fostering dependency and undermining local capacities (Dalen and McFerrin, 2023). Short-term funding cycles exacerbate power imbalances (Peace Direct, 2022, 2023; Sandvik, 2019) and grant recipients can often be too afraid to voice their concerns for fear of loss of funding.

Although the discourse around these issues has evolved significantly in recent years, funders continue to face criticism for their reluctance to speak about and address issues of power (Peace Direct, 2023). Movements for racial justice have prompted critical reflection on institutions and practices that perpetuate structural inequalities and white supremacy, and philanthropy is no exception. Philanthropic funders are having to grapple with how colonial legacies have shaped their wealth and how their practices contribute to inequalities in the distribution of wealth and power (Williams, 2019). There have been calls for increased accountability (Moran and Stone, 2016), including calls for measurements of success to shift away from simplistic impact metrics to encompass how well power is shifted (Williams, 2019; Shift the Power, 2019).

Recognising and addressing power imbalances is a central component of effective safeguarding but until recently, the role of philanthropic funders was rarely considered. Funders often have very limited interactions with people and communities, and as such, they have viewed safeguarding as a purely programmatic concern. This began to shift in 2018 when an inquiry into high-profile failures in safeguarding criticised funders for failing to prioritise safeguarding as 'core to delivering a safe and proper service' and treating it as an optional 'add-on' (IDC, 2018, p. 40). The media and political scrutiny that followed prompted a new focus on the role of funders in raising safeguarding standards. Leading agencies revised their requirements to make clear that those distributing funds had a responsibility to ensure recipients had effective safeguarding measures in place (Charity Commission, 2018; DfID, 2018) and 22 governments from around the world signed commitments to raise standards on safeguarding in their own organisations and in the organisations they fund (DfID, 2018).

This chapter explores the role of philanthropic funders in supporting efforts to keep people safe and examines the complexities of donor power and trust within this. Given the relatively recent focus on safeguarding within philanthropy, there are still very few empirical studies examining this issue. To date, the only in-depth study to focus exclusively on this issue was conducted by the Funder Safeguarding Collaborative (FSC) in 2021 and written by one of the authors of this chapter (Walker-Simpson, 2021a). The Collaborative is a global network of grant-making organisations committed to strengthening organisational cultures and practices that keep people safe. The study considered the challenges and opportunities for funders to integrate safeguarding within their grant-making and included a desktop literature review as well as an online survey and focus groups with funders, grant recipients, and sector experts across Africa, Asia, Europe, Latin America, and North America. This chapter outlines potential challenges in the way funders use their power to influence safeguarding as well as the positive practices that showed potential for replication. Insights from the FSC study are supplemented by research from others working in the humanitarian and development sector as well as from within the philanthropic eco-system.

Terminology

Safeguarding is defined differently from funder to funder (Sandvik, 2019). The definition of safeguarding used in this chapter is the one adopted by the Funder Safeguarding Collaborative. It considers measures aimed at preventing and responding to all forms of harm, abuse, and exploitation. The definition is not restricted to the protection of any specific group but includes efforts to safeguard all individuals who come into contact with funders and the organisations they support (Walker-Simpson, 2021a).

Funders refers to agencies involved in philanthropic giving through a variety of vehicles, including family foundations, corporate foundations, donor advised funds, intermediaries who receive funding from the previous categories and grant onwards to non-profit organisations, movements or individuals. Although FSC focuses on the work of philanthropic funders, the challenges and positive practice highlighted in this chapter are also highly relevant to bilateral and government funders.

Grantee Partners refers to all organisations who receive grant funding to support their work, irrespective of location. This term encompasses service delivery and non-service delivery organisations. It also includes organisations of different sizes and structures, from small community-based groups to large international organisations.

Underlying challenges

The FSC study identified four cross-cutting challenges that have the potential to undermine the effectiveness of funder efforts to strengthen safeguarding within their own institutions and the organisations that they fund.

A particular issue is compliance over contextualisation, impeding organisational ownership of safeguarding within grantee organisations. Compliance is further complicated by inconsistent expectations which leave grantee partners having to guess what is expected of them and use valuable resources to satisfy funder requirements. There is a lack of recognition of the knowledge of grantee partners and the communities they support, along with the limited knowledge of funders when it comes to serious safeguarding incidents, which may result in survivors being placed at further risk.

All of these challenges are compounded by the assumption that the resourcing of safeguarding should be shouldered by grantee partners and with little to no support from funders and the inherent power inequalities in the funder-grantee relationship.

Compliance not ownership

Due diligence checks play an important role in philanthropy. They help ensure funding has the desired impact by checking eligibility and ensuring appropriate controls are in place to prevent the misuse of funds (Chukwudi, 2023). Increasingly, safeguarding forms an important component of due diligence, with applicants expected to demonstrate that they have specific measures in place to qualify for funding. These requirements act as powerful incentive and have been identified as 'the most significant' factor in motivating improvements in safeguarding (Rhind and Owusu-Sekyere, 2018, p. 125). Despite the value of due diligence, several challenges still exist.

The FSC study found that the pressure to distribute money in a timely manner can make it difficult to conduct meaningful assessments at the application stage.

This challenge is accentuated by the fact that very few funders have dedicated safeguarding personnel, so checks are often conducted by individuals with a limited knowledge of safeguarding. Often these personnel are not on the ground and not familiar with the context, which complicates things further. In the absence of time and expertise, funders may resort to a reductive 'tick box' approach where safeguarding is assessed by measuring compliance against a generic checklist of policies and procedures. While policies and procedures have an important role to play in safeguarding, what exists on paper may not accurately reflect practice (Walker-Simpson, 2021a; IDC, 2018; Feather et al., 2020). Organisations may simply cut and paste policies to ensure they can access funding, while failing to implement and embed safeguarding in practice (Walker-Simpson, 2021a; Bond, 2019). Conversely, some organisations with strong practice may miss out on funding simply because they haven't documented their practice into the required procedures (Walker-Simpson, 2021a).

Similar problems persist once funding is approved. Where gaps are identified at assessment stage, some funders may require grantee partners to develop policies or implement new safeguarding measures as a condition of funding. Grantees can feel as though they have little control over the changes and feel compelled to comply, even if the measures appear unrealistic and unsustainable in their context (Walker-Simpson, 2021a). Too often, existing good practice is overlooked, and changes are determined by the funder rather than the organisation themselves (Walker-Simpson, 2021a; Bond, 2019). This undermines local ownership and contributes to the perception of safeguarding as a funder-driven, compliance issue rather than a means to strengthen organisations and their programmes (Walker-Simpson, 2021a; Bond, 2019).

Inconsistent expectations

Although many funders now impose safeguarding requirements, the lack of consistency in how 'safeguarding' is defined (Sandvik, 2019) inevitably leads to inconsistency in the assessment criteria that are established. While some funders refer exclusively to 'child safeguarding', others require applicants to have measures in place that safeguard both children and adults. Over recent years, many funders have placed particular emphasis on the prevention of sexual exploitation and abuse, and more recently harassment, often referred to as PSEA or PSEAH, while others take a more holistic approach that encompasses all forms of harm. These inconsistencies create confusion and uncertainty for organisations applying for funding and increase the pressure on organisational resources as applicants must fulfil different requirements depending on the demands of each individual funder (Walker-Simpson, 2021a).

This challenge is accentuated when funding organisations across diverse geographical contexts. The term safeguarding originates in the UK and is often poorly understood in other contexts (Walker-Simpson, 2021b). Although organisations may already take steps to keep people safe, they do not necessarily recognise these as 'safeguarding' measures and so struggle to demonstrate compliance with funder requirements simply because they are unclear about what is expected (Walker-Simpson, 2021a; Bond, 2019). Small grassroots organisations are disproportionally affected as they often have less contact with international agencies and may therefore be completely unfamiliar with the concept of safeguarding as defined by international agencies (Walker-Simpson, 2021a). While funder requirements can motivate action, the failure to listen to those who are implementing the work, and recognise how they keep people safe, can lead to resentment and may ultimately undermine the effectiveness of safeguarding if it is discounted as an alien concept that lacks relevance in other contexts.

Inadequate resources

Research by Brunel University identified 'resources' (time, human, financial) as instrumental in shaping 'the nature, and crucially, the quality of safeguarding within an organisation' (Rhind and Owusu-Sekyere, 2018, p. 156). Within international development, the availability of resources is largely determined by the policies and practices of international donors (Anderson et al., 2012). Ironically, although donors have increased their expectations around safeguarding, they rarely provide the resources necessary to do this effectively (IDC, 2018; Walker-Simpson, 2021b). This was underlined in a report by Humentum (2022) which found that safeguarding was the least resourced function within the organisations of study participants, with 54% of organisations reporting that they were unable to secure funding for safeguarding and a quarter saying this meant they were unable to implement the required safeguarding measures.

Even where funding is provided, funders often don't recognise the true costs associated with effective safeguarding. While some funders allow organisations to include one-off costs such as policy development or training in their budget, the ongoing cost of employing staff with safeguarding expertise is frequently excluded. This can seriously undermine the effectiveness of safeguarding as organisations simply can't afford suitably skilled staff or ensure existing staff have the time and capacity to embed safeguarding or respond to safeguarding incidents. Resource challenges are particularly acute for smaller organisations as, unlike larger NGOs, they are unable to absorb the cost of safeguarding into overhead budgets across multiple sources of funding (Walker-Simpson, 2021b). This can undermine the effectiveness of safeguarding as managers and front-line staff can be reluctant to implement measures that they perceive as unrealistic given local resource constraints (Austin and O'Neil, 2013; Rhind and Owusu-Sekyere, 2018).

In fact, the way that funders approach safeguarding can inadvertently add to the pressure on already limited resources. The FSC study found that bureaucratic assessments can mean that applicants divert resources away from service delivery to ensure that they can demonstrate compliance with funder requirements. Where improvements are required, funders often impose unrealistic timescales leading to superficial changes which fail to shift the organisational culture or day-to-day practices. Perhaps the area of greatest concern is around the reporting of safeguarding incidents.

Reporting to funders can divert time and resources away from active case management, particularly where strict timescales exist or where organisations have multiple funders to inform. While the intention may be to improve accountability and ensure an effective response, funder requirements can actually have the inverse effect with the funder's need being prioritised over those of the survivor as organisations fear that failure to comply will result in funding being withdrawn (Walker-Simpson, 2021a).

Lack of knowledge and understanding

While funders emphasise the importance of safeguarding policies and procedures in the organisations they fund, they often fail to implement similar policies and procedures in their own organisations. Although attitudes are changing, the FSC study found that many senior leaders within funder organisations still perceive safeguarding as primarily the responsibility of service delivery organisations. This leads to a lack of priority being placed on safeguarding, and insufficient resources being allocated for training or employing staff with relevant expertise. The failure to implement safeguarding in their own organisations can undermine the credibility of funders and lead to a mistrust around funder motivations including further exacerbating the power differential as different standards are being required. In addition, the absence of training or support for grant managers can limit their ability to both assess and support safeguarding in the organisations they fund (Walker-Simpson, 2021a).

The lack of knowledge and expertise within funders is most worrying in relation to their response to safeguarding incidents as funders may require actions that expose survivors to further harm (Walker-Simpson, 2021a). In the FSC study, concerns were raised about the amount of personal information that funders request, as this compromises confidentiality and may increase risks as many funders did not have adequate protocols in place to manage such sensitive data (Walker-Simpson, 2021a). Grantee partners were particularly worried that funders might require them to report cases to the authorities without understanding that in some contexts, this can expose both survivors, organisations, and witnesses to additional harm (IDC, 2018). Unfortunately, the power imbalance inherent in the funding relationship may mean that NGOs feel compelled to follow funder instructions even where these may not be in the best interest of those involved, as they risk losing their funding if they do not comply (Walker-Simpson, 2021a, 2021b).

Positive practices

Despite these challenges, philanthropy has the opportunity to do things differently. Recent trends have shown that there is flexibility to involve and learn from grantee partners and find solutions to difficult and complex problems (Dalen and McFerrin, 2023). Given the level of power held by funders, they have the ability to set the tone, including around safeguarding (ICVA, 2024) and lead the way by recognising the knowledge and expertise held by grantee partners (Shift the Power, 2019), responding to partner requests to adequately resource safeguarding, and importantly, adding credibility by developing safeguards in their own organisations.

The FSC study identified four positive practice principles which, if applied by funders, can help address many of the challenges highlighted above, and allow a more constructive and meaningful approach to strengthening safeguarding within philanthropic institutions and in the organisations that they fund.

Organisational ownership

In recent years, there have been increasing calls for a move towards trust-based philanthropy that emphasises the knowledge and expertise that exist in people and communities, and the organisations serving them (Scott et al., 2020). This doesn't mean that funders remove their checks and accountability expectations altogether but rather that they approach these differently by de-centring themselves to instead centre local knowledge and promote local ownership (Chukwudi, 2023; Scott et al., 2020; Shift the Power, 2019). This message emerged strongly from the FSC study into safeguarding, which emphasised the need to move away from imposing one-size-fits-all requirements towards a strength-based approach that values and supports existing good practice (Walker-Simpson, 2021a; Bond, 2019). Focusing on strengths not only increases organisational ownership but ensures changes are more relevant and sustainable as they are founded on existing ways of working (Walker-Simpson, 2021a, 2021b).

To achieve this, the FSC study emphasised the need for 'curiosity not compliance' (Walker-Simpson, 2021a, p. 13) when assessing safeguarding. Criteria or standards should act as framework to help assessors explore safeguarding rather than a rigid checklist that ignores the specificities of the local context (Rhind and Owusu-Sekyere, 2018; Kaviani Johnson and Sloth-Nielsen, 2020; Walker-Simpson, 2021b). Indeed, funders can often gain a better understanding of how measures are implemented by asking questions, requesting practical examples, and providing space for organisations to explain how they approach safeguarding in their context (Walker-Simpson, 2021a). In engaging in dialogue, funders need to demonstrate willingness to listen and learn, accepting that they do not understand the nuances of safeguarding in different organisational and geographical contexts. Even if funders choose to review policies, they should look for evidence that the policy has been tailored to the specific organisation and recognise that effective safeguarding requires a holistic approach where it is integrated into organisational systems and routines (Walker-Simpson, 2021a; James, 2020; Rhind and Owusu-Sekyere, 2018).

When supporting organisations to strengthen safeguarding, it is also important not to rely on a checklist of tangible outputs such as policies and training. Instead, the aim should be for safeguarding to be internalised within the organisation's culture and day-to-day practice, which takes time. Accordingly, action plans and timescales need to be flexible, acknowledging the other demands on the grantee and adjusting project milestones as needed (Walker-Simpson, 2021a; James, 2020; Bond, 2019). It is important that support is provided by experts who are familiar with the organisation's area of programmatic intervention and that they understand the operating context (Walker-Simpson, 2021a; James, 2020). In regions where it is challenging to find safeguarding specialists, peer-to-peer learning can be helpful, ensuring learning is grounded in practical realities, and can open up space for more honest dialogue (Walker-Simpson, 2021a). However, these spaces need to be properly facilitated and the competitive funding environment means that peer learning tends to be more effective where participants can build relationships of trust over time (Walker-Simpson, 2021a).

Two-way communication

Building trust requires clarity in expectations, honesty, and transparency (Chukwudi, 2023). To avoid confusion, it is important that funders are transparent about their expectations around safeguarding by publishing their requirements and taking care to ensure these are understood (Walker-Simpson, 2021a; James, 2020). In order to move safeguarding away from compliance, the FSC study repeatedly heard about the importance of conveying 'why' funders viewed safeguarding as important rather than simply dictating 'what' measures organisations had to have in place. This is particularly important when it comes to requiring grantee partners to report safeguarding incidents, as this involves highly sensitive data and funders need to have a justifiable rationale that is consistent with their priorities and values (Walker-Simpson, 2021a).

Effective communication is not one way, however. Too often, funders are viewed as remote institutions who provide funding but without engaging in meaningful dialogue with the organisations they fund. Opening a space for two-way communication emerged in the study as one of the most effective ways for funders to understand and improve safeguarding. At the assessment stage, adopting a discussion-based approach helps shift the focus away from compliance and helps ensure a shared understanding of what is meant by safeguarding and why it is important. Normalising discussions about keeping people safe during ongoing monitoring helps to ensure safeguarding is a critical component of programme delivery and allows progress to be acknowledged which then increases motivation (Walker-Simpson, 2021a; James, 2020). While Dalen and McFerrin (2023) argue that funders should approach due diligence as part of relationship building, the FSC study suggests that more relational approaches are beneficial at all stages of the grant cycle as it helps demonstrate the funder's willingness to listen and learn which, in turn, builds mutual understanding and trust and balances out power relations.

Realistic resources

Alongside more opportunities to discuss safeguarding, trust also relies on the provision of resources and funders 'putting their money where their mouth is' (Walker-Simpson, 2021b). If funders acknowledge that safeguarding is a critical component of safe and effective project delivery, this confers on them the responsibility to provide funding for safeguarding, as standard (Walker-Simpson, 2021a; IDC, 2018). Funding should extend beyond the development of policies to cover the costs associated with implementation, and there should be a recognition that small grassroots organisations may have higher costs and require higher levels of assistance. Although some funders have already begun to address this by providing unrestricted funding, supplementary grants, or allowing a percentage of the main grant to be allocated to safeguarding, there is need for greater flexibility and trust in an organisations' ability to use funding where it is needed most (Panorama Global, 2023).

Trust is particularly important where funders expect grantees to inform them of safeguarding incidents which requires proactive efforts to build a relationship of trust, including steps to address the perception that funding will be removed if cases are reported. While some funders felt the right to suspend or withdraw funding was important, most respondents to the FSC study felt that funding should not be removed if the grantee is taking the issue seriously and initiating action to address the concerns (Walker-Simpson, 2021a). Equally, if cases highlight gaps in organisational safeguarding, funders should also consider providing resources and support to address these gaps. In some regions, strengthening the quality of response does not simply imply providing funding to cover the grantee's costs but wider investment to improve the availability of services for survivors (Walker-Simpson, 2021b).

Even in cases where suspending funding is deemed necessary, decisions should be based on a clear assessment of risk, including the risks that might be generated to the survivor, programme participants and communities by the removal of funds. This may mean that funders release some funds to allow critical work to continue or to ensure the organisation has sufficient resources to ensure the safeguarding incident is investigated and addressed (Walker-Simpson, 2021a).

Walking the talk

Although funders generally have less direct contact with people and communities, the imposition of requirements without addressing safeguarding in their own organisations can lead to resentment and mistrust (Walker-Simpson, 2021b). Rather than simply requiring changes in the organisations they fund, there is a need for 'mutual accountability' in which funders 'walk the talk' (Anderson et al., 2012; Walker-Simpson, 2021b). Although funders have a different role, the safeguarding measures that should be in place are not dissimilar to those that many already require of their grantees. Funders need to develop their policies and procedures to demonstrate their commitment to safeguarding and to guide practice. There should be awareness raising and training, although this should be tailored to needs of funders as this helps staff see how safeguarding is relevant to their day-to-day work as a grant-making organisation (Walker-Simpson, 2021a). The engagement of senior leadership is critical, and it is particularly important for funders, as leaders, to articulate why keeping people safe should be a priority even though the funder may not be engaged in direct service delivery.

The FSC study further emphasised the need for designated staff who hold safeguarding responsibilities to have higher levels of training and support. Grant assessors are likely to need specific training so they can make informed judgements about what types of safeguarding measures are reasonable and appropriate across different organisational and geographical contexts. While grant managers should be encouraged to discuss safeguarding as part of their monitoring, they should not feel under pressure to become safeguarding experts. Rather, they should act as a champion for safeguarding and can help signpost grantees to any support they may need (James, 2020). Given the risks involved, it is particularly important that staff who receive safeguarding reports have adequate knowledge and experience. It may not be possible or proportionate for all funders to employ a designated safeguarding lead, but care is needed to ensure staff managing concerns have additional learning opportunities and that they have access to support and advice when needed (Walker-Simpson, 2021a).

Conclusion

This chapter has explored the complexities surrounding the power held by funders and the implications this has on the application of safeguarding requirements of grantee partners. The traditional narrative of philanthropy, rooted in altruism and benevolence, has been challenged by critiques highlighting the inherent tensions around funders setting the agenda. Despite recent shifts in discourse towards increased accountability and recognition of power imbalances, funder approaches on safeguarding can still be improved.

The study conducted by the Funder Safeguarding Collaborative (FSC) in 2021 shed light on key challenges faced by philanthropic funders in their efforts to support safeguarding initiatives. These challenges include compliance mentalities, inconsistent expectations, inadequate resources, and lack of knowledge and understanding, which underscore the need for re-evaluation of existing approaches and a new way forward.

However, amidst these challenges, positive practices have emerged, offering pathways for a more constructive and meaningful approach to safeguarding within philanthropic funders and the organisations they fund. These positive practices, rooted in principles of organisational ownership, two-way communication, realistic resource provision, and walking the talk, offer promising avenues for addressing the intricacies of safeguarding, gradual release of funder power and increased trust.

Central to these positive practices is a shift towards trust-based philanthropy, which acknowledges and values the knowledge and expertise of grantee partners and communities. By ceding power and adopting strength-based approaches that centre local knowledge and promote local ownership, funders can foster more meaningful and sustainable safeguarding practices. Moreover, fostering two-way communication, transparency, and clarity in expectations can enhance trust and understanding between funders and grantee partners, paving the way for more effective collaboration and ultimately, higher impact.

Ensuring realistic resource provision for safeguarding in grantee organisations, including funding for policy development, implementation, and ongoing support, is essential for the success of safeguarding efforts. Funders must demonstrate their commitment to safeguarding by investing in their own internal policies, procedures, and staff training, thus leading by example and fostering mutual accountability.

While the challenges surrounding funder power and safeguarding in philanthropy are significant, the emergence of positive practices offers hope for a new way forward. By embracing principles of trust, communication, realistic resource provision, and internal accountability, philanthropic funders can let go of power, reshaping their roles and fostering safer and more empowering environments for grantee partners and the communities they serve.

Key messages that we would leave you with are that:

- Philanthropy aims to enhance social good but often imposes funder-driven priorities that can constrain grant recipients. This can lead to dependency, undermine local capacities, and create power imbalances.
- Funders are criticised for not addressing power dynamics and colonial legacies. Recent scrutiny has pushed funders to prioritise safeguarding, ensuring grant recipients have measures to prevent harm, abuse, and exploitation.
- Compliance-focused funder approaches hinder grantee ownership of safeguarding. Inconsistent expectations and rigid requirements can lead to resource strain and superficial compliance, rather than the implementation of meaningful, context-specific safeguarding practices.
- Effective safeguarding needs adequate funding. However, funders often fail to consider, provide, or prioritise adequate resources that allow grant recipients to successfully implement safeguarding measures.

- Safeguarding is enhanced when funders embrace the values of trust-based philanthropy, grantee expertise, and promote organisational ownership. Clear communication, flexible support, and mutual accountability are crucial. Funders must also implement robust safeguarding within their own organisations to build trust and credibility.

Further reading

- For those interested in a step-by-step approach for funders to consider their approach to safeguarding, the *ACF & FSC Safeguarding framework* (2021) offers helpful questions for consideration and discussion. https://fundersafeguardingcollaborative.org/resources/acf-fsc-safeguarding-framework-for-foundations-2/
- Humentum's report *Breaking the starvation cycle: How international funders can stop trapping their grantees in their starvation cycle and start building their resilience* (2022) makes a convincing case that unrestricted funding contributes to keeping people safe. https://humentum.org/wp-content/uploads/2022/03/Humentum-ACR-Research-Report-FINAL.pdf
- Catalyst 2030 brings together funders 'walking the talk' in their open letter to shift funding practices. Their ten principles include building trust and transparency, sharing power, and supporting the whole organisation, all contributing to safer ways of working. https://shiftingfundingpractices.catalyst2030.net/

References

Anderson, M., Brown, D., and Jean, I. (2012) *Time to Listen: Hearing People on the Receiving End of International Aid,* Cambridge, Massachusetts: CDA Collaborative Learning Projects.

Austin, L., and O'Neil, G. (2013) The Joint Standards Initiative Global Stakeholder Consultation. London: ODI. [online]. Available at: https://alnap.org/help-library/resources/the-joint-standards-initiative-global-stakeholder-consultation-report/ (accessed 3 March 2024).

Bond (2019) *Safeguarding in successful partnerships – change statement* [online]. Available at: www.bond.org.uk/wp-content/uploads/2022/03/safeguarding_in_successful_partnerships_-_change_statement.pdf (accessed 4 April 2024).

Charity Commission for England and Wales (2018) *Safeguarding and protecting people for charities and trustees* [online]. Available at: www.gov.uk/guidance/safeguarding-duties-for-charity-trustees (accessed 29 April 2024).

Chukwudi, O. (2023) *Philanthropy: What's trust got to do with it?* [online]. Available at: https://shiftthepower.org/2023/05/23/philanthropywhats-trust-got-to-do-with-it/ (accessed 28 January 2024).

Dalen, K. B., and McFerrin, T. L. (2023) Relational Philanthropy. *Stanford Social Innovation Review*, 22(1), 61–62. https://doi.org/10.48558/D66X-ZS15

Dark Matter Labs (2022) *Beyond the Rules. Funding public good in complexity: four interrelated propositions*.[online]. Available at: https://drive.google.com/file/d/1NIw_EUu6cDevJyBN9xQmoyYLrWWY7igg/view (accessed 21 August 2025).

Department for International Development (DfID) (2018) *Commitments made by donors to tackle sexual exploitation and abuse and sexual harassment in the international aid sector* [online]. Available at: https://assets.publishing.service.gov.uk/government/uploads/system/uploads/attachment_data/file/749632/donor-commitments1.pdf (accessed 3 March 2024).

Feather, J., Martin, R., and Neville, S. (2020) *Global Evidence Review of Sexual Exploitation and Abuse and Sexual Harassment (SEAH) in the Aid Sector*, London: Resource and Support Hub [online]. Available at: https://safeguardingsupporthub.org/sites/default/files/2021-03/RSH_Global_Evidence_Review_Final_Design_V5.pdf (accessed 3 March 2024).

Harvey, C., Maclean, M., and Suddaby, R. (2019). Historical Perspectives on Entrepreneurship and Philanthropy. *Business History Review*, 93(3), 443–471.

Humentum (2022) *Breaking the starvation cycle: How international funders can stop trapping their grantees in their starvation cycle and start building their resilience* [online]. Available at: https://humentum.org/wp-content/uploads/2022/03/Humentum-ACR-Research-Report-FINAL.pdf (accessed 2 April 2024).

ICVA (2024) *Funding well: A path towards values-aligned, trust-based solidarity* [online]. Available at: https://d1h79zlghft2zs.cloudfront.net/uploads/2024/02/CHS-Alliance-Funding-Well-report.pdf (accessed 12 April 2024).

International Development Committee (IDC) (2018) *Sexual Exploitation and Abuse in the Aid Sector: Eighth Report of Session 2017–19*, London: International Development Committee [online]. Available at: https://publications.parliament.uk/pa/cm201719/cmselect/cmintdev/840/840.pdf (accessed 2 April 2024).

James, C. (2020) *Oak Child Safeguarding Learning Review, Technical Report*, Oak Foundation (unpublished).

Kaviani Johnson, A., and Sloth-Nielsen, J. (2020) Safeguarding Children in the Developing World—Beyond Intra-Organisational Policy and Self-Regulation. *Social Sciences*, 9(6): 98. https://doi.org/10.3390/socsci9060098

Moran, M., and Stone, D. (2016) The New Philanthropy: Private Power in International Development Policy? In Grugel, J., Hammett, D. (eds) *The Palgrave Handbook of International Development*. London: Palgrave Macmillan.

Panorama Global (2023) *Insights: A nonprofit wishlist for funders* [online]. Available at: www.panoramaglobal.org/publications/insights-a-nonprofit-wishlist-for-funders?utm_source=website&utm_medium=social&utm_campaign=nonprofit_wishlist (accessed 7 January 2024).

Peace Direct (2022) *Race, power, and peacebuilding. Insights and lessons from a global consultation.* [online]. Available at: www.peacedirect.org/content/uploads/2023/09/Race-Power-and-Peacebuilding-report.v5.pdf (accessed 21 August 2025).

Peace Direct (2023) *Transforming partnerships in international cooperation. A practical resource for civil society, donors, INGOs and intermediaries.* [online]. Available at: www.peacedirect.org/content/uploads/2025/04/Peace-Direct-Transforming-Partnerships-philanthropists-and-funders-extract.pdf (accessed 21 August 2025).

Rhind, D., and Owusu-Sekyere, F. (2018) *International Safeguards for Children in Sports: Developing and Embedding a Safeguarding Culture*, Abingdon: Routledge.

Sandvik, K. (2019) 'Safeguarding' as Humanitarian Buzzword: An Initial Scoping. *Journal of International Humanitarian Action* 4, 3.

Scott, K., Bray, S., and McLemore, M. (2020) First, Do No Harm: Why Philanthropy Needs to Re-Examine Its Role in Reproductive Equity and Racial Justice. In *Health Equity*. Dec 2020. pp. 17–22 [online]. http://doi.org/10.1089/heq.2019.0094

Shift the Power (2019) *Manifesto for change* [online]. Available at: https://shifttthepower.org/more-than-a-hashtag/manifesto-for-change/

Walker-Simpson, K. (2021a) *Funder approaches to safeguarding. Challenges, positive practices and opportunities for collaboration.* Available at: https://fundersafeguardingcollaborative.org/resources/funder-approaches-to-safeguarding/ (accessed 21 August 2025).

Walker-Simpson, K. (2021b) *Protection in practice: 'What works' to support non-governmental organisations in Tanzania to respond to child abuse.* Professional Doctorate Thesis: University of Bedfordshire. Available at: https://uobrep.openrepository.com/handle/10547/625977 (accessed 3 March 2024).

Williams, T. (2019) Generosity and impact aren't enough. Let's judge philanthropy on how well it shifts power. *Inside Philanthropy* [online]. Available at: www.insidephilanthropy.com/home/2019/9/6/why-impact-and-generosity-arent-enoughtoward-judging-philanthropy-on-how-well-it-shifts-power (accessed 7 January 2024).

Chapter 5

The challenge of a standards-based approach to safeguarding

Karen Walker-Simpson

Chapter objectives

By the end of this chapter, you will:

1 Understand the origins of international standards and the events that prompted their creation.
2 Be aware of some of the key findings from the author's research into the application of safeguarding standards in Africa and the challenges that NGOs may encounter.
3 Understand the author's analysis of how definitions of harm and safeguarding vary across contexts, and the implications this has for the effectiveness of international standards.
4 Understand the author's analysis of resource constraints within Global Majority countries and the implications this has for compliance with international standards.

5 Be aware of some of the strategies identified in the author's research to strengthen safeguarding through valuing and supporting the knowledge and expertise of local practitioners.

Introduction

International standards can play an important role in ensuring the accountability of non-governmental organisations (NGOs), particularly in humanitarian and development settings. In countries affected by poverty, conflict and natural disaster governments may be unable or unwilling to intervene and NGOs are often relied upon to deliver a wide range of essential services (Johnson and Sloth-Nielsen, 2020). State regulation of these services, however, is often weak or may be entirely absent (Neubert, 2009; Wheatley, 2009). Within this context, international standards can represent a form of *'soft law'* (Peters et al., 2009, p. 7), establishing clear expectations and incentivising compliance through their inclusion in requirements from international donors (UNICEF, 2016; Rhind and Owusu-Sekyere, 2018).

Over the past two decades, there has been a proliferation of safeguarding standards designed to ensure that NGOs working in the international development sector do not cause harm to the communities they work with. The initial catalyst was the 2002 report exposing widespread abuse and exploitation by aid workers in West Africa (UNHCR and Save the Children, 2002). The intense media attention which followed prompted international agencies to revise existing codes of practice and develop new standards to increase accountability and prevent abuse and exploitation by staff and volunteers. While compliance with these standards is voluntary, international donors increasingly require evidence that safeguarding measures are in place, and funding can be refused or withdrawn if NGOs fail to meet the required standards.

Despite their increasing influence, however, there is very little evidence of the effectiveness of these standards (DfID, 2018b; Feather et al., 2020). This was vividly illustrated in 2018 when the sector was rocked by new allegations of misconduct within leading international agencies who arguably had the required safeguarding measures in place. An inquiry by the UK's parliamentary International Development Committee (IDC) acknowledged the efforts made by NGOs to implement the policies and procedures required by international standards but concluded that these measures had failed to produce tangible results (IDC, 2018). Although the events of 2018 prompted another flurry of activity to restore confidence in the sector, few substantial changes emerged. Instead, politicians, donors and international agencies simply issued renewed commitments to ensure compliance with existing standards (DfID, 2018a; Bond, 2018).

In 2017, I published an article inviting critical reflection on the effectiveness of international safeguarding standards when applied in different contexts (Walker-Simpson, 2017). This was prompted by the concerns of local practitioners in Africa and Asia who raised questions about the effectiveness of the recommended measures when applied in their local context. Their concerns prompted me to undertake doctoral research to explore this issue further. The aim was not to prove or disprove the effectiveness of safeguarding standards, but to test the assumption that they could improve practice irrespective of context. This chapter shares some of the findings from that research (Walker-Simpson, 2021).

The chapter begins by highlighting the limited involvement of local practitioners in the development of international standards. I then raise questions about how this impacts the way safeguarding is understood and the effectiveness of standards in addressing the real-life challenges faced by NGOs. Do safeguarding standards adequately reflect the complex harms that NGO have to navigate? Are the recommended measures adequate to mitigate these risks? To answer these questions, I share insights from the small pool of research into safeguarding, as well as drawing on my own in-depth analysis of international standards and donor requirements. To illustrate the practical challenges facing local practitioners, I share examples from research conducted in sub-Saharan Africa as well as excerpts from my interviews with standard setting bodies, international agencies and local NGOs in Tanzania. I conclude with some practical recommendations to improve the effectiveness of safeguarding when applied across diverse contexts.

Who sets the standards?

Over the last five years, there have been increasing calls for the decolonisation of the international development sector (e.g. Dickenson et al., 2023, Peace Direct, 2021; Shift the Power, 2023). As discussed in Chapter 1, international agencies have been criticised for *'white saviourism'* (Dickenson et al., 2023) and for privileging the knowledge of white experts while ignoring the expertise, leadership and agency of local actors (Peace Direct, 2021). Although calls for the decolonisation of aid have garnered more attention in recent years, the underlying concerns have existed for decades. As early as 1981, James Midgley was criticising international agencies for engaging in *'professional imperialism'* (Midgley, 1981, p. xiii) by privileging knowledge generated in the West while marginalising endogenous practices that may be better suited to local needs.

While international safeguarding standards stress the importance of adapting measures to the local context, the prioritisation of knowledge generated in the Global North is clearly evident. During my interviews with representatives from standard setting bodies, a number of them described their intentions in strikingly similar terms.

> We've been doing this in the UK for years. What can we do to translate that internationally to see if we can support improved practice elsewhere?
> (Representative from a standard setting body)

> We were wrestling with 'How do you translate child protection and child safeguarding from the UK context into working internationally?'
> (Representative from a standard setting body)

Across the board, the committees responsible for developing the standards were dominated by agencies based in Europe and North America. While the standards developed for use in humanitarian settings involved extensive global consultations, decision-making power was still held in the Global North and the resulting standards have been criticised for failing to take into account local realities (Austin and O'Neil, 2013).

Although their development may have been dominated by agencies in the Global North, most standards stress the importance of contextualising measures through consultation with local practitioners and communities. Unfortunately, achieving this can be challenging. While international agencies acknowledge the importance of contextualisation, meaningful adaptation takes time and resources. The limited budget allocated to safeguarding (IDC, 2018) and competing pressures from international donors often means that efforts to engage local staff and communities is deprioritised (Anderson et al., 2012; Bond, 2022). As one international NGO explained,

> There's never sufficient time and space allowed. There's no time to go into the community or even get everyone in one place to talk about it. All of my safeguarding space gets cut in favour of discussions on monitoring and evaluation, value for money and financial reporting.
> (International NGO)

It is perhaps not surprising, therefore, that the IDC inquiry repeatedly heard how the rhetoric of contextualisation was not matched by reality. Submissions to the inquiry indicated that all too often safeguarding policies and practice were written by agencies in the Global North and then simply communicated to country offices and local NGO partners to implement. While this may achieve superficial compliance, it can also lead to resentment and may result in the measures being discounted as impractical or culturally inappropriate (Rhind and Osuwu-Sekyere, 2018; Austin and O'Neil, 2013).

Are we speaking the same language?

English remains the dominant language in international development and language barriers represent a significant obstacle to effective safeguarding (Austin and O'Neil, 2013; Rhind and Owusu-Sekyere, 2018). Although most standards are now available in major languages such as Spanish and Arabic, these translations don't adequately reflect the diversity of languages both within and between countries. Even where translations are available, it can be difficult to accurately translate technical terminology, particularly where there are no equivalent terms in other languages (Rhind and Owusu-Sekyere, 2018).

The word *safeguarding* is particularly problematic. The term originates in the UK where it has been enshrined in legislation since 1989. Internationally, however, the concept is relatively new (Bond, n.d.) and has no legal basis in the countries where the standards are applied. In the absence of law and regulation, safeguarding has been defined by international agencies but there is a striking lack of consistency. My review of international standards and donor requirements identified over 20 different definitions. Some standards restrict safeguarding to the protection of children, while others aim to safeguard anyone receiving support or services from NGOs. High-profile cases of sexual harassment in the workplace have prompted some organisations to include protection from workplace bullying and harassment under the safeguarding umbrella. One donor even includes the prevention of harm to the environment within their definition.

This lack of conceptual clarity inevitably leads to confusion and uncertainty. Respondents in my research felt that the introduction of the term had actually detracted from their efforts to improve safeguarding as they had to dedicate so much time to clarifying concepts. As one international NGO explained,

> It's over-complicated it, and it's created more confusion...how can I get a person or a community to even conceptualise what safeguarding is if I don't have the linguistic means to communicate that? It's just not feasible.
>
> (International NGO)

In addition, the imposition of foreign terminology can leave NGOs feeling as though they have nothing in place simply because they do not recognise existing systems and processes as *safeguarding*. This can contribute to the perception that local practitioners lack knowledge or expertise, perpetuating the dependence on *experts* from the Global North to *explain* or *educate* those working in other contexts.

The fact that international definitions of safeguarding focus on the prevention of abuse and exploitation by staff and volunteers is also problematic. Although some reports suggest that abuse by aid workers is widespread (Csaky, 2008; IDC, 2018; DfID, 2018b), it only actually accounts for a small proportion of abuse and exploitation globally. Respondents in my study were far more concerned about abuse in the community, as this is reported more frequently and is often much more difficult to resolve. Addressing this within the scope of safeguarding is particularly important as evaluations of international standards suggest that NGOs who implement safeguarding measures are likely to receive an increase in reports of abuse from the community, while reports of abuse by workers are likely to remain low (GCPS Consulting, 2013; Rhind and Owusu-Sekyere, 2018).

The narrow focus on abuse by aid workers creates a number of problems. Firstly, implementing safeguarding measures may prompt a high number of reports that NGOs simply do not have the capacity to respond to. I heard about an NGO in Ethiopia that had established feedback boxes as part of their safeguarding and were receiving up to 300 reports per month. While very few of these would be classified as *safeguarding*, as they didn't relate to the conduct of NGO staff, many involved clear examples of abuse that necessitated a response.

The need to respond brings a second challenge, that the narrow focus on abuse by aid workers means the standards provide very little guidance on how to deal with issues beyond the NGO. Representatives from standard setting bodies recognised this problem but explained that they had intentionally avoided tackling it because it was simply too context specific.

> We really focused on within the walls of the organisation. We did talk a lot about what do you do if someone discloses something that is happening beyond your organisation… I think that's where it gets really tricky, honestly. What do you do in the best interests of a child that is being raped by her father every day in a community where that person is the head of the community? I think very honestly, we've dodged that issue a little bit because it is quite context specific.
> (Representative from a Standard Setting Body)

Although case management guidelines exist to help NGOs manage these types of issues, case management is generally viewed as separate from safeguarding and therefore not included in the standards or associated guidance. For many, the failure to address these issues breeds resentment and adds to the perception that *safeguarding* is designed to protect the reputation of international actors rather than addressing the realities on the ground.

How do we overcome contested definitions of abuse?

Achieving a shared understanding of what constitutes abuse can also be challenging. Although a number of international standards include definitions, these may not align with national legislation and may be contested at a local level. One issue to emerge strongly from the empirical literature in Africa is that certain forms of violence may be normalised and therefore may not be recognised as abuse (e.g. Jewkes et al., 2005; Frankenberg et al., 2014; Murove et al., 2010). Although current research tends to focus on attitudes within the wider community, cultural norms inevitably affect workers' perceptions too (Murove et al., 2010; Plummer and Njugana, 2009; Pierce and Bozalek, 2004). As one international explained,

> What's in the community is within the organisations. We have to realise that organisations are peopled by humans. We have the same issues as the one that are on the outside.
> (International NGO)

My research indicated that cultural norms can severely inhibit the recognition of abuse, but this is given very little attention within international standards. Other than UK safeguarding charity Keeping Children Safe, who dedicate almost an entire manual to exploring how *'cultural practices, traditions and faith influence workers' perceptions, values and behaviours'* (Keeping Children Safe, 2014, p. 18), underlying values and beliefs are largely ignored in the other standards.

The limited attention given to underlying beliefs and attitudes inevitably impacts the effectiveness of efforts to increase workers' awareness and understanding of abuse. Although all respondents in my study thought training played an important role in improving safeguarding, they were cautious about its ability to change worker's beliefs, attitudes or behaviours. Rather than simply telling people what constitutes abuse, achieving change requires an open discussion where workers can unpick their understanding and explore any disconnect between culturally accepted practices and safeguarding expectations (Rhind and

Owusu-Sekyere, 2018; Walker-Simpson, 2021). This can be challenging as exploring deeply held beliefs requires care and sensitivity, and training by external *experts* can engender strong resistance. In practice, I heard repeated examples of trainers relying on generic PowerPoint slides and theoretical definitions of abuse without encouraging any meaningful reflection or discussion. At the end of such trainings, workers may be able to recite the categories of abuse, but their beliefs and behaviours are likely to remain unchanged (Sen, 2019; Walker-Simpson, 2021).

Rather than simply providing one-off training, my research indicates that a more holistic approach is needed. This process starts at recruitment, with importance placed on an individual's values and beliefs, not simply their qualifications and professional experience. While induction and training are important, change is unlikely to be achieved in one-off workshops, rather a *'temporal approach'* to learning is required (Rhind and Owusu-Sekyere, 2018, p. 144). As one respondent explained,

> It's taken a lifetime to get that personality, why do you think you can undo it in one workshop? No, it takes being constant, going over the same things time and time again and trying the message differently.
>
> (International NGO)

Rather than simply providing one-off training, my study suggests that change is best achieved through ongoing discussion, with the opportunity to explore what definitions mean in practice. This type of learning is best facilitated by individuals based within the NGO, or at least living and working in the same context, as they can draw on practical case examples and are available to provide guidance on an on-going basis.

Although elements of a more holistic approach are included in international standards, it is far from consistent. Most standards recommend that NGOs conduct interviews as part of the recruitment process but very few highlight the importance of exploring values and attitudes. Although Keeping Children Safe emphasise the impact of values and beliefs, they focus almost exclusively on training with very little attention given to other forms of discussion and learning. The approach taken by donors is perhaps the most concerning as they tend to only require safeguarding training at induction stage, which suggests that learning is a one-off event rather than an ongoing process. While one off training may satisfy donor requirements, its ability to ensure the recognition and reporting of abuse and exploitation is likely to be limited.

Do international standards help NGOs navigate complex risks?

While raising awareness of abuse and exploitation by aid workers is undoubtedly important, a narrow focus on traditional forms of harm means that other types of risks are given very little attention. International standards are based on the principle of *do no harm* but in many contexts, encouraging survivors to report abuse can actually expose them to a range of secondary harms. Indeed, my own research was prompted, in part, by an NGO working in Somalia who were worried that implementing measures to encourage reporting might expose women and girls to fatal harm due to the reactions of their family and community. Although they raised this concern with their international donor, they were simply told that reporting procedures were one of their required standards and if they didn't comply then funding would be withdrawn.

While community actors play a critical role in ensuring protection in many humanitarian and development settings (Krueger et al., 2014; Wessels et al., 2015), the *'communal shame problem'* (Boayke, 2009, p. 961) still represents a very real risk. In many contexts, reporting abuse is seen as bringing shame on the family and wider community and disclosure can results in discrimination, stigma and even violent backlash (DfID, 2018b; Davey et al., 2010; Lattu, 2008; Csaky, 2008). The risk of violent backlash was a real concern for international respondents, particularly in settings where the police and authorities are unwilling or unable to take action (DfID, 2018b; Rhind and Owusu-Sekyere, 2018; Csaky, 2008; IDC, 2018).

Although the risk of violent backlash is real concern in some contexts, it is important not to over-generalise. In Tanzania, the potential for violence was not identified as a concern by local practitioners and the perceptions of international respondents did not reflect the reality on the ground. Instead, Tanzanian respondents were more worried that the stigma associated with abuse could damage relationships and compromise the support offered to survivors. The expectation that NGOs report cases to the authorities can exacerbate tensions as formal protection services are often seen as alien and in conflict with local values (Krueger et al., 2014; Wessells, 2015).

> At the community level, they don't want all those kinds of things to be reported. They don't want it. Maybe they would discuss it among themselves and resolve the issue at a grassroots level, but without going to the police or government authorities.
> (Tanzanian NGO)

Tanzanian respondents repeatedly stressed the importance of working with survivors in the context of their family and wider community and yet this is given very little attention in the standards. Indeed, many worried about reporting concerns to international agencies as they feared they would impose individualistic responses that discounted the significance of social harms, and consequently risked the long-term support and welfare of the survivor.

The risk of reporting abuse is not restricted to the reactions within the community, however. While it is important that NGOs do not act in isolation, contact with the authorities can actually result in further harm. In many countries, inadequate training and entrenched beliefs can lead to victim blaming and insensitive handling of cases (e.g. DfID, 2018b; Kisanga et al., 2010; Rhind and Owusu-Sekyere, 2018; IDC, 2018; Schiller, 2017). Poor co-ordination between services also means that survivors may be forced to tell their stories to multiple professionals, increasing the risk of re-traumatisation (Schiller, 2017). Although rarely acknowledged in the standards, the reality of secondary harm was highlighted during the IDC Inquiry which criticised international donors for imposing a blanket requirement on NGOs to report abuse to statutory services as they believed this had '*the potential for subjecting victims and survivors to further harm*' (IDC, 2018, p. 31).

Although risk assessments are included in a number of the standards, these tend to focus on the risk of harm by the NGOs staff, volunteers and operations and the risks associated with intervening to address the abuse are rarely explored. Instead, international standards tend to rely on pre-defined, linear procedures that fail to take into account the complexity involved in safeguarding cases. This was even acknowledged by those who had written the standards.

> I've always said to people, you can write it down on paper, it's nice and neat and somebody will come and speak to this person, and they'll speak to that person and this is what happens next. It never happens like that.
> (Representative from a standard setting body)

Rather than relying on procedures, my study suggests that the best way to navigate these complex risks is through a collaborative dialogue between team members. This allows for a broad range of perspectives and expertise to be accessed while reducing the pressure on any one individual. While many respondents felt that their partners in Africa naturally took a more collaborative, discussion-based approach, the importance of internal case discussions is not emphasised in the standards. Case discussions and the on-going, holistic assessment of risk are a key component of case management but, as already noted, this is seen as separate from safeguarding and so the benefits of this approach are often missed.

The active involvement of survivors in assessing risks and determining the best course of action is also essential. Respondents repeatedly stressed that you '*can't force them*' (Tanzanian NGO), and without listening to the survivors, professionals may engage in actions that cause further harm or prompt the survivor to withdraw from the process. While there have been repeated calls from the international community to listen and learn from survivors (e.g. DAC, 2019; Bond, 2018a; DfID, 2018a), this is still not adequately reflected in the standards. Although the standards emphasise the importance of engaging communities to promote reporting, there is a tendency to view survivors as passive recipients once the report has been made and survivor-centred decision-making is rarely emphasised (Walker-Simpson, 2021). This can undermine the willingness of survivors to come forward as well as limiting the ability of the NGO to successfully navigate complex risks.

How realistic is safeguarding in low resource settings?

Within the standards, the emphasis on standardised procedures also extends to how the NGO interacts with other agencies. In order to ensure an effective response to concerns, international standards recommend that NGOs conduct a mapping or stakeholder analysis so that they are aware of other services in their area. Most also recommend that NGOs develop formal referral pathways to ensure the smooth handling of cases when they arise. While these referral procedures may ensure that NGOs in the Global North are able to access services and support, the acute resource constraints in many Global Majority countries can undermine their effectiveness in other contexts.

In Africa, for example, inadequate resources represent the '*predominant challenge*' facing protection services (Schmid, 2018, p. 1357). Persistent lack of investment means that statutory services are often hampered by inadequate staffing, high caseloads and a lack of basic equipment (e.g. Schmid, 2018; Krueger et al., 2015; Schiller, 2017). In some areas, resource constraints are so acute that police officers and social workers lack insufficient funds to pay for something as basic as the petrol to go and follow up a case (Cooper, 2012; Kisanga et al., 2010; Muleya, 2006). Consequently, NGOs are often relied upon to accompany survivors to medical appointments and court appearances in addition to providing them with psychosocial, financial and other support. The need for ongoing intervention is rarely recognised within the standards which appear to assume that statutory services will intervene when cases are referred.

The need to follow-up cases inevitably places pressure on NGO resources. This is exacerbated by the fact that NGOs are often relied upon to cover any associated costs as neither the survivor, their family nor statutory services have the financial resources to do so. This was a common challenge for the Tanzanian NGOs in my study.

> Now the social welfare officer is intervening to make sure the child is safe, and we are following up on that. So, the child is taken to hospital. She stayed there for a week without any improvement. So, we need to transfer the child to the national hospital because the situation is worse. No money. Social welfare – they don't have. The police say, 'we don't have'. The family – 'we don't have'. So, what is the situation now? We have to provide the support and make sure the child is safe.
> (Tanzanian NGO)

Although NGOs may want to provide support, most lack dedicated funding for safeguarding (Walker-Simpson, 2021; IDC, 2018) and the additional cost of accessing services for survivors is rarely recognised. This can leave NGOs with a difficult choice between using resources allocated to other areas of programming or compromising the support they are able to provide to survivors.

Despite '*resources*' being identified as one of the pillars of effective safeguarding (Rhind and Owusu-Sekyere, 2018, p. 156), they are given very little attention in the standards. A number of implementation guides highlight the importance of allocating adequate resources to safeguarding, but they give very little guidance on how NGOs can access these critical funds. The PSEA handbook produced by CHS Alliance is the most explicit and advises NGOs to include safeguarding costs in project proposals and to '*not be afraid*' of approaching donors (CHS Alliance, 2017, p. 20). While this type of practical advice is welcome, the findings from my study suggest that approaching donors can be challenging and may have limited possibility for success. Indeed, the IDC inquiry found that a lack of funding for safeguarding was the '*main obstacle*' to progress and they criticised donors for treating safeguarding as an '*add on*' (IDC, 2018, p. 5).

The lack of attention paid to resources has the potential to significantly undermine the effectiveness of safeguarding standards. Managers and frontline staff can be reluctant to implement measures that appear unrealistic given local resource constraints (IDC, 2018; Rhind and Owusu-Sekyere, 2018; Austin and O'Neil, 2013). Even where NGOs attempt to implement the measures, inadequate resources can limit their ability to follow up concerns and provide support. This, in turn, can lead to disappointment and frustration among survivors which undermine their willingness to report concerns in the future (DFID, 2018b; Csaky, 2008; Davey et al, 2010; Lattu, 2008). Within this context, a number of respondents from standard setting bodies actually felt that it was unwise for small NGOs to implement reporting procedures, even though they had recommended them in their standards, as encouraging reporting without the capacity to respond could potentially lead to further harm.

Where next?

While my research found value in many of the measures set out in international standards, it also identified a significant disconnect between the theoretical model of safeguarding offered by international standards and the lived reality of local practitioners. It was notable that very few international NGOs actually shared the international standards and accompanying guidance with their local partners as they were not confident that they would see their relevance or be able to apply them successfully in their local context. While more investment in locally developed standards and guidance would be welcome, my research suggests that a more dynamic and interactive approach is required.

Rather than relying on generic guidance or external *experts*, my research suggests there is a need to place much greater value on the knowledge and experience held within NGOs. Although NGOs in the Global Majority may be less familiar with the term *safeguarding*, many are dealing with issues of protection every day and have a deep understanding of the risks and how to keep people safe. Local practitioners are able draw on practical examples and real-life experience which helps bring concepts to life and reduces the risk that safeguarding is discounted as a foreign concept being imposed by those from the Global North.

In recommending this, it is important to acknowledge that many NGOs may not have the expertise needed to facilitate these types of discussions. This does not mean, however, that the knowledge and expertise is not available locally. Respondents in my study emphasised the value of peer-to-peer learning opportunities, particularly for smaller NGOs who are unable to afford external training or employ specialist staff. These spaces not only create an opportunity for shared learning, but they also help foster inter-agency relationships and can lead to collaboration to tackle shared challenges. Respondents stressed the importance of inviting statutory agencies into these learning spaces as a way to educate and influence them with the aim of improving the handling of cases and reducing the risk of harm when cases are referred. This is an area where international donors can add real value by connecting the organisations they fund and providing the investment needed to ensure these spaces are well-facilitated and sustainable.

This doesn't mean that international standards have no place but rather that there is a need to *'flip the conversation'* (International NGO). Rather than starting with international models of best practice and then identifying gaps, the aim should be to understand the context, identify existing good practice and then build from there. While standards can provide a useful framework for these discussions, international agencies should avoid reductive approaches which reduce safeguarding to a rigid checklist of requirements that apply equally irrespective of context. Although evaluations of international standards emphasise the need for *'facilitation not dictation'* (Rhind and Owusu-Sekyere, 2018, p. 38), implementing this change depends on the willingness of international agencies to accept that there are different ways of approaching safeguarding and trusting NGOs to define which approach fits best in their context.

Key messages that I would leave you with are that:

- While international standards aim to ensure organisations *do no harm*, the limited involvement of local practitioners in developing and contextualising safeguarding can lead to measures that are poorly understood or discounted as impractical given local realities.
- Ensuring adequate resources is one of the pillars of effective safeguarding. Resource constraints within local NGOs and the wider protection system can limit the ability of organisations to implement safeguarding measures and comply with international standards.
- Individual values and cultural beliefs influence what is considered to harmful and how workers respond to abuse. While training is valuable, there is a need to explore underlying beliefs and discuss any potential disconnect between culturally accepted practices and safeguarding expectations.
- When responding to abuse, NGOs must consider and mitigate a broad range of risks, including secondary harm from authorities, communities and damage to personal relationships. Safeguarding risk assessments must consider the broad range of potential harms and include survivors in assessing risk and determining the best course of action.
- While standards can provide a useful framework, much greater value should be placed on the knowledge and experience held within NGOs. Rather than simply identifying gaps in compliance with international standards, the aim should be to understand the context, identify existing knowledge and good practice and build from there.

Further reading

- For those who wish to find out more about the author's research which underpins this chapter, a summary of the research findings can be accessed at: https://fundersafeguardingcollaborative.org/resources/safeguarding-in-practice-tanzania-response/
- To better understand the available evidence and the gaps that exist, the Global Evidence Review by Feather, Martin and Neville (2020) provides a comprehensive summary of available evidence on measures to address Sexual Exploitation and Abuse and Sexual Harassment in the Aid Sector.
- For those looking to support people and organisations to implemented international standards, the research by Rhind and Owusu-Sekyere (2018) identifies eight simple pillars which can support effective change.

References

Anderson, M, Brown, D and Jean, I (2012) *Time to Listen: Hearing People on the Receiving End of International Aid*, Cambridge, Massachusetts: CDA Collaborative Learning Projects.

Austin, L and O'Neil, G (2013) *The Joint Standards Initiative Global Stakeholder Consultation*, London: ODI. Available at: https://alnap.org/help-library/resources/the-joint-standards-initiative-global-stakeholder-consultation-report/ (Accessed 21 August 2025).

Boayke, K (2009) 'Culture and nondisclosure of child sexual abuse in Ghana: A theoretical and empirical exploration', *Law and Social Enquiry*, 34(4), pp. 951–979.

Bond (2022) Safeguarding in successful partnerships – Change statement. London: Bond. [online]. Available at: www.bond.org.uk/wp-content/uploads/2022/09/safeguarding_in_successful_partnerships_-_change_statement_v7_final.pdf (Accessed 21 August 2025).

Bond (2019.) *Safeguarding Definitions and Reporting Mechanisms for UK NGOs*, London: Bond. Available at: www.bond.org.uk/resources-support/uk-ngo-safeguarding-definitions-and-reporting-mechanisms (Accessed 3 March 2024).

Bond (2018) *UK Non-Governmental Organisations: Commitments to Tackle Sexual Exploitation and Abuse and Sexual Harassment in The International Aid Sector*, London: Bond. Available at: https://assets.publishing.service.gov.uk/government/uploads/system/uploads/attachment_data/file/749772/NGO_Commitments_-_final.pdf (Accessed 3 March 2024).

CHS Alliance (2017) *PSEA Implementation Quick Reference Handbook*, Geneva: CHS Alliance. Available at: https://d1h79zlghft2zs.cloudfront.net/uploads/2019/07/PSEA_Handbook.pdf (Accessed 3 March 2024).

Cooper, E (2012) 'Following the law but losing the spirit of protection in Kenya', *Development in Practice*, 22(4), pp. 498–509.
Csaky, C (2008) *No One to Turn To: The Under-Reporting of Child Sexual Exploitation and Abuse by Aid Workers and Peacekeepers*, London: Save the Children. Available at: https://resourcecentre.savethechildren.net/node/2732/pdf/no_one_to_turn_to_1.pdf (Accessed 3 March 2024).
Davey, C, Nolan, P and Ray, P (2010) *Change Starts With Us, Talk to Us!* Geneva: Humanitarian Accountability Partnership International. Available at: https://alnap.org/help-library/resources/change-starts-with-us-talk-to-us/ (Accessed 21 August 2025).
Department for International Development (DfID) (2018a) *Commitments Made by Donors to Tackle Sexual Exploitation and Abuse and Sexual Harassment in the International Aid Sector*. Available at: https://assets.publishing.service.gov.uk/government/uploads/system/uploads/attachment_data/file/749632/donor-commitments1.pdf (Accessed 3 March 2024).
Department for International Development (DfID) (2018b) *Victim and Survivor Voices: Main Findings from a DFID-led Listening Exercise*, London: DfID. Available at: https://assets.publishing.service.gov.uk/government/uploads/system/uploads/attachment_data/file/749741/Listening-Exercise1.pdf (Accessed 3 March 2024).
Development Assistance Committee (DAC) (2019) *DAC Recommendation on Ending Sexual Exploitation, Abuse, and Harassment in Development Co-Operation and Humanitarian Assistance: Key Pillars of Prevention and Response*. Available at: https://legalinstruments.oecd.org/en/instruments/OECD-LEGAL-5020 (Accessed 3 March 2024).
Dickenson, K, Khan, T and Sondarjee, M (2023) 'Introduction: Why White Saviorism?', in Khan, T, Dickenson, K, and Sondarjee, M (eds) *White Saviorism in International Development: Theories, Practices and Lived Experiences*, Quebec: Daraja Press, pp. 1–24.
Feather, J, Martin, R and Neville, S (2020) *Global Evidence Review of Sexual Exploitation and Abuse and Sexual Harassment (SEAH) in the Aid Sector*, London: Resource and Support Hub. Available at: https://safeguardingsupporthub.org/sites/default/files/2021-03/RSH_Global_Evidence_Review_Final_Design_V5.pdf (Accessed 3 March 2024).
Frankenberg, S, Holmqvist, R and Rubenson, B (2014) 'In earlier days everyone could discipline children, now they have rights': Caregiving dilemmas of guidance and control in urban Tanzania, *Journal of Community and Applied Social Psychology*, 24, pp. 191–204.
GCPS Consulting (2013) *KCS Impact Study Report*. Internal Keeping Children Safe Report. Unpublished.
International Development Committee (IDC) (2018) *Sexual Exploitation and Abuse in the Aid Sector: Eighth Report of Session 2017–19*, London: International Development Committee. Available at: https://publications.parliament.uk/pa/cm201719/cmselect/cmintdev/840/840.pdf (Accessed 3 March 2024).
Jewkes, R, Penn-Kekana, L and Rose-Junius, H (2005) '"If they rape me, I can't blame them": Reflections on gender in the social context of child rape in South Africa and Namibia', *Social Science & Medicine*, 61, pp. 1809–1820.

Johnson, A and Sloth-Nielsen, J (2020) 'Safeguarding children in the developing world—Beyond intra-organisational policy and self-regulation', *Social Sciences*, 9(6), 98

Keeping Children Safe (2014) *Understanding Child Safeguarding: A Facilitator's Guide*, London: Keeping Children Safe. Available at: https://resourcecentre.savethechildren.net/node/8560/pdf/kcs_understanding_2014.pdf (Accessed 3 March 2024).

Kisanga, F, Mbwambo, J, Hogan, N, Nystrom, L, Emmelin, M and Lindmark, G (2010) 'Perceptions of child sexual abuse – a qualitative interview study with representatives of the socio-legal system in urban Tanzania', *Journal of Child Sexual Abuse*, 19(3), pp. 290–309.

Krueger, A, de Vise-Lewis, E, Thompstone, G and Crispin, V (2015) 'Child protection in development: Evidence-based reflections and questions for practitioners', *Child Abuse & Neglect*, 50, pp. 15–25.

Krueger, A., Thompstone, G. and Crispin, V. (2014) 'Learning from child protection systems mapping and analysis in West Africa: Research and policy implications', Global Policy, 5(1), pp. 47–55.

Lattu, K (2008) *To Complain or Not To Complain: Still The Question – Consultations with Humanitarian aid Beneficiaries on Their Perceptions of Efforts to Prevent and Respond to Sexual Exploitation and Abuse*, Geneva: Humanitarian Accountability Partnership International. Available at: https://reliefweb.int/sites/reliefweb.int/files/resources/4FB40B9AB3F8708B852574780059ACEB-HAP_To%20Complain%20or%20Not%20to%20Complain.pdf (Accessed 3 March 2024).

Midgley, J (1981) *Professional Imperialism*, London: Heinemann.

Muleya, W (2006) 'A comparative study of social work intervention in context in Zambia and England', *International Social Work*, 49(4), pp. 445–457.

Murove, T, Forbes, B, Kean, S, Wamimbi, R and Germann, S (2010) 'A discussion of perceptions of community facilitators from Swaziland, Kenya, Mozambique and Ghana: Cultural practices and child protection', *Vulnerable Children and Youth Studies*, 5(S1), pp. 55–62.

Neubert, D (2009) 'Local and regional non-state actors on the margins of public policy in Africa', in Peters, A, Koechlin, L, Forster, T and Zinkernagel, G (eds) *Non-State Actors as Standard Setters*, New York: Cambridge University Press, pp. 35–60.

Peace Direct (2021) *Time to Decolonise Aid Insights and Lessons from a Global Consultation*, London: Peace Direct. Available at: www.peacedirect.org/wp-content/uploads/2023/09/PD-Decolonising-Aid_Second-Edition.pdf (Accessed 3 March 2024).

Peters, A, Koechlin, L and Zinkernagel, G (2009) 'Non-state actors as standard setters: Framing the issue in a multidisciplinary fashion', in Peters, A, Koechlin, L, Forster, T and Zinkernagel, G (eds) *Non-State Actors as Standard Setters*, New York: Cambridge University Press, pp. 1–32.

Pierce, L and Bozalek, V (2004) 'Child abuse in South Africa: An examination of how child abuse and neglect are defined', *Child Abuse & Neglect*, 28, pp. 817–832.

Plummer, C and Njugana, W (2009) 'Cultural protective and risk factors: Professional perspectives about child sexual abuse in Kenya', *Child Abuse & Neglect*, 33(8), pp. 524–532.

Rhind, D and Owusu-Sekyere, F (2018) *International Safeguards for Children in Sports: Developing and Embedding a Safeguarding Culture*, Abingdon: Routledge.

Schiller, U (2017) 'Child sexual abuse allegations: Challenges faced by social workers in child protection organisations', *Practice: Social Work in Action*, 29(5), pp. 347–360.

Schmid, J (2018) 'Social service workforce strengthening in Sub-Saharan Africa', *British Journal of Social Work*, 48, pp. 1351–1369.

Sen, P (2019) *What Will It Take? Promoting Cultural Change to End Sexual Harassment*, New York: UN Women. Available at: www.unwomen.org/sites/default/files/Headquarters/Attachments/Sections/Library/Publications/2019/Discussion-paper-What-will-it-take-Promoting-cultural-change-to-end-sexual-harassment-en.pdf (Accessed 3 March 2024).

Shift the Power (2023) *#Shift the Power Manifesto for Change*, Belfast: Shift the Power. Available at: www.shiftthepowersummit.org/shiftthepower-manifesto-for-change (Accessed 3 March 2024).

UNHCR and Save the Children UK (2002) *Sexual Violence and Exploitation: The Experience of Refugee Children in Liberia, Guinea and Sierra Leone – Report of Assessment Mission Carried Out From 22 October To 30 November 2001*, Geneva: UNHCR and Save the Children UK. Available at: www.parliament.uk/documents/commons-committees/international-development/2002-Report-of-sexual-exploitation-and-abuse-Save%20the%20Children.pdf (Accessed 3 March 2024).

UNICEF (2016) *Changing Minds, Policies and Lives Improving Protection of Children in Eastern Europe and Central Asia Improving Standards of Child Protection Services*. Available at: www.unicef-irc.org/publications/pdf/improving.pdf (Accessed 3 March 2024).

Walker-Simpson, K (2017) 'The practical sense of protection: A discussion paper on the reporting of abuse in Africa and whether international standards actually help keep children safe', *Child Abuse Review*, 26, pp. 252–262.

Walker-Simpson, K (2021) *Protection in Practice: 'What Works' to Support Non-Governmental Organisations in Tanzania to Respond to Child Abuse*. Professional Doctorate Thesis: University of Bedfordshire. Available at: https://uobrep.openrepository.com/handle/10547/625977 (Accessed 3 March 2024).

Wessells, M (2015) 'Bottom-up approaches to strengthening child protection systems: Placing children, families and communities at the center', *Child Abuse and Neglect*, 43, pp. 8–23.

Wheatley, S (2009) 'Demographic governance beyond the state: The legitimacy of non-state actors as standard setters', in Peters, A, Koechlin, L, Forster, T and Zinkernagel, G (eds) *Non-State Actors as Standard Setters*, New York: Cambridge University Press, pp. 215–240.

Chapter 6

The HR professionals' dilemmas – and how to resolve them

Kathryn Gordon

Chapter objectives

By the end of this chapter, you will:

- Be more confident in dealing with a safeguarding incident when it arises.
- Understand a structure to begin to address the process which needs to occur.
- Be able to create a framework to help prepare for the next occasion a safeguarding concern arises.

You're always busy, your inbox is bulging, there is a Board paper to write, the budget is not adding up, the engagement survey results were a shocker, there is no thinking time and someone in your team, in your organisation is managing a safeguarding case. Does this sound familiar?

Perhaps, one of your team members is responding to a concern raised by an employee, perhaps a member of the public has accused a member of your staff of inappropriate behaviour. It could even be that someone who worked for the organisation you happen to work for today, but who worked there or engaged with the company as a supplier 30 years ago, now wants to tell you something.

In any of these instances, you know what is coming: dilemmas, challenges, the need for some thinking time, a desire for more information, a wish for a straightforward solution.

How do we know this? Is there another way?

We know because, we have already experienced it, this thing "safeguarding, #metoo, sexual harassment, sexual abuse," it is happening in our workplace, as much as it is happening in others. Globally, studies indicate that a significant percentage of women and men have experienced sexual violence and harassment at work. A 2023 poll from the Trades Union Congress (TUC) found that three in five women have experienced harassment at work (TUC, 2023).

We know because the individuals dealing with the concern or complaint will get stuck, these are human problems created by human beings, so they will be complex and messy; the investigation may be inconclusive, someone will decide to no longer talk, some things won't add up, or perhaps the employee is one of the senior managers and the whole process is coloured by that.

Eventually someone will say "we need to make a decision, someone will need to decide who is right, who is wrong, what to do next". Someone will need to be brave and make the next right decision for your organisation. That person is likely to be you, the HR Manager, the leader, and it will not be possible to tie everything up in a neat package, with a bow and present it as a complete solution, or send it on its way, done and dusted.

This chapter will address some of the things we can do to help us make the next right decision when we find ourselves in this place. It aims to help leaders find the strength and resilience to make brave decisions in the face of behaviour that is disrespectful to others and indeed humanity.

Making decisions can be hard enough, there is lots of advice, many principles, the list is endless. Here, I want to simplify it to one thing choice – choosing to make a decision is often the best choice.

This is not to minimise the challenge; making decisions that will allow individuals who have been subject to harm feel they can be resilient enough to get up the next day, continue with their lives and not be paralysed by trauma or ongoing fear, is not a small step. As an HR professional who has learnt to guide and direct based on balancing both company/organisation and employee's interest, this might seem to be choosing neither. That is not the case.

This chapter will outline how we as organisation leaders can prepare and find the confidence to hold on to the integrity we brought into our roles, the licences to work given to us by those whose lives we are impacting.

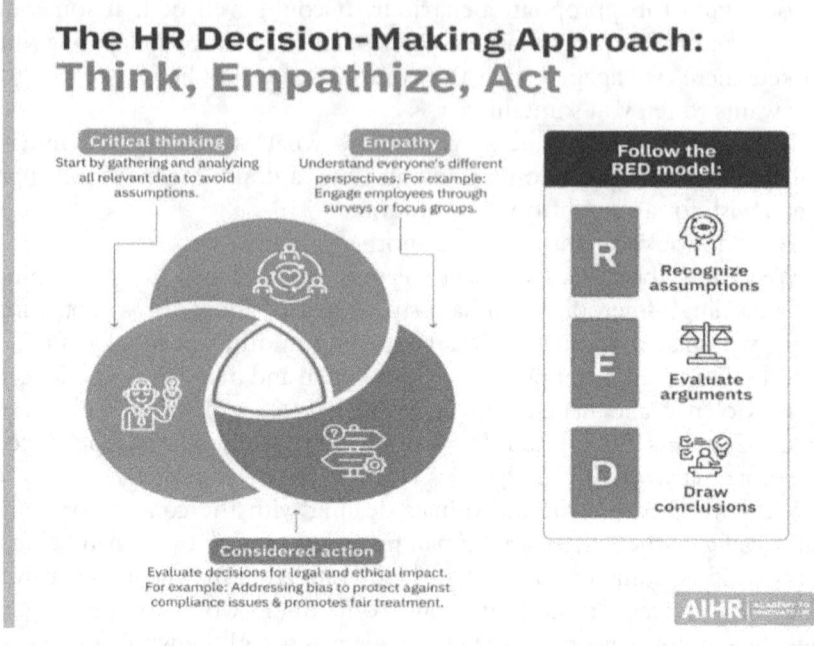

Figure 6.1 The HR Decision-Making Approach (Academy to Innovate HR, Decision-Making in HR: How To Take the Right Approach – AIHR).

This model – the HR Decision-Making Approach; Think, Empathise, Act can help frame some of the practical steps we can take (Figure 6.1).

Outlined are some of the steps we can take when presented with the dilemma of a concern, a complex case, or a complaint and provides some examples which will help you with the confidence to find your "C," your choice to act.

These steps are for you, if you manage one person, if you are acting independently, if you work with 10,000 people, if you are leading them or supporting a subgroup of people as their HR Manager. They are for you if you have an HR professional alongside you, or if you are the one with many hats, including that of HR, in your role as a manager or a leader.

When you first get the news

Let's look at what to do when you first get the news, the email, the phone call, the instant message, the look from a colleague; what should your response be when you know there is a live safeguarding issue on your to do list?

Think – who will be able to give me the information; is it the person telling me now, or do I need to contact other people? Take time to work that out.

Empathise – be clear with the messenger, you appreciate them sharing what they know with you, explain if you need further information, tell them what you are going to do next.

Act – make sure that the person who is, or might be, at risk is safe from further harm, is there distance between them and the alleged subject of complaint?

These steps don't spell TEA just because those letters are the first letter of each word, but also because often these situations need tea. Tea, or whatever is your way of introducing a pause into a hectic conversation or giving yourself time to process what you've heard, can be a strategic ally in the hectic work of people management and support.

Let's now work through what you can do to be prepared for this moment:

1 Understand your organisations' Code of Conduct; if there is no such document think about it as what you model for people about respect and dignity through your words and actions. As the HR Manager you may have written the Code of Conduct; as a leader you might have contributed to sharing it, or expectations of behaviour, during induction of new employees.

   Your preparation – be sure to have worked through in your own mind what behaviour is acceptable and what is not in the workplace. Read some #metoo stories, read them on social media, think about how those dynamics might play out in your organisation, recognise that "situations" rarely occur at the desk.

   Be brave, ask in your network, with colleagues. In doing this, you will have some backup already in place – you will know other people who have got through these situations and be confident that you can too.

   Know where to find your company policies; know how to find out what legal processes you are working within. This might involve using your company's database, file sharing or customer relationship management (CRM) system to look up "legal". In a bigger organisation it might mean talking to your HR professional, your in-house legal professional, your Head of Risk, your internal auditor; if those options are not available, it might mean asking a knowledgeable friend or doing an online search.

2 Knowing how to access professional support is key to any form of incident management. You are not expected to know everything, you are expected to know how to get appropriate inputs to help you with your "C" – the choice you need to make to act.

3   Know how reporting and governance works in your organisation; who needs to know, how do decisions get made? Be aware of incident management protocols, who are the decision-makers, be able to distinguish between the noise makers and the decision-makers, whose job is it to know, whose job is it to report? If you are unsure keep asking. Is there a correct order, how do you get in touch with people in a different country, do not rely on just being able to send an email.

If we have done this preparation work, we are better equipped, after a cup of tea of course, to take some considered action. A handy checklist for this first stage might include:

(a) Check with complainant or the investigator that there is adequate protection in place – are the parties distanced, are there measures in place to protect against further harm?
(b) Absorb the information you have received in whatever form, a first-hand report, or a completed investigation. Take the time to read the notes you have taken, or the case review or investigation report presented to you. Make your list of clarifying questions, ask them, remember why you are asking, you will have to make a choice, an informed choice – this is why it is on your desk. Asking questions can only help you understand.
(c) Map all the parties involved; their relationship with one another, with your organisation and with the legal context. For this latter point, you need to know what country they are in, what is their status with the organisation, employee, volunteer, member of the public, and what age they are.
(d) Confirm reporting requirements – what needs to be done, what has been done, do you need to inform law enforcement, the donor, other people?
(e) Brief out and up – who else needs to know, are there others who are going to have to help with decision-making, do others need to know to maintain protective action, who else is responding, what follow up will be needed? Prepare your briefs in writing; name the audience; who you are briefing, what is the message, how will you tell them. Start with what has happened, not what you have done.

Your organisation response

Now you are ready to go again with another TEA.

Think – what information do I have, can I determine what information is useful, remembering that not all evidence is created equal, can I see patterns that validate or contradict?
Empathise – have I considered all the stakeholders, have I checked for bias and been objective, looking at the range of perspectives and aspects?
Act – what are the risks and ethical factors I need to take account of, how do these apply to the evidence, the human impact and consequences to allow me to conclude?

Whether you are responsible for everything or you are acting based on an investigation report, all these steps are important, they are not duplicating, they are helping you get to your "C," the choice you need to make to act.

Let's look now at the preparation work we can do to generate a different culture of response through the way in which we apply our HR practice. It will require of us to explore critically the employment approaches, the ethical challenges, and the myriads of legal jurisdictions that make up how we carry out our professional roles on a day-to-day basis. We will look at three areas: global standards of conduct, legal compliance and organisation culture.

Maintaining global standards of conduct

Hands up if you've ever had a safeguarding case where the people involved were all the same nationality, employed on the same terms and from within 5 km of one another?

Yes, the statistics tell us that the majority of survivors of sexual abuse knew the alleged perpetrator, yet in our global organisations, there is a high probability that this will not mean they are permanently in the same location. In our workplaces, connectivity and engagement opportunity is created from within diverse teams, labour mobility, international conferences, basically the circumstances of working in humanitarian aid and development. This means incidents involve people who are employed under different contractual terms and conditions, subject to different legal jurisdictions.

Add to this, as human nature is to retreat when something awful happens it could well mean that the person making the complaint or allegation has left your workplace, gone home, moved to somewhere they thought they could forget and chances are the alleged perpetrator is in a different place, perhaps also in a different part of your organisation.

Why does this matter?

You are being asked what to do next, can we fire someone, can the complainant sue us, what will we tell the press, do we need to tell anyone else? You are presented with a range of items to take account of; the employment contracts, in different countries, with different companies or structures of your organisation and most likely, not in the same place as your organisation registration, your Board of Directors, Trustees and best of all, in a different country from the donor.

One of the things that can help you with your "C", the choice you need to make to act, is a framework that allows you to straddle all these complexities for your organisation.

A global standard of conduct will give you the reference from which to:

- identify the behavioural and ethical standards, the acceptable conduct expected of people engaged with your organisation
- determine the levels of respect, integrity and professionalism, with which to report and execute decisions which will contributing to a positive and inclusive workplace atmosphere
- balance compliance with legal and regulatory requirements, and the risk of further employee misconduct
- define the actions necessary for resolving conflicts and addressing behavioural issues, helping to maintain stability in employee, manager relationships going forward

Top tip – If you do not yet have a global standard of conduct, get one.

Legal compliance: avoiding legal challenge, navigating absent, inconsistent national employment/labour laws and law enforcement.

We are taught that legal compliance is necessary to protect both your business, your organisation and your employees. What happens though when one part of the legal environment conflicts with another, or there are gaps in the system, the governance structures, or the rules and regulations are not designed to support the complexity of safeguarding cases?

Back to the tea, put the kettle on and this time make sure you attach a "C" to the T.

Again, we will Think, Empathise and Act, this time ensuring our thinking is critical thinking; understanding the context, testing our reasoning and clarifying our purpose.

What can our preparation in this area involve?

- Understanding the context – the employment law parameters in each country for investigating, suspending, disciplining, terminating. This one takes time, remember you will be fortunate if you are only dealing with one nation's legislation. Even if that is the case you will have at least two parties involved, a subject of complaint and a harmed individual. Your map of all the characters, where they are and how they relate to one another and to the organisation, will be helpful. Ask the same question more than once, be curious, play devil's advocate, ask what if, again and again.

- Testing the reasoning – ask yourself what it will take for me to keep going to reach a decision and get to my "C" the choice to act. Are all the terms defined, have I made sure there is no room for misinterpretation, is everyone referring to the same thing, e.g., differentiating between terms such as abuse and harassment, even if individuals are using different language. How much risk can I actively manage?

  This question is answered by naming the dilemmas and contradictions you might run into, e.g., the complainant has a right to keep their personal information private, the alleged perpetrator has a right to know what the allegations are before you can invite them to a disciplinary hearing, or there is no fair dismissal for misconduct of this kind but your disciplinary policy says this is gross misconduct. Preparation for this might involve preparing a "character map" – some reading and analysis of who, what parties and jurisdictions were involved. Your reasoning will allow you to identify where there are clear anomalies, divergent requirements, perhaps around disclosing evidence or the nature of complaints or making a report to a statutory body.

- Clarifying your purpose: having tested your reasoning you have your first round of questions which need to be answered, you can set these alongside your purpose to decide how you will answer them. There will be more than one purpose of course and more than one action to take, but breaking it down will prepare you to take action. The range of purposes might include: am I doing what I can to support a conclusion for the individual who has been harmed or am I minimising the number of people who know about this incident or am I trying to keep this from the board/the public/the donor?

  Your actions are unlikely to be mutually exclusive, for example – removing the complainant from the situation that led to the complaint may require the removal of the subject of complaint from that setting. This might be through a role consolidation, a change in contract status or even dismissal. Minimising the number of people who know and appropriately reporting may require summaries or for information only briefings. All these options can be done compliantly.

Now your TEA is ready, the thinking has got you to recognise where empathy is needed; not everyone is going to agree or be happy with your actions, but your critical thinking means you can explain your "C," your choice to act.

Organisation culture

Finally, let us consider what does it mean in terms of preparation to respond in a responsible way to a safeguarding incident using organisation culture as our framework?

There are as many types of organisation culture as there are organisations, the one common thread is that culture is dynamic – it is reflected in the ways in which people behave, how people understand how work gets done. As HR professionals, we know that identifying characteristics of the culture and working with them to influence and shift behaviour is imminently preferable to railing against it.

There are two key elements that we must recognise:

1 That the organisation's culture is ever present, from the tough employees who think "I always do my own thing, no-one can tell me what to do," to the responsible thoughtful and diligent employees who want to get things done and remain compliant; both types contribute to the culture.
2 That the dynamic nature of culture, the very fact that it is determined by individual and collective behaviour, means that it can be influenced and changed for the good, often by single actions.

If we bear in mind these key elements, we can prepare well by introducing some practical steps to include a perspective and practice on safeguarding into our culture.

1 Start before the beginning, before anyone joins your organisation – what do they hear or see about your organisation, does any of your promotional material actually say that you value respect of other individuals, that you do not tolerate inappropriate behaviour, that you will report incidents?
2 Start at their beginning – every employee enters the organisation somehow. At each of these doors, do you have a sign, we will expect you to behave appropriately, if you do not we will call it out?
3 Continue with everybody – ask your managers to ask people are they witnessing inappropriate behaviour, do they know what to do if that is the case?
4 Share information – tell people there were incidents, explain you had to deal with them, it is not a secret that there are cases, this is life, we know it happens.
5 Make reporting easy – make sure everyone knows what to say and practice – a good place to start is giving everyone permission to say "thanks for being able to share this with me, shall we think about who else might help us?"

6 Explain to the finance team – there will be costs involved, they may not want to recognise them, that does not mean you can respond to an incident for free, get a code generated, or explain how to use the account codes you already have.

Remember, it is your "C," your choice to act, your decision to make… HR professionals and leaders are well placed within organisations to align, shape, influence, be aspirational as well as inspirational. We can be the ones who know how things get done, what or who drives action from others. We can work with one another in our own organisation, with those in other organisations to move forward, get things done, cover each other's back, stand up for what is right.

If you are still challenged by all of this, maybe you are reading this and thinking "*the culture in my organisation is driven clearly from the top, this organisation has been here for 60 years, the culture is ingrained, we are results driven no one pays attention to the culture*" – those thoughts are all valid. A helpful sentiment to bear in mind in such situations is that "*Though no one can go back and make a brand-new start, anyone can start from now and make a brand-new ending*" (Sherman, 1982).

Although every organisation is uniquely shaped by its vision, mission and leadership, cultures can be dissected and described both broadly and more granularly. Let us look at some examples of dominant culture types and how a safeguarding perspective might be integrated.

In research published in Harvard Business Review, Groysberg, Lee, Price and Cheng (2018) named an identifiable range of organisational culture:

- **Purpose culture:** In companies with a purpose-driven culture, employees share the organisation's (often altruistic) values of improving the world and ensuring global resources are more equally distributed with those who live in the margins.

  From a safeguarding perspective, the argument can be that those in whose interests we work, those who live in the margins, are those to whom we owe a greater respect and commitment to doing no harm. Action must therefore be taken if there is any indication that our work is "doing harm" this may involve sacrifice, including terminating employment contracts.

- **Learning organisational culture:** In organisations with a learning culture, learning (and development) is at the forefront of the company's values and strategy.

  In this environment, leaders can encourage people to grow through the response to a complaint or concern, providing opportunity to role model and showcase alternative behaviours.

- **Result organisational culture:** In a result culture, there is a strong emphasis on meeting targets, achieving goals and high performance overall.

    Here, the need to demonstrate achievement can be linked to the success, growth or continuation of the work that comes from managing an incident well. Demonstrating that in today's environment, when it is apparent to all that there will be incidents of a safeguarding nature, we can demonstrate outcomes from support to complainants, increase responsibility for prevention and protection, lead to changed behaviour and a managed response that does no further harm.

- **Authority organisational culture:** Companies with an authority culture typically boast a competitive working environment with strong leaders, a top-down management style, clear objectives and expectations, and employees who strive to be the best in their field. This is perhaps both the easiest and the hardest to work with. If your preparation work is with the leaders and they perceive a strong response to safeguarding concerns is their responsibility and a behaviour they should demonstrate, then job done, if the boss says so, then we have to do it.

    Alternatively, if the boss disregards the need to respond and dismisses claims or concerns raised you will need to go back to each preparation step and get your network to support you. Remember organisations don't have just one culture characteristic, and there will be other key aspects: reputational implications, the consequences of continuing harm, the cost of claims that will help you with convincing the leadership.

- **Safety organisational culture:** A safety culture fosters a work environment focusing on thorough strategic planning and carefully calculated, low-risk decisions.

    Here, the ability to influence through preparation is high, and organisations with a safety culture try to be prepared for the unexpected as much as possible. The introduction of risk assessments, mitigation plans and contingency plans for a range of safeguarding scenarios will be well within the bounds of possibility.

- **Order organisational culture:** In organisations with an order culture, everything is clear; processes, policies, rules and even people's roles are clearly defined.

    When order is a characteristic of your culture, preparation can take the form of pre-empting whose role is it to do what, when and how. Building responsibility for reporting, responding, incident management, prevention into the role descriptions of key individuals will support stronger safeguarding.

- **Caring organisational culture:** In a caring organisational culture, the organisation prioritises the total wellbeing of its people. It is an environment characterised by trust, mutual respect and collaboration that often leads to strong engagement and loyalty among the organisation's employees.

    What better culture to inculcate a safeguarding culture; mutual respect for individuals will be well understood, the concepts of a strong response to an individuals' vulnerability will be expected, promoting this type of practice should land well.

Being able to recognise the characteristics of the culture in your organisation takes time and perspective, sometimes gained by looking at other organisations, often reinforced through critical thinking and reflection on the response to a particular incident. Hopefully, you will recognise something or some part of your organisation in these examples, to allow you to start or improve; take the steps to go from the current to the desired organisational culture and shift from conceptual to live tangible and visible practice. Paying attention to culture, talking across your organisation about what does and what does not support a respectful safeguarding response and environment where no harm is done does not require a budget, it requires a voice. Yours, your "C", your choice to act and speak up.

Key preparations

Preparation remains key. You will be feeling the burden of the choices you have to make; preparation will allow for more informed, thoughtful and strategic approach whilst reducing the risk of having to make and remake decisions. This is normal, remember wanting to do the right thing by people, finding ways for everyone to be their best selves is why we chose these roles, to lead people, to support the leadership of people, to do the right thing, no-one ever said that would be easy (Figure 6.2).

For now, resources related to things which might be helpful to initiate at this stage or to already have in place.

(a) links to employment law guidance or lawyers in each jurisdiction that your organisation operates in. Misconduct disclosure scheme, https://misconduct-disclosure-scheme.org/legal
(b) a Code of Conduct, that defines behaviour standards can be found here [Free] Code of Conduct Template and Guide (With Examples) – AIHR and for safeguarding polices more generally
(c) www.bond.org.uk/resources/safeguarding-policy-templates/

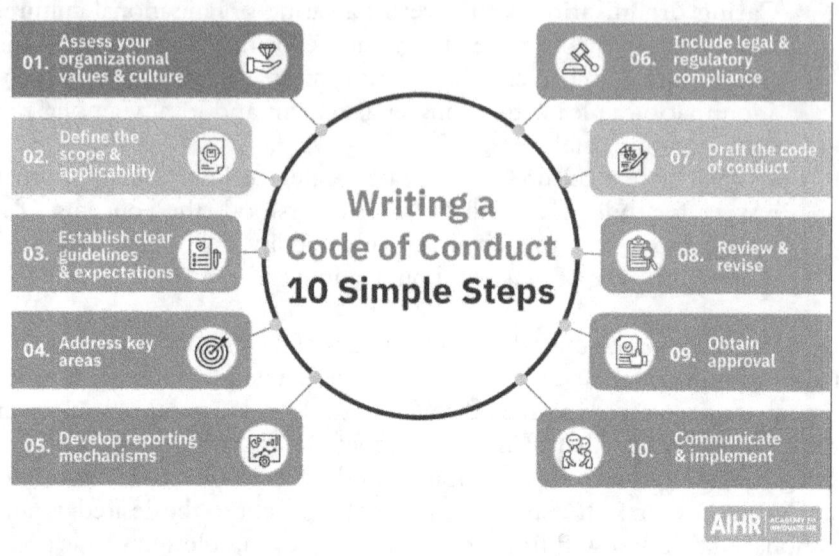

Figure 6.2 Writing a Code of Conduct: 10 Simple Steps (Academy to Innovate HR, Decision-Making in HR: How To Take the Right Approach – AIHR).

Conclusion

When writing the first draft of this chapter, the international aid/NGO sector was operating in an environment of a well-established ODA (Oversea Aid Assistance) mechanism for funding, in many countries funding was index-linked either morally or in legislation to economic growth of the nation. There was international co-operation based approach to share resources more globally. This brought with it an environment of regulation; spending of public money came with conditions, a need to comply with ever increasing frameworks for policy, practice and reporting. These requirements included many addressing how safeguarding incidents are reported and managed.

In the years since the public scrutiny of NGO's in this area, following the issues outlined in Appendix 1, it had been those who were not subjected to this regulatory environment who were relieved not to have to conform in a prescribed way; the organisations, [faith based and single cause] who relied instead on private donations from members of the public. Some would say they were slower to change, their "saviour phenomena" remaining strong and allowing them to continue with employment practices that are unlikely to bring about the respectful changes necessary to safeguard those with whom we work.

The ODA environment is now irrevocably changed, government funders, who have switched on/off project funding without regard for the impact on those whom the work is serving or the employees of the agencies to which they have granted the funding, will no longer be able to hold the moral ground of funding with integrity. International development work, if it still continues, is likely to become less regulated.

More than ever, it will be for HR professionals and leaders to make the choice to act with integrity, to maintain their licence to operate to practise development work that does no harm. Let's make this #metoo, "#you too" can operate in a brave responsible way. With preparation you will be more confident to take the small steps you can, to contribute to generating safer environments for vulnerable individuals.

We can be more deliberate in some of our thinking, we can pause and consider some of our actions, knowing that the safeguarding of children and vulnerable people will be a live issue on our desk, in our inboxes or swirling around in our messy brains someday.

Further reading

(a) links to employment law guidance or lawyers in each jurisdiction that your organisation operates in. Misconduct disclosure scheme, https://misconduct-disclosure-scheme.org/legal
(b) a Code of Conduct, that defines behaviour standards can be found here [Free] Code of Conduct Template and Guide (With Examples) – AIHR and for safeguarding polices more generally
(c) www.bond.org.uk/resources/safeguarding-policy-templates/

References

Groysberg B., Lee, J., Price, J., and Cheng, Y. (2018) *The Leader's Guide to Corporate Culture: How to Manage the Eight Critical Elements of Organizational Life.* Harvard Business Review. Accessed April 4, 2025.

Sherman, J. (1982) *Rejection: How to Survive Rejection and Promote Acceptance.* Golden Valley, Pathway Books.

TUC. (2023) 2 in 3 young women have experienced sexual harassment, bullying or verbal abuse at work. www.tuc.org.uk/news/new-tuc-poll-2-3-young-women-have-experienced-sexual-harassment-bullying-or-verbal-abuse-work. Accessed April 4, 2025.

Chapter 7

Gender as a lens into safeguarding

Mayumi Fuchi

Chapter objectives

By the end of this chapter, you will:

1 Explore how safeguarding challenges in the international aid and development sector are influenced by gendered power imbalance deeply embedded within the structure of the sector and within the communities we operate in.
2 Understand how gender norms and stereotypes, deeply ingrained in many societies, influence both the distribution of aid and the protection of beneficiaries. These norms dictate the expected behaviours and roles of men, women, boys, and girls, which can lead to varying experiences of violence, exploitation, and access to resources.
3 Be able to understand powercube analysis and use it to evaluate how gender power imbalance manifests themselves within the fragile context of refugee camps.

Introduction

The safeguarding scandal of 2018 (see Appendix 1) marked a pivotal moment in the aid sector, drawing intense global attention to the issue of NGO accountability in preventing sexual exploitation and abuse (SEA). Reports of SEA had surfaced with increasing frequency over the previous decade, exposing both non-recent and ongoing cases. The issue first gained significant attention in 1999 during peacekeeping missions (Whitworth, 2004). It was further amplified in 2002 when UNHCR and Save the Children documented widespread abuse in West Africa, including cases involving children (Defeis, 2008; DFID, 2018). These incidents revealed the alarming scale of the problem and led to the establishment of accountability and safeguarding standards within the sector. However, the 2018 Oxfam Haiti scandal, along with allegations against Save the Children UK and Médecins Sans Frontières, highlighted the sector's ongoing struggles to effectively manage and prevent SEA, stressing the urgent need for reform (see Appendix 1).

This chapter critically examines the pervasive safeguarding challenges within the international aid sector, exploring how these issues are deeply rooted in gendered power imbalances. It analyses how such power imbalances create environments where abuse and exploitation can occur with impunity, often leading to the normalisation of such behaviours. The chapter uses a case study of Sudanese refugee camps to illustrate these dynamics, employing a gender-sensitive powercube framework to examine power relations at various levels, spaces, and forms of power. The analysis provides actionable insights for practitioners and emphasises the need for a more robust, context-sensitive approach to safeguarding. The chapter concludes by calling for NGOs to prioritise ethical conduct and accountability. It stresses the importance of addressing deep-rooted power imbalances that enable abuse and exploitation within vulnerable communities.

Power dynamics and SEA

Power dynamics between aid workers and affected populations significantly shape their relationships, often leading to a culture of silence around SEA. The fear of losing critical aid or facing retaliation prevents many from raising concerns or reporting SEA (New Humanitarian, 2023). This power disparity is particularly evident when transactional sex becomes entrenched in local economies, with aid workers exploiting their authority to exchange essential resources for sexual favours (CHS Alliance, 2022; Westendorf, 2020). Affected populations, with limited bargaining power, find it difficult to voice concerns or challenge exploitative practices, leading to failures in safeguarding. Documented cases show how these imbalances enable SEA, as vulnerable populations are coerced into compromising positions due to their dependence on aid (Kovatch, 2016; Lopez, 2015).

These power imbalances not only obstruct accountability but foster an environment where victims feel disempowered and unable to report abuses. When individuals are coerced into exchanging sexual favours for essential resources it highlights broader structural inequalities within the aid sector that perpetuate abuse (Westendorf & Searle, 2017; Daoust & Dyvik, 2021). The failure to address these deep-rooted power dynamics creates a permissive environment where those in authority exploit vulnerable communities. The intersection of race and gender complicates the issue further, as marginalised groups—especially women of colour—are the most vulnerable and the least empowered to report abuses or challenge systemic exploitation.

In addition, patriarchal and racial hierarchies within the aid sector exacerbate these issues, with leadership dominated by white males while frontline workers and affected populations are predominantly people of colour (Champion, 2023). This racial and gender imbalance fosters a culture where perpetrators are seen as "humanitarian saviours" and abuses go unchecked, allowing sexism and racism to thrive (Crewel & Fernando, 2006; Turner, 2020; Narayanaswamy, 2024). Feminist and intersectional analyses have long highlighted the need to dismantle these entrenched power structures to foster a more equitable aid sector (Harrington, 2022; Daoust & Dyvik, 2021). Recent debates on intersectionality, localisation, and decolonisation of aid emphasise the need for a fairer distribution of power that addresses both racial and gender-based inequalities (Patel, 2020; Miller, 2020; Krause, 2021).

Introduction to Gaventa's powercube

Understanding power dynamics is crucial for addressing complex issues like SEA within the aid sector. Power is not just about authority; it encompasses the processes by which decisions are made, the inclusion or exclusion of voices, and the subtle forces that shape behaviour and perceptions. Gaventa's powercube offers a comprehensive framework for analysing these dynamics, categorising power into three dimensions: forms, spaces, and levels.

The powercube explains three forms of power: visible, hidden, and invisible. **Visible power** refers to the formal decision-making processes typically controlled by those in authority (Bradley, 2020). **Hidden power** operates behind the scenes, influencing agendas and excluding marginalised voices (Gaventa, 2005). **Invisible power** is the most subtle yet pervasive, embedded in social norms and beliefs that unconsciously shape behaviour and perceptions (Scott-Villiers & Oosterom, 2016). These forms of power manifest in various **spaces**: closed spaces where decisions are made without external input, invited spaces where marginalised groups are included but within predefined limits, and claimed spaces where these groups actively create their own opportunities to influence outcomes (VeneKlasen, 2020). The powercube also examines power across multiple **levels**, from the global and national to the local and even within household dynamics.

In this chapter, the powercube framework is applied to analyse power dynamics among stakeholders in refugee camps, with a focus on gender-sensitive perspectives. By exploring how different forms and spaces of power affect the effectiveness of complaint mechanisms, the analysis aims to uncover the structural inequalities that heighten the vulnerability of women and girls to SEA. The goal is to identify ways to shift these power dynamics to enhance accountability and safeguarding measures within these vulnerable communities.

Applying the power cube to analyse SEA in refugee camps

In refugee camps, power imbalances are fundamental drivers of vulnerability to SEA. The **visible power** within these settings is often held by the host states and United Nations agencies such as UNHCR (Wilde, 1998; Farmer, 2006; Pallis, 2005). Their power allows the host states and UNHCR to manipulate the law enforcement, leading to discrepancies between laws and their enforcement (Kinchin, 2016; Verdirame, 2011). Research by Harrell-Bond and Verdirame (2005) on refugee rights violations in Kenya and Uganda shed the light into how the authority of host states and UNHCR can be misused, exacerbating the vulnerabilities of refugees. When these entities fail to responsibly exercise their visible power, they create an environment ripe for exploitation and abuse.

Hidden power reveals the subtle, often behind-the-scenes influences exerted by stakeholders such as UNHCR, NGOs, and community leaders. This form of power operates away from the formal decision-making arenas, shaping agendas and influencing outcomes in less visible ways (Kamanzi, 2012). Community leaders, intended to represent refugee voices, often fail to address the full spectrum of needs, including those related to SEA. This hidden power contributes to a culture where discussing SEA is stigmatised, reinforcing silence and maintaining power imbalances. Victims face stigma, fear of reprisal, and threats of rejection from their families and communities, which further complicates their ability to seek

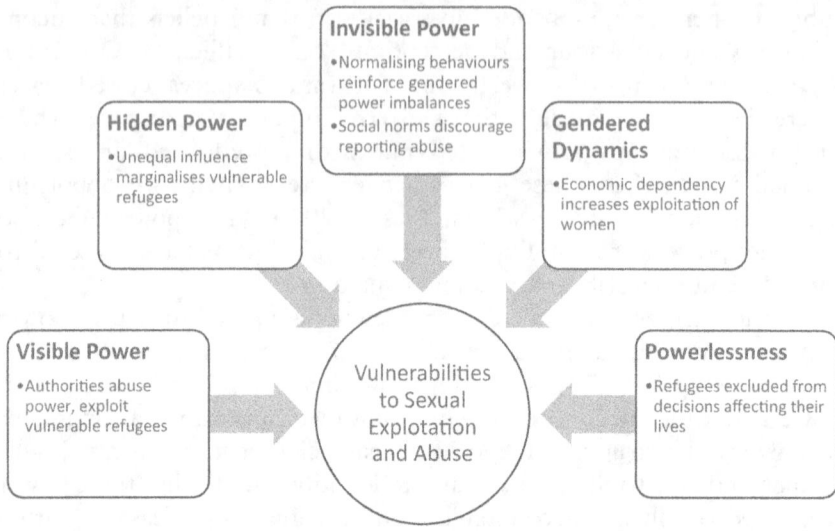

Figure 7.1 Vulnerabilities to Sexual Exploitation and Abuse in Sudanese Refugee Camps.
Source: Created by the author.

justice (Aubone & Hernandez, 2013; Hossain et al., 2018; Muuo et al., 2020). Muuo et al. (2020) highlighted how cultural norms in Dadaab refugee camp influence the recognition and response to gender-based violence.

Invisible power plays a crucial role in shaping social norms and perceptions, both within institutions and in everyday interactions among refugee populations. This form of power is embedded in underlying cultural dynamics and structural inequalities that influence daily life and interactions (Abdi, 2006; Behera, 2006). According to Bradley (2020), invisible power operates subtly, often unconsciously shaping beliefs and behaviours in ways that perpetuate existing hierarchies. By normalising certain behaviours and reinforcing gendered power imbalances, invisible power heightens the vulnerability of marginalised groups, such as refugees, to exploitation and SEA (Figure 7.1).

Overall, the interplay of these power dynamics—visible, hidden, and invisible—creates a complex environment within refugee camps. Confined spaces, limited resources, and dependence on external aid converge to foster conditions where SEA can proliferate, demonstrating the need for a nuanced understanding of power to effectively address and prevent abuse.

Gendered power dynamics of stakeholders and SEA at refugee camps

Accountability in refugee camps involves various actors—host states, UNHCR, and NGOs—each wielding different levels of power that impact the creation and effectiveness of accountability mechanisms, such as complaint systems (Fox, 2016). These power differentials often result in an unequal influence over decision-making processes and resource allocation (Capjon, 2007; Bondokji, 2016; McGee, 2019), marginalising vulnerable refugee populations, particularly women, girls, and people with disabilities, from meaningful participation in shaping their welfare.

The host states' responsibility and abuse of power

The host states are entrusted with the responsibility of providing a safe haven for refugees and are legally and morally accountable to a diverse array of stakeholders, including NGOs, refugees themselves, and the global community at large (UNHCR, 2010). In the case of Sudan, the Sudanese governmental department for the protection of refugees, Commissioners of Refugees (COR) bears the primary responsibility for the protection of refugees. This includes refugee safety, access to asylum procedures, and fulfilment of basic human rights.

The power imbalances within the system often lead to abuse, with women and girls being disproportionately affected due to their heightened vulnerability in such environments (UNHCR, 2010). The visible power wielded by authorities, such as the Commissioners of Refugees (COR) in Sudan, exacerbates these vulnerabilities, particularly for women. Empirical evidence and interviews by this author illustrate how women are subjected to sexual coercion by COR staff, as highlighted by one female refugee volunteer:

> Some guys from COR are violating women's dignity ... When female refugees go to COR to complain, they always ask them for a favour. They use their power and money for sexual violence ...
> (Interview with B4. See Fuchi, 2024: 160)

This gendered exploitation highlights the intersection of power abuse and gender inequality, as male officials leverage their authority to manipulate women, often withholding essential resources like shelter until women comply with sexual demands (Fuchi, 2024: 174).

This abuse reflects a broader issue of patriarchal structures within refugee camps, where women are more vulnerable to SEA due to their economic dependence and the absence of protective mechanisms. The lack of accountability and oversight allows these abuses to persist unchecked, mirroring findings from other contexts like Guinea's refugee camps, where similar power dynamics resulted in SEA without repercussions (Farmer, 2006). To address this, host states must adopt gender-sensitive policies that prioritise the protection of women and girls, establish transparent complaint mechanisms, and enforce accountability for perpetrators of SEA.

UNHCR's quasi-state role

As the first point of contact for refugees, UNHCR has significant control over resources, protection, and decision-making processes within camps, acting in a governmental capacity (Pallis, 2005; Farmer, 2006). However, refugee testimonies from my research reveal a troubling absence of UNHCR staff within the camps, except in emergencies, leaving refugees, particularly women, vulnerable to exploitation.

Multiple interviews (B9, B2, B6, B10, C1, C3, C4, C8, C9, C12; see Fuchi, 2024) indicate that UNHCR is often perceived as a distant authority, visible only at the transition centre, which fosters a lack of trust and confidence in their ability to provide ongoing protection. This detachment becomes even more problematic for women and girls, who face heightened vulnerability to SEA due to their gender and socio-economic status. The interviews suggest that some UNHCR staff abuse their power by soliciting sexual favours from female refugees in exchange for necessary services. One refugee (C7) made a disturbing comment:

> When my friend approached UNHCR for a permission to move from one camp to another because of ethnic conflicts within the camp, UNHCR staff asks for a favour. If you are a boy, they ask for money. If you are a girl, they ask for sex. They are corrupted
> (Interview with C7. See Fuchi, 2024: 162)

This behaviour reinforces the patriarchal structures already present in refugee camps, where women are often economically dependent and lack access to justice, making them more susceptible to SEA.

A lack of a functional complaint mechanism to address such abuses further aggravates the situation. This issue is not new; scholarly research has consistently criticised UNHCR for its failure to hold staff accountable for misconduct and for the absence of sanctions against those who exploit their authority (Sandvik & Jacobsen, 2016; Harrell-Bond, 2000). For women, who are often already marginalised and disempowered, this unchecked power creates an environment where they are treated as subjects rather than individuals with rights.

NGO aid workers and power: Rhetoric vs. practice discrepancies

NGOs hold significant operational roles in refugee camps and function as frontline agencies to organise and deliver aid distribution (Murray, 1999). While they assert their commitment to accountability towards affected populations, evidence from refugee participants reveals a considerable gap between this rhetoric and the realities on the ground. Numerous refugee accounts indicate troubling instances of SEA involving NGO aid workers, which contradicts the NGOs' stated accountability goals. Refugee participants (C2, C7, C9, C10; see Fuchi, 2024: 162) frequently identified and commented on nominally consensual yet exploitative relationships between refugees and aid workers—describing them as "boyfriends and girlfriends". It is seen as widely accepted and common knowledge among refugees that those refugees who are engaged in a consensual relationship with aid workers as "boyfriend" or "girlfriend" receive a greater quantity and/or better quality of aid (Interview with B11, B14; see Fuchi, 2024: 162).

As Ferris (2007) critically analyses, refugees are controlled by "moneyed elites—UN, aid workers, peacekeepers—whose resources are 10×, 100×, 1000× more than what the refugees have. They can afford to exploit this extreme disparity and pay for sex when they want and with whom they want" (2007: 586). In exploitative relationships, direct cash payments for sex may not always be the norm; instead, aid workers may wield their discretionary power to selectively distribute aid, providing benefits and preferential treatment to those engaged in such relationships. Aid workers essentially exercise discretion, using their hidden power to choose who gets what, in order to channel benefits to those being exploited in return for sex or preferential treatment.

Verbal sexual abuse is another common type of SEA that was disclosed during interviews. Inappropriate conversations such as "you are pretty, I will give you more supplies if you come with me" (Interview with B13; see Fuchi, 2024) are frequently reported. One national aid worker who visits Tunaybah Camp daily described the situation as follows:

> Some NGO workers like to have chit chat with refugees. Through aid distribution, a relationship sparks between NGO

worker and refugees. They start with getting to know each other's names, then catch up over coffee. They hug in the public and flirt with each other, but nobody cares. Then if you see alcohol and woman in provocative outfit in their hands, you know what happens next because of sexual conversations they are having

(Interview with B8. See Fuchi, 2024: 163)

Such occurrences are often visible around cafes within the camps. The interviewees made general observations about uncomfortable social interactions and unwelcome remarks made by males on the appearance of female refugees selling tea (Interview with B3, B8, B9, B16, B21; see Fuchi, 2024). For example, an aid worker described the experience of one 17-year-old female refugee who works as a community incentive volunteer for NGO in the camp. She met an aid worker at the distribution point where she collected non-food items. Subsequently, the aid worker maintained friendly conversations with her whenever they saw each other on the camp. One day, the aid worker visited her tent. It was soon after her father and husband left the camp for work in the morning. The interviewee reported that the refugee felt afraid, and this was exacerbated by pressure from the aid worker to sleep with him in exchange for employment at his agency. As demonstrated above, women refugees are often left with limited materials and financial resources, increasing their vulnerability to exploitations. With no alternatives, they are coerced into "bartering their only remaining possessions: their bodies and their dignity" (Murray, 1999: 1015).

The situation described above demonstrates gender roles and vulnerabilities of girls influenced by power at the household level. Female refugees' vulnerability was exacerbated by traditional gender roles and the lack of economic opportunities for women. Girls' sense of coercion and fear highlight the unequal power relations and the exploitative environment they navigate. On the one hand, the absence of male family members, who might traditionally be seen as protectors, may leave women and girls more exposed to exploitation within the household. However, men can also pose threats, often exacerbated by the hidden and private nature of these spaces. Consequently, this situation results in heightened gendered vulnerabilities within displacement contexts, such as refugee camps.

This is a clear manifestation of abuse of *visible* and *hidden* power of NGO staff over refugees. The desperation of refugees to do anything to meet their basic needs underlines the profound impact of power differentials within these contexts. Many aid workers acknowledged these power dynamics, with one stating:

> We all know that that is the line – there is a line you cannot cross. It is not negotiable, in terms of power dynamics. Aid workers we have power so we need to be responsible
> (Interview with B21. See Fuchi, 2024: 165)

The issue of SEA committed by aid workers against vulnerable populations highlights a disturbing breach of trust and downward accountability, resulting in a grave violation of ethical principles of NGOs as well as a failure to comply with the CHS. The challenges within refugee camps, however, extend beyond aid workers, as the empirical evidence also sheds light on incidents of SEA within host communities, or SEA committed by host community members in the refugee camps. These camps, often characterised by cramped living conditions and scarce resources, can become breeding grounds for further misconduct by surrounding communities, including SEA.

Power(lessness) of refugees

Refugees in camps are often positioned at the bottom of the power hierarchy, which exacerbates their vulnerability to exploitation. They are trapped in closed spaces of power, where they are systematically excluded from decision-making processes that directly affect their lives (Arendt, 2006; Griek, 2009; Holzer, 2013). Bender (2021) highlights a scenario involving female SEA refugee victims who were unable to advocate for changes in camp layouts that exposed them to risks, such as poor lighting near communal latrines. In many refugee camps, where the supposed protectors, including aid workers, are often the perpetrators of abuse, the lack of accountability combined with the refugees' lack of power underscores the structural inadequacies that leave refugees vulnerable. This powerlessness contributes to an environment in which SEA can flourish, with misconduct going unaddressed and victims left without adequate recourse or support.

While some refugees may be invited into decision-making spaces, their involvement is often superficial, placing them in what Gaventa (2019) terms a "claimed" space of power. For example, UNHCR mandates the creation of camp management committees, intended to include refugee voices in decision-making and ensure that programs address the needs of vulnerable groups (UN Refugee Agency et al., 2015). However, my research reveals the limitations of these structures, as demonstrated by the minimal influence of a female committee member. A female refugee in my research was never invited to the community leaders' meetings even after her appointment as a female community leader in the camp (Fuchi, 2024). Hidden power, particularly in the form of male leadership within the committee, continues to marginalise women's voices, reducing their ability to advocate for the needs of vulnerable groups, including those affected by SEA.

A critical issue that emerges in these camps is the prevalence of transactional sex, raising the difficult question: Do female refugees engage in transactional sex out of necessity or as a social choice? In the camps studied, Ethiopian social norms appear to influence these dynamics. Empirical evidence points to the existence of a designated prostitution area, where transactional sex has become normalised. This normalisation likely reflects the broader societal norms from Ethiopia, a country where prostitution is widespread, often driven by extreme poverty and entrenched from a young age (Ni Raghallaigh et al., 2017; Lalor, 2000). Tadele et al. (2021) recognise prostitution as common among women in various settings, including refugee camps (Abebe, 2016).

While not all interactions at or around the prostitution areas involve direct cash transactions for sex, ample evidence indicates frequent flirtatious exchanges with individuals who possess financial means or power, often in exchange for preferential treatment and benefits. At the region these refugees fled from in Tigray, Ethiopia, widespread prostitution has been reported (The Guardian, 2022) as a means of survival due to extreme poverty. Similarly, at the refugee camps in Gadaref, the dire lack of food and materials, essentially poverty, has compelled refugees to turn to transactional sex.

The powerlessness of refugees, especially their exclusion from decision-making, directly contributes to their vulnerability within camps. Lacking control over their lives and subjected to the visible and hidden power of host states, UNHCR, and NGOs, refugees are left exposed to exploitation. This disempowerment, particularly of women, girls, and marginalised groups, amplifies their risk of SEA. The next section explores how structural inequalities and the harsh living conditions within camps further heighten refugees' vulnerabilities to SEA, as they face limited protection and resources.

Vulnerabilities of female refugees to SEA

Gender dynamics play a crucial role in the context of displacement, with women and girls emerging as particularly vulnerable groups. The intersection of economic dependency, physical insecurity, and pervasive patriarchal norms intensifies their exposure to SEA within refugee settings (Mootz et al., 2017). Displacement not only impedes the fulfilment of basic needs but also disrupts familial and communal structures, compounding vulnerabilities.

Research by Murray (1999) highlights that the loss of male family members due to conflict often results in women assuming the role of household heads. This transition can lead to a severe loss of financial stability and increases the likelihood of exploitation. Women, now navigating precarious situations alone, may resort to transactional sex as a means of survival due to limited economic opportunities (Fuchi, 2024). A poignant testimony from a female refugee volunteer (C1) illustrates the severe insecurity faced in refugee camps:

> No, I don't feel safe. So many strangers can hold knives and can harm us. Someone can come in anytime. I'm afraid people will come and steal things from my tent...You see, I used to be a computer engineering student back home. I really hate this place but I have no option. I've seen people being killed in front of us ...
> (Interview with C1. See Fuchi, 2024: 152)

This statement highlights the pervasive fear among refugees and the harsh realities of SEA within refugee camps, which, while intended as safe havens from conflict, often perpetuate their own forms of violence and exploitation. Interviews with various individuals (B13, B21, C3, C6, D1, D6) further reveal that women traveling alone, female-headed households, child-headed households, and orphaned children face the highest levels of vulnerability.

Intersectionality of vulnerabilities for women and girls

The Women's Refugee Commission (2010) emphasises the intersectionality of these vulnerabilities, noting that women with disabilities are at heightened risk of SEA due to a combination of disability, gender, and refugee status. This "triple marginalisation" is exacerbated by impoverishment, language barriers, and a pervasive fear of authorities, including police and legal institutions (Murray, 2000). These factors inhibit their ability to seek and obtain protection and redress, reinforcing existing patriarchal vulnerabilities (Farmer, 2006).

Unaccompanied minors are also at increased risk, vulnerable to exploitation, trafficking, and abuse (Achilli, 2023). The lack of strict enforcement of protective laws in refugee camps exacerbates these dangers, allowing SEA to thrive. As a result, there is a surge in unwanted pregnancies among refugee women, and aid workers report a rising demand for abortion services. The high number of gender-based violence cases, including forced pregnancies, highlights the pervasive nature of SEA in these settings.

Deeply entrenched cultures of impunity and economic survival

Research reveals a deeply entrenched culture of impunity surrounding SEA in and around refugee camps, perpetuated by host states, UNHCR, NGO aid workers, and local communities. Factors such as corruption in Sudan's law enforcement, a culture of alcoholism, and the historical development of Um Rakuba Camp, now a hub for prostitution, exacerbate the issue. Corruption in the legal system allows perpetrators to avoid accountability while victims struggle to seek justice, leaving refugees vulnerable and empowering abusers to continue unchecked (Brysk, 2018).

Transactional sex within refugee camps presents a complex issue, often driven by economic necessity. The Ethiopian community managing the camp has normalised a designated area for prostitution, reflecting norms from their home country. Women frequently engage in transactional sex for survival, exchanging favours for basic necessities. Aid workers (B26, B19) who have long observed the circumstance refugees are put in suggest that there is also a need to eliminate activities that force refugees to make money to meet their basic needs and in doing so may force them into transactional sex. One refugee explained that they believe transactional sex persists because NGOs are not meeting the needs of refugees:

> For example, we distribute sorghum that need to be grained. But refugees don't have grinders. They don't have money to grind. To get money, some inevitably put themselves into prostitution
> (Interview with B26. See Fuchi, 2024: 172)

This example illustrates the practical challenges and unintended consequences of aid delivery practice to identify and act upon potential or actual intended negative effects. The oversight in the sorghum distribution case reflects a failure to fully engage with the needs and capacities of the refugee population, suggesting a broader issue of insufficient accountability. They are then placed in positions where they must seek additional resources outside the aid received. It then exacerbates power imbalance between aid providers and affected populations, increasing their vulnerability to exploitation including SEA. The intersection revealed here between extreme poverty, transactional sex, and the practices of those managing and delivering goods and services in the camps highlights the harsh realities faced by those affected by civil war and trapped in cycles of vulnerabilities.

Conclusion

This chapter has presented a snapshot of accountability gaps in safeguarding and identified risks and vulnerabilities around SEA, particularly for women and girls. Using Gaventa's powercube framework, the analysis has illuminated the complex intersections between power dynamics and fragmented accountability mechanisms within the aid sector. The empirical evidence, sourced from aid workers and refugees, reveals the interplay of visible, hidden, and invisible forms of power, creating an environment conducive to various forms of SEA. These SEAs manifest as exploitative relationships, verbal sexual abuse, transactional sex, and forced pregnancy.

The intersection of gendered power dynamics across multiple levels profoundly impacts the lives of women and girls. Gendered power dynamics intersect with broader social and economic structures, heightening the vulnerabilities of women and girls. This intersectionality demonstrates that gendered power is not isolated but deeply interwoven with other systemic structures, leading to compounded disadvantages for women. These dynamics manifest in visible forms of power within formal decision-making processes, where women are often excluded or marginalised, and in hidden biases and cultural norms that perpetuate unequal relations and increase susceptibility to SEA. The interplay of these various power dynamics highlights the complex and multifaceted nature of gender inequality, making it essential to address all levels of power to mitigate the risks faced by women and girls.

By addressing invisible forms of power, the analysis reveals deep-seated societal attitudes and institutional practices that marginalise women. These ingrained beliefs and practices further entrench gender inequality and hinder women's access to protection and resources. The hidden power dynamics, such as biases and cultural norms, though less apparent, significantly impact women's lives by maintaining unequal relations and increasing their vulnerability to SEA. This gender-sensitive approach therefore stresses the compounded risks faced by women due to the pervasive and interconnected nature of power dynamics, emphasising the need to dismantle these entrenched inequalities and promote gender equality.

Key messages and learning: calls for NGOs

- **Embed safeguarding in organisational culture:** NGOs must integrate safeguarding measures into their core operations, ensuring these practices are not just compliance exercises but are deeply rooted in organisational culture. This includes establishing a zero-tolerance stance on exploitation, implementing transparent reporting procedures, and holding perpetrators accountable.
- **Empower women and address vulnerabilities:** Implement gender-responsive strategies that address the unique vulnerabilities of women and girls. This involves providing gender-sensitive training for all staff, particularly those on the front lines, and empowering women within refugee communities through leadership opportunities and inclusion in decision-making processes.
- **Strengthen legal and policy frameworks:** Collaborate with governments, international bodies, and local organisations to reform policies that perpetuate gender-based discrimination. Strengthening legal accountability mechanisms, such as independent bodies to oversee SEA cases, is essential to breaking the cycle of abuse and impunity.
- **Promote economic independence:** Focus on providing women and girls with tools for economic self-reliance, including access to education, vocational training, and livelihood programs. Ensure essential services like safe spaces, healthcare, and psychosocial support are available to help survivors recover and reintegrate without stigma.

Calls for donors

- **Fund safeguarding and accountability systems:** Prioritise funding for robust safeguarding mechanisms that prevent SEA, monitor power dynamics, and ensure clear reporting and accountability procedures. Require detailed safeguarding plans as part of grant applications and support continuous monitoring and independent audits.
- **Demand transparency:** Insist on regular public reporting from NGOs regarding SEA incidents and their handling. This transparency fosters a culture of accountability and discourages cover-ups, while ensuring NGOs adhere to ethical standards.
- **Support gender-responsive strategies:** Make gender-responsive approaches a funding requirement. This includes conducting gender audits, ensuring gender equality in program design, and allocating funds specifically for initiatives that empower women and girls. Support leadership opportunities and community-based approaches that amplify women's voices in decision-making.

References

Abdi, A. M. (2016). Refugees, gender-based violence and resistance: A case study of Somali refugee women in Kenya. In *Women, migration and citizenship* (pp. 231–252). Routledge.

Abebe, M. (2016). *Factors Affecting Exiting Behaviour of Prostitute Life Style. In the Case of Gerji Area, Addis Ababa*. Addis Ababa, Ethiopia: Addis Ababa University.

Achilli, L. (2023). 'Protection' on my own terms: human smuggling and unaccompanied Syrian minors. *Journal of Ethnic and Migration Studies*, 49(13), 3289–3307.

Arendt, H. (2006). *The Origins of Totalitarianism*. Harcourt, Brace, New York: Indiana University Press.

Aubone, A. & Hernandez, J. (2013). Assessing refugee camp characteristics and the occurrence of sexual violence: a preliminary analysis of the Dadaab complex. Refugee Survey Quarterly, 32(4), 22–40.

Behera, N. C. (2006). *Gender, Conflict and Migration. Women and Migration in Asia, Volume 4*. London: SAGE Publications.

Bender, F. (2021). Should refugees govern refugee camps? *Critical Review of International Social and Political Philosophy*. 27(4), 441–464. https://doi.org/10.1080/13698230.2021.1941702

Bondokji, N. (2016). The expectations gap in humanitarian operations: field perspectives from Jordan. *Asian Journal of Peacebuilding*, 4(1), 1–28.

Bradley, A. (2020). Did we forget about power? Reintroducing concepts of power for justice, equality and peace. In: R. McGee & J. Pettit (Eds.), *Power, Empowerment and Social Change* (pp. 101–116). Abingdon: Routledge.

Brysk, A. (2018). *The Struggle for Freedom from Fear: Contesting Violence Against Women at the Frontiers of Globalization*. Oxford: Oxford University Press.

Capjon, A. (2007). *Coordinating the Humanitarian Response to Refugee Situations: The Role of Power and Trust in Humanitarian Networks*. Working Paper 42. Brighton: University of Sussex Centre for Migration Research.

Champion, S. (2023). In my view: Is the aid sector racist?. In *Development Co-operation Report 2023: Debating the Aid System*. Paris: OECD Publishing. https://doi.org/10.1787/708f5472-en.

CHS Alliance. (2020). *Humanitarian Accountability Report 2020. Are We Making Aid Work Better For People Affected by Crisis*. Available at https://d1h79zlghft2zs.cloudfront.net/uploads/2020/10/01450-CHS-2020-HAR-Report-FA2-WEB2.pdf

CHS Alliance (2022). Humanitarian Accountability Report 2022: Accountability is Non-Negotiable – Ending sexual exploitation, abuse and harassment. Available at https://d1h79zlghft2zs.cloudfront.net/uploads/2022/11/Chapter-4-PSEAH.pdf.

Crewel, E. & Fernando, P. (2006). The elephant in the room: racism in representations, relationships and rituals. *Progress in Development Studies*, 6(1), 40–54.

Daoust, G. & Dyvik, S. L. (2021). Reconceptualizing vulnerability and safeguarding in the humanitarian and development sector. *Social Politics: International Studies in Gender, State and Society*, 29(1), 355–378.

Defeis, E. F. (2008). U.N. *peacekeepers and sexual abuse and exploitation: an end to impunity. Global Studies Law Review*, 7(2). Washington University.

Available at https://openscholarship.wustl.edu/law_globalstudies/vol7/iss2/2.

DFID Safeguarding Unit. (2018). *Sexual Exploitation, Abuse and Harassment (SEAH) in the International Aid Sector. Victim and Survivor Voices: Main Findings from a DFID-led Listening Exercise*. DFID. Available at https://assets.publishing.service.gov.uk/government/uploads/system/uploads/attachment_data/file/749741/Listening-Exercise1.pdf.

Farmer, A. (2006). Refugee responses, state-like behavior, and accountability for human rights violations: a case study of sexual violence in Guinea's refugee camps. *Yale Human Rights and Development Law Journal*, 9, 44.

Ferris, E. (2007). Abuse of power: sexual exploitation of refugee women and girls march 2007. *Journal of Women in Culture and Society*, 32(3), 584–591.

Fox, J. (2016). Doing accountability differently: Vertically integrated civil society policy monitoring and advocacy. *Going vertical: citizen-led reform campaigns in the Philippines*, p. 15–33. Quezon City, Philippines: G-Watch, Accountability Research Center.

Fuchi, M. (2024). *NGO Accountability and Power Dynamics in Safeguarding: The Core Humanitarian Standard in Theory and Practice in Refugee Camps in Sudan*. University of Birmingham. Doctor of Philosophy thesis.

Gaventa, J. (2005). *Reflections on the Uses of the 'Power Cube' Approach for Analyzing the Spaces, Places and Dynamics of Civil Society Participation and Engagement. Prepared for Dutch CFA Evaluation 'Assessing Civil Society Participation as Supported In-Country by Cordaid, Hivos, Novib and Plan Netherlands'*.

Gaventa, J. (2019). Applying power analysis: using the 'powercube' to explore forms, levels and spaces. In Rosemary McGee & Jethro Pettit (Eds.), *Power, Empowerment and Social Change* (pp. 117–138). Abingdon: Routledge.

Griek, I. (2009). The 'rights turn' in refugee protection: an analysis of UNHCR's adoption of the human rights-based approach. *Deusto Journal of Human Rights*, 6, 73–90.

Harrell-Bond, B. E. (2000). *Aid Evaluation of the Tanganyika Christian Refugee Service Refugee Project in Kibondo District, Tanzania: 5–19 Jan. 2000: Report and Recommendations (Feb. 2000)*.

Harrell-Bond, B. & Verdirame, G. (2005). *Rights in Exile: Janus-Faced Humanitarianism*. New York: Berghahn Books.

Harrington, C. (2022). *Neoliberal Sexual Violence Politics: Toxic Masculinity and #MeToo*. Palgrave Macmillan, New York: Springer Nature. https://doi.org/10.1007/978-3-031-07088-4

Holzer, E. (2013). What happens to law in a refugee camp? *Law & Society Review*, 47(4), 837–872. The Law and Society Association.

Hossain, M., Izugbara, C., McApine, A., Stella, M., Bacchus, L., Muuo, S., Kohli, A., Egesa, C., Pearson, R., Franchi, G., & MacRae, M. (2018). *Violence, Uncertainty, and Resilience Among Refugee Women and Community Workers: An Evaluation of Gender-based Violence Case Management Services in the Dadaab Refugee Camps*. London: Department for International Development (DFID).

Kamanzi, A. (2012). *Power Analysis: A Study of Participation at the Local Level in Tanzania*. Research paper/ASC Working Paper Series. Issue 105.

Kinchin, N. (2016). The implied human rights obligations of UNHCR. *International Journal of Refugee Law*, 28(2), 251–275.

Kovatch, B. (2016). Sexual exploitation and abuse in UN peacekeeping missions: a case study of MONUC and MONUSCO. *The Journal of the Middle East and Africa*, 7(2), 157–174.

Krause, U. (2021). Colonial roots of the 1951 refugee convention and its effects on the global refugee regime. *Journal of International Relations and Development*, 24(3), 599–626.

Lalor, K. (2000). The victimization of juvenile prostitutes in Ethiopia. *International Social Work*, 43(2), 227–242.

Lopez, L. E. (2015). Corruption and international aid allocation: a complex dance. *Journal of Economic Development*, 40(1), 35.

McGee, R. (2019). Rethinking accountability: a power perspective. In Rosemary McGee & Jethro Pettit (Eds.), *Power, Empowerment and Social Change* (pp. 50–67). Abingdon: Routledge.

Miller, B. (2020). *Stepping into the Intersection: The Unintended Consequences of Presenting a 'Latina Educational' at a Feminist Health Organisation. Social Work & Policy Studies: Social Justice, Practice and Theory*, 3(1). Sydney: University of Sydney.

Mootz, J. J., Stabb, S. D., & Mollen, D.. (2017). Gender-based violence and armed conflict: a community-informed socioecological conceptual model from northeastern Uganda. *Psychology of Women Quarterly*, 41(3), 368–388. https://doi.org/10.1177/0361684317705086

Murray, R. (1999). Sex for food in refugee economy: human rights implications and accountability. *Georgetown Immigration Law Journal*, 14(4), 985–1026.

Muuo, S., Muthuri, S. K., Mutua, M. K., McAlpine, A., Bacchus, L. J., Ogego, H., Bangha, M., Hossain, M., & Izugbara, C. (2020). Barriers and facilitators to care-seeking among survivors of gender-based violence in the Dadaab refugee complex. *Sexual and Reproductive Health Matters*, 28(1), 245–260.

Narayanaswamy, L. (2024). Chapter 15: race, racialisation, and coloniality in the humanitarian aid sector; in the book. In S. Roth, B. Purkayastha, & T. Denskus (Eds.), *Handbook on Humanitarianism and Inequality*. Cheltenham: Edward Elgar Publishing.

New Humanitarian. (2023). *Q&A: How to Fix the UN's Sex Abuse Problem? 'If We're Going to be Successful in Combating Sexual Exploitation and Abuse, We Need to Leave Our Logos and Egos at the Door.'* Available at www.thenewhumanitarian.org/interview/2023/04/24/qa-how-fix-uns-sex-abuse-problem

Ní Raghallaigh, M., Morton, S., & Allen, M. (2017). HIV transmission as a form of gender based violence: experiences of women in Tigray, Ethiopia. *International Social Work*, 60(4), 941–953.

Pallis, M. (2005). The operation of UNHCR's accountability mechanisms. *New York University Journal of International Law & Politics*, 37(4), 869–918.

Patel, K. (2020). Race and a decolonial turn in development studies. *Third World Quarterly*, 41(9), 1463–1475. https://doi.org/10.1080/01436597.2020.1784001.

Sandvik, K. B. & Jacobsen, K. L. eds. (2016). *UNHCR and the Struggle for Accountability: Technology, Law and Results-Based Management*. London: Taylor & Francis Group.

Scott-Villiers, P. & Oosterom, M. (2016). Power, Poverty and Inequality. The Institute of Development Studies and Partner Organisations. Report.

Tadele, G., Nencel, L., & Sabelis, I. (2021). Problematizing the 'prostitution problem' in Ethiopia. The stigmatization of sex workers through moral discourses and their representations. In J. Bionness, L. Nencel, & M. L. Skilbrei (Eds.), *Reconfiguring Stigma in Studies of Sex for Sale*. 1st Edition. London: Routledge.

The Guardian. (2022). *'Ethiopia: Tigray on brink of humanitarian disaster, UN says'*. Available at www.theguardian.com/global-development/2022/jan/14/ethiopia-tigray-on-brink-of-humanitarian-disaster-un-says?s=09 (Accessed: 6 September 2024).

The Women's Refugee Commission. (2010). *Disabilities Among Refugees and Conflict-affected Populations*. Published January 31, 2010. Available at www.womensrefugeecommission.org/research-resources/disabilities-among-refugees-and-conflict-affected-populations/

Turner, L. (2020). 'Refugees can be entrepreneurs too!' humanitarianism, race, and the marketing of Syrian refugees. *Review of International Studies*, 46(1), 137–155.

UNHCR. (2010). *Submission by the United Nations High Commissioner for Refugees for the Office of the High Commissioner for Human Rights' Compilation Report – Universal Periodic Review: SUDAN*. Division of International Protection. Human Rights Liaison Unit. Available at www.ohchr.org/sites/default/files/libdocs/HRBodies/UPR/Documents/Session11/SD/UNHCR_UnitedNationsHighCommissionerforRefugees_-eng.pdf.

UNHCR, IOM, NRC, & CCCM Cluster (2015). Camp Management Toolkit. Available at https://data.unhcr.org/en/documents/download/51887.

Westendorf, J. (2020). *Why Transactional Sex is Difficult to Stop in the Aid Sector: 'Safeguarding Experts Have Been Hired in Droves.' Opinion*. The New Humanitarian. Available at www.thenewhumanitarian.org/opinion/2020/10/06/sexual-abuse-aid-workers-again.

Westendorf, J. & Searle, L. (2017). Sexual exploitation and abuse in peace operations: trends, policy responses and future directions. *International Affairs* (London), 93(2), 365–387.

Whitworth, S. (2004). *Men, Militarism, and UN Peacekeeping: A Gendered Analysis*. Boulder, USA: Lynne Rienner Publishers. https://doi.org/10.1515/9781685851330

Wilde, R. (1998). Quis Custodiet Ipsos Custodes?: Why and how UNHCR governance of 'development' refugee camps should be subject to international human rights law. *Yale University Human Rights & Development Law Journal*, 1, 107–119.

VeneKlasen, L. (2020). Plus ça change? Shifting power in a disorienting moment. In R. McGee & J. Pettit (Eds.), *Power, Empowerment and Social Change* (pp. 19–36). New York, NY: Routledge.

Verdirame, G. (2011). *The UN and Human Rights: Who Guards the Guardians?* New York: Cambridge University Press.

Part Two

Chapter 8

Sexual violence as a weapon of war

Céline Bardet and Léa Darves-Bornoz

Chapter objectives

By the end of this chapter, you will:

- Have an awareness of the latest understanding of the use of sexual violence by state actors as a weapon of war.
- Understand the fact that a good proportion of aid work is delivered in contexts where gender-based violence and sexual violence are seen as a legitimate tactic to achieve strategic outcomes.

Introduction

Conflict-related sexual violence (CRSV) is as old as war itself. A key shift in contemporary thinking on war and gender has been the recognition that wartime rape is not merely a by-product of conflict but often a deliberate, strategic policy. Over the past 30 years, advocacy around "rape as a weapon of war" has underscored the systematic, pervasive, and orchestrated nature of such violence, positioning it as integral rather than incidental to armed conflict.

CRSV is brutal, intentional, and serves to humiliate or punish individuals and their communities, leaving lasting trauma. It is used both as a weapon of war and a tactic of terrorism (UNDPO, 2019). While its scale varies, CRSV rarely occurs in isolation, often accompanying other atrocities such as killings, child recruitment, looting, and the destruction of property (UNDPO, 2019). Its recognition has been shaped by the testimonies of survivors and the relentless work of local and international actors, leading to several UN resolutions that define CRSV as requiring a direct or indirect link to the conflict, whether temporal, geographical, or causal (United Nations Security Council, various). Beyond their recognition through international resolutions, a significant milestone has been their legal qualification as intentional crimes. International humanitarian and criminal law now classify sexual violence as a war crime, a crime against humanity, and, in some cases, a constitutive act of genocide (Office of the Prosecutor, International Criminal Court, 2014). Yet, despite these legal advancements, impunity remains the norm, posing a major challenge for international justice and humanitarian organisations striving to support victims. Moreover, the continuous questioning of women's and girls' human rights—though they are the primary but not the sole victims of these crimes—undermines efforts to ensure recognition, protection, and accountability.

In this context, understanding the strategic use of sexual violence by state and non-state actors, its evolving dynamics, and its profound humanitarian impact is critical. Addressing CRSV requires an innovative, inclusive approach that rethinks traditional humanitarian responses. Medical, psychosocial, and judicial support mechanisms must be adapted to reach survivors proactively and extend assistance to their communities. Outreach and confidence-building efforts are essential to encourage survivors to come forward, ensuring that their experiences are acknowledged, and justice is pursued.

Rape as a weapon of war: a deliberate and organised strategy

CRSV can arise from opportunistic acts by individual combatants, particularly in contexts of weakened command structures and general impunity. However, extensive documentation has demonstrated that in many conflicts, sexual violence is systematically used as a strategic tool to achieve military, political, and economic objectives (Wood, 2006). This distinction is crucial for understanding the patterns of such crimes, as well as the legal and humanitarian challenges they present. Sexual violence includes acts of a sexual nature, which are perpetrated against a person without his or her consent, often by force or coercion.

A mechanism for community destruction and social control

One of the most severe consequences of CRSV is its capacity to destabilise and dismantle families, communities, and societies. Unlike conventional weapons that primarily target infrastructure or combatants, sexual violence directly affects individuals while also inflicting long-term damage on the social fabric. In many societies, particularly those with patriarchal norms, survivors face stigma, ostracisation, and, in some cases, forced displacement. This dynamic is exploited by perpetrators who use sexual violence as a means to instil fear, weaken social cohesion, and facilitate the forced movement of populations.

The Bosnian War (1992–1995) provides a well-documented example of the systematic use of rape as a tool of ethnic cleansing. The organised sexual violence committed against Bosnian women in so-called "rape camps" was not incidental but part of a broader strategy to terrorise communities, forcibly alter demographics, and prevent future generations through forced impregnation (Trial International, Vive Žene & GSF, 2022). This case became a landmark in international criminal law when the International Criminal Tribunal for the former Yugoslavia (ICTY) recognised rape as a form of torture and for sexual enslavement as crime against humanity (Koenig, Lincoln & Groth, 2011).

A tactic for political repression and terrorism

Sexual violence is also employed as a tool of political control, particularly in authoritarian regimes and conflict settings where opposition groups are targeted. State security forces, intelligence agencies, and paramilitary groups have used it to punish dissent, intimidate political opponents, and suppress resistance movements. In Syria, since the outbreak of the civil war in 2011, reports have extensively documented the use of sexual violence by state actors, including in detention centres, as a means of torture and coercion. Survivors have described systematic rape, sexual humiliation, and other forms of abuse used to extract confessions, break the will of detainees, and spread fear among opposition communities (Nassar et al., 2023). The United Nations and independent human rights organisations have classified these acts as crimes against humanity. These crimes have been documented by the International, Impartial, and Independent Mechanism for Syria (IIIM) of the UN Human Rights Council, as well as prosecuted under universal jurisdiction by several national courts.

Notably, in Germany, a landmark case led to the conviction of former Syrian intelligence officers for crimes against humanity, including sexual violence committed in Syrian detention centres (ECCHR, undated).

In recent years, a new form of CRSV has emerged, particularly among global jihadist groups with a Salafist ideology. Several terrorist organisations have systematically and institutionally incorporated sexual violence into their operational strategies, not only as a weapon of war but as a fundamental component of the societal model they seek to establish. The self-proclaimed Islamic State (ISIS) exemplified this approach by integrating sexual slavery into its governance structure. Unlike many other conflicts where sexual violence is committed covertly, ISIS openly institutionalised it as a legally sanctioned practice within its so-called caliphate. The enslavement of Yazidi women was not only used as a recruitment tool for fighters but also regulated through official decrees, judicial rulings, and administrative departments within the organisation (United Nations Human Rights Council, 2016). Courts within ISIS-controlled territories justified and facilitated the organised sale, trade, and systematic rape of Yazidi women, reinforcing the group's ideological narrative and asserting control over conquered population. The large-scale abduction, sexual enslavement, and trafficking of Yazidi women in Iraq in 2014 demonstrated how sexual violence can be weaponised for ideological domination. These acts were not incidental, but part of a broader genocidal strategy aimed at eradicating the Yazidi community.

An instrument of economic exploitation

Beyond its use as a method of social destruction and political repression, sexual violence has also been deployed as a tactic for economic exploitation and control. In resource-rich conflict zones, armed groups have used sexual violence to exert dominance over populations, facilitating forced labour, extortion, and the appropriation of land and assets. The case of the Democratic Republic of the Congo (DRC) illustrates this economic dimension. Various armed groups, including those controlling lucrative mining regions, have used sexual violence to subjugate local communities, displace populations, and establish dominance over resource-rich territories. The widespread and systematic nature of these crimes has been extensively documented by international investigations, underscoring the role of sexual violence in reinforcing war economies.

The challenges of accountability and response

Despite increasing international recognition of CRSV as a serious crime under international law, accountability remains the exception rather than the rule. The prosecution of these crimes faces significant structural, legal, and political barriers, leaving survivors without redress and allowing perpetrators to operate with impunity.

Structural and legal barriers to justice

One of the primary challenges in prosecuting CRSV is the difficulty of collecting evidence that meets the high legal standards required for criminal convictions. Survivors often face significant obstacles in coming forward, including stigma, social ostracisation, and fear of retaliation. In conflict zones, the destruction of medical and forensic infrastructure further limits the ability to document crimes and secure reliable testimony. Additionally, legal systems in many affected countries lack the necessary frameworks or political will to prosecute sexual violence effectively, particularly when state actors or allied militias are implicated.

Internationally, while institutions such as the International Criminal Court (ICC) have made progress in recognising sexual violence as a war crime, a crime against humanity, and an act of genocide, enforcement mechanisms remain weak. Many perpetrators continue to evade justice due to political constraints, the refusal of states to cooperate with international courts, and the complexity of gathering admissible evidence in active conflict settings. Universal jurisdiction, which allows national courts to prosecute international crimes regardless of where they occurred, has provided some avenues for accountability, as seen in recent cases against Syrian intelligence officers. However, such efforts remain limited in scope and highly dependent on the political will of states.

Beyond legal justice: the need for holistic responses

While legal accountability remains essential, addressing CRSV requires a broader, survivor-centred approach that goes beyond prosecutions. Justice for survivors must include reparations, psychosocial support, and long-term reintegration into their communities. In many cases, the stigma associated with sexual violence is so severe that survivors are rejected by their families or communities, exacerbating their vulnerability and furthering the cycle of violence.

Comprehensive response mechanisms must prioritise accessibility, confidentiality, and trust-building. Traditional humanitarian responses often fail to account for the specific needs of sexual violence survivors, particularly in conflict settings where state institutions are weak or complicit.

Survivor-led initiatives, mobile legal and medical clinics, and community-based reconciliation programs have shown promise in bridging this gap. The next section explores the growing humanitarian consequences of CRSV and the urgent need for innovative, survivor-focused interventions that address both immediate and long-term needs.

The growing humanitarian impact of CRSV

Humanitarian needs related to CRSV have been increasing steadily as sexual violence is increasingly used as a tactic of war (United Nations Secretary-General, 2025). The scale and systematic nature of these crimes place a significant burden on humanitarian actors, who must respond to both immediate and long-term consequences. Survivors require access to urgent medical care, psychological support, legal assistance, and socio-economic reintegration, yet these services remain severely underfunded and often inaccessible in conflict zones.

CRSV has devastating and far-reaching consequences, not only for survivors but also for their families and communities. Unlike many other forms of violence in war, its impact is deeply intertwined with social structures, cultural perceptions, and long-term psychological and economic repercussions. Addressing these crimes requires a humanitarian response that is both inclusive and adapted to the specific needs of survivors, while ensuring that it remains an integral part of broader relief efforts.

A humanitarian challenge requiring a renewed approach

The medical consequences of CRSV are severe, including genital injuries, obstetric fistulas, sexually transmitted infections, and unwanted pregnancies. In many conflict zones, healthcare services are either destroyed or inaccessible, leaving survivors without emergency or long-term medical support. The psychological impact is equally profound. Survivors frequently suffer from post-traumatic stress disorder, depression, anxiety, and suicidal ideation. In many cultures, they face stigma, social ostracisation, and rejection by their families and communities, further isolating them from essential services. Traditional humanitarian structures, such as medical camps in displacement sones, are often inadequate for reaching survivors, as many avoid these spaces due to fear of exposure and further victimisation. A new approach is needed, one that does not rely on survivors seeking help but instead actively reaches out to them in a way that is both discreet and culturally sensitive.

The importance of outreach and trust-building

Due to the shame and fear associated with sexual violence in conflict, survivors are often reluctant to seek medical or psychological support. Unlike other war-affected populations who may openly access humanitarian aid, many survivors prefer to remain invisible, fearing judgement, reprisals, or further harm (Rubini et al., 2023). This makes outreach a fundamental component of any effective humanitarian response.

Rather than relying on fixed aid structures, humanitarian actors must adopt mobile and community-based strategies to identify and assist survivors. This means working with trusted local intermediaries, including community leaders, health workers, and survivors themselves, to create safe channels of access. Confidentiality and trust-building are key, as survivors are more likely to seek help when services are brought to them rather than requiring them to come forward publicly. An effective model involves creating integrated support spaces where survivors can access medical, psychological, and legal aid in a single, discreet location. These centres, adapted to conflict zones, would allow survivors to seek care without having to navigate multiple systems or expose themselves to risk. Building trust within communities is essential, as survivors will only engage with humanitarian services if they feel safe and respected.

Innovation in documentation and access to justice

One of the major challenges in responding to sexual violence in conflict is the collection and preservation of evidence, particularly in conflict zones where medical and legal infrastructure is weak. Many cases of sexual violence go undocumented due to fear, lack of medical access, or destruction of records. New technologies offer potential solutions to these barriers. For example, blockchain-secured medical certificates could provide a tamper-proof record of injuries, allowing survivors to seek justice without fear of their evidence being lost or manipulated. Digital platforms could enable survivors to anonymously report crimes and access legal or psychological support remotely, reducing the risk of retaliation. Additionally, technology can improve outreach efforts. Secure communication tools can connect survivors with legal aid and support networks, while AI-driven risk mapping can help identify areas where sexual violence is most prevalent, ensuring that humanitarian resources are deployed where they are most needed. These innovations must be designed with survivors in mind, ensuring that they enhance access to services rather than create new risks or barriers.

Conclusion

Sexual violence in conflict is not just an individual tragedy—it is a structural weapon of war that requires equally strategic and sustained responses. Innovation, survivor-centred approaches, and long-term investments in outreach, justice, and recovery mechanisms are essential to breaking cycles of violence and ensuring that survivors receive the dignity, protection, and support they deserve.

References

European Center for Constitutional and Human Rights (ECCHR) (undated) *Survivors: Sexual Violence by Syrian Intelligence Services Are Crimes against Humanity*. Available at: www.ecchr.eu/en/case/survivors-sexual-violence-by-syrian-intelligence-services-are-crimes-against-humanity/ (accessed January 30, 2025).

Koenig, K. A., Lincoln, R., and Groth, L. (2011) *The Jurisprudence of Sexual Violence*. Berkeley: Human Rights Center, University of California.

Nassar, A., The Global Survivors Fund (GSF), Woman Now for Development (WND), and the Association of Detainees and the Missing in Sednaya Prison (2023) *Syria Study on Opportunities for Reparations for Survivors of Conflict-Related Sexual Violence*, pp. 19–27, available at: www.globalsurvivorsfund.org/fileadmin/uploads/gsf/Documents/Resources/Global_Reparation_Studies/GSF_Report_SYRIA_EN_Sept2023_WEB.pdf

Office of the Prosecutor, International Criminal Court (2014) *Policy Paper on Sexual and Gender-Based Crimes*, pp. 12–21, available at: www.icc-cpi.int/sites/default/files/Policy_Paper_on_Sexual_and_Gender-Based_Crimes-20_June_2014-ENG.pdf

Rubini, E., Valente, M., Trentin, M., Facci, G., Ragazzoni, L., and Gino, S. (2023) Negative Consequences of Conflict-Related Sexual Violence on Survivors: A Systematic Review of Qualitative Evidence. *International Journal for Equity in Health*, 22: 227.

Trial International, Vive Žene, and GSF (2022) *Study on Opportunities for Reparations for Survivors of Conflict-Related Sexual Violence*, pp. 14–20, available at: www.globalsurvivorsfund.org/fileadmin/uploads/gsf/Documents/Resources/Global_Reparation_Studies/GSF_Report_BiH_EN_March2022_WEB.pdf

United Nations Department of Peace Operations (UNDPO) (2019) *The Handbook for United Nations Field Missions on Preventing and Responding to Conflict-Related Sexual Violence*, Chapter 1: Conceptual Foundation and the Evolution of the CRSV Mandate, p. 6, available at: www.un.org/sexualviolenceinconflict/wp-content/uploads/2020/06/2020.08-UN-CRSV-Handbook.pdf

United Nations Human Rights Council (2016) *They Came to Destroy: ISIS Crimes Against the Yazidis*, Report (A/HRC/32/CRP.2), pp. 25–31, available at: www.ohchr.org/sites/default/files/Documents/HRBodies/HRCouncil/CoISyria/A_HRC_32_CRP.2_en.pdf

United Nations Security Council (2008) *Resolution 1820 (S/RES/1820(2008))*, New York; United Nations Security Council. (2009). *Resolution 1888 (S/RES/1888(2009))*, New York; United Nations Security Council. (2010). *Resolution 1960 (S/RES/1960(2010))*, New York; United Nations Security Council. (2013). *Resolution 2106 (S/RES/2106(2013))*, New York;United Nations Security Council. (2015). *Resolution 2242 (S/RES/2242(2015))*, New York; United Nations Security Council. (2016). *Resolution 2331 (S/RES/2331(2016))*, New York.

United Nations. (2025, 14 August) *'Help Us Live With Dignity, Not Just Survive': New UN Report Calls for Scaled-Up, Comprehensive Services amid Unprecedented Levels of Conflict-Related Sexual Violence*. New York: United Nations, Secretary-General's Office, available at: www.un.org/sexualviolenceinconflict/press-release/help-us-live-with-dignity-not-just-survive-new-un-report-calls-for-scaled-up-comprehensive-services-amid-unprecedented-levels-of-conflict-related-sexual-violence/

Wood, E. J. (2006) Rape as a Practice of War: Toward a Typology of Political Violence. *Politics & Society*, 34(3): 307–341.

Chapter 9

Sexual violence among humanitarian aid workers

No wind of change

Melanie Sauter

By the end of this chapter, you will understand that:

- Sexual violence against humanitarian aid workers remains underreported, under-researched, and often silenced within organisations.
- Aid organisations tend to focus on sexual violence perpetrated by staff *against* affected populations, neglecting internal dynamics of violence among staff.
- Organisational cultures and structures – including gender hierarchies, impunity, and precarious employment – contribute to the persistence of sexual violence.
- Institutional responses often prioritise organisational reputation over survivor support and accountability.
- Policy responses focus on individual wrongdoing instead of structural change in the sector.

Introduction

In July 2016, during intense fighting in Juba, South Sudanese soldiers attacked the Terrain Hotel. During the attack, they killed a journalist and sexually assaulted at least five international aid workers (Ingber, 2018).

When discussing sexual violence in the aid sector, the first thought often turns to brutal assaults by armed groups or military personnel against aid workers. While such incidents do occur – like the case in Juba – they remain relatively rare. The more pervasive issue lies within the sector itself, where colleagues rather than external actors often perpetrate abuse.

The humanitarian aid sector is built on principles of compassion, service, and protection for vulnerable populations. However, over the past two decades, repeated reports of sexual exploitation, abuse, and harassment (SEAH) by aid workers have shown a troubling paradox: those sent to protect sometimes perpetrate harm. The fact that most perpetrators work for aid agencies raises concerns about their responsibility to prevent misconduct within their ranks (Nobert, 2017).

Sexual violence in humanitarian aid takes two forms: abuse of beneficiaries and misconduct within organisations. Chapter 8 covers the first; this chapter examines the second. It explores SEAH prevalence, institutional failures, structural dynamics, and policy responses. The sector often ignores internal gender issues, creating a permissive culture for abuse.

The scope of the problem

Research on violence against aid workers focuses on individual misconduct (Fast, 2014), opportunistic crime (Buchanan and Muggah, 2005; Fast, 2014), and aid politicisation (Sauter, 2024b; Stoddard, Harmer and DiDomenico, 2009). However, these studies mainly explore external threats, neglecting internal organisational dynamics that contribute to sexual violence.

Instead, sexual violence within aid organisations can be understood as opportunistic or as an institutionalised tolerated practice (Wood, 2014) reinforced by masculinity norms (Kreft, 2020). A key analytical lens for understanding sexual violence in humanitarian contexts is situational permissiveness. This concept, drawing from criminology and gender studies, argues that sexual violence does not occur in isolation but is facilitated by structural and environmental conditions that allow perpetrators to act with impunity (Reike, Sharma and Welsh, 2015; Sauter, 2024a). Table 9.1 summarises the facilitative conditions that foster a permissive environment.

Table 9.1 Facilitative Conditions of Misconduct

Power imbalances	Humanitarian organisations have strict hierarchical structures; women and local staff fill lower ranks.
Masculine work cultures	Hypermasculine work environments normalise sexual violence and protect perpetrators through group cohesion.
Legal and jurisdictional challenges	Aid workers often operate beyond local legal jurisdictions. Weak legal frameworks in host countries and no enforcement mechanisms in home countries enable impunity for perpetrators.
Weak accountability mechanisms	Lack of vetting and reporting mechanisms allow perpetrators to move undetected. Bureaucratic inertia and reputational concerns discourage proactive investigations.
Organisational culture and complicity	A culture of silence discourages reporting. The humanitarian exceptionalism creates reluctance to scrutinise aid workers' misconduct.

Workplace culture and power dynamics

Humanitarian crises inherently create power asymmetries. Feminist scholars argue that these power imbalances mirror broader patriarchal structures (Kreft, 2020). Humanitarianism is not immune to the same gendered dynamics found in other institutions. However, the notion of humanitarian exceptionalism – where aid workers are seen as altruistic actors – creates a reluctance to question their behaviour.

Many feminist critiques suggest that the aid sector operates within a colonialist framework. Western-led organisations reinforce hierarchies that enable abuses of power against local populations but also within an organisation (Clarke, 2021; Daigle, 2022). Senior staff are usually white male expatriates, while women and local staff fill lower ranks. The #AidToo movement has highlighted how existing duty-of-care policies mainly protect expatriate staff, leaving local staff more vulnerable (Bian, 2022; Daigle, Martin and Myrttinen, 2020).

A culture of silence and complicity discourages whistleblowing, particularly among junior staff. Aid organisations prioritise reputation management, sometimes covering up allegations rather than addressing them transparently. The sectors' temporary contracts, hierarchical structures, and limited oversight create an enabling environment for abuse (Shaw, Hegewisch and Hess, 2018). Group cohesion among male colleagues often silences survivors and shields perpetrators, reinforcing an implicit code of silence within organisations (Moser and Moser, 2005). Hypermasculine work environments, such as in the military, contribute to the normalisation of sexual violence (Zippel, 2006; Fitzgerald et al., 1995). Aid workers face similar stressors and dangers as soldiers. Intense and often dangerous fieldwork environments foster a prevailing "machismo" culture (Nobert, 2017). These hierarchical structures, gendered power imbalances, and workplace norms perpetuate a permissive environment for sexual violence (Zippel, 2006).

Security manuals traditionally focus on external threats, assuming sexual violence comes from outsiders (Gillespie, Mirabella and Eikenberry, 2019; Nobert and Williamson, 2017). They focus on victim-based measures, like advising women on dress codes and behaviour, reinforcing victim-blaming cultures while failing to hold perpetrators accountable.

For example, one aid worker recounted that her organisation questioned her for not disclosing her rape to her male colleagues.

> On the last night before I left for R&R, a program manager from another organisation came into my tent while I was asleep, climbed into my bed naked and raped me. I was questioned as to why I hadn't reported it directly to the staff of the local agency (all men, some of who reported to the man who raped me) or tell my driver or programme officers (all male and all my subordinates). They wanted to know why my tent hadn't been locked, why I didn't call and report it immediately as it happened, why I didn't fight back more.
> (Nobert, 2017)

Legal barriers to justice

Aid workers operate in fragile political contexts with weak legal systems, limiting survivors' access to justice. International humanitarian law (IHL) theoretically protects aid workers as civilians under the Geneva Conventions and the 1998 Rome Statute (Heintze, 2011). However, IHL applies only when violence involves conflict parties, leaving grey areas for sexual violence between aid workers (Gaggioli, 2014). Outside of conflict, only non-binding human rights treaties apply, meaning national laws largely determine justice outcomes (Seelinger, 2014). Domestic courts in conflict settings may be unreliable or inaccessible, leaving survivors with no viable legal recourse (Lake, 2014).

In the case of South Sudan, the victims faced significant obstacles in their pursuit of justice. A military court convicted ten soldiers for their roles in these crimes and sentenced them to prison terms in September 2018. In 2019, a crucial case file had gone missing after being sent to President Salva Kiir for confirmation, hindering the appeals process for both the victims and the convicted soldiers (Amnesty International, 2019).

Humanitarian organisations operate across multiple jurisdictions, complicating legal accountability. Many aid workers have diplomatic or legal immunities, shielding them from prosecution in host countries (Fleck, 2013). Relying on home countries to prosecute offenders has failed, as many states lack the political will or legal frameworks to address transnational sexual violence cases (Reinisch, 2008).

In 2022, several victims filed a lawsuit in the United States against the Republic of South Sudan, seeking compensation for the injuries and trauma they suffered during the attack. They argued that South Sudan had waived its sovereign immunity, allowing the case to proceed in U.S. courts. However, in August 2023 the U.S. District Court dismissed the case, ruling that South Sudan retained its sovereign immunity, thereby preventing the lawsuit from moving forward (Bunch, 2023). At the time of writing (January 2025), the missing case file continues to impede the appeals process within South Sudan, leaving the victims without adequate legal recourse.

Accountability and organisational duty of care

Many organisations relocate offenders rather than hold them accountable (Nobert, 2016). Expatriate staff often escape prosecution by using legal immunities and relocating between duty stations. Unlike local staff, they can more easily leave a country when facing allegations. While location does not determine criminal charges, moving away hinders evidence collection and witness testimonies, making legal proceedings more difficult and costly (Gaggioli, 2014).

Aid agencies have a duty of care to their staff but often fail to implement gender-sensitive policies. The Dennis vs. Norwegian Refugee Council case set a precedent by holding aid organisations legally responsible for staff security (Kemp and Merkelbach, 2016). However, humanitarian security policies mainly focus on expatriate staff (Bradley, 2019). The Beijing Platform for Action (BPFA) recognised non-state actors' responsibility for workplace safety, yet aid agencies remain largely unaccountable (Gardam and Jarvis, 2000).

Policy responses and reforms

Humanitarian organisations have introduced reforms to address SEAH, but progress is slow. The following examples show how institutional responses often focus on individual cases rather than fixing systemic power imbalances.

INTERPOL's project soteria

Launched in 2022, Project Soteria aims to keep sexual predators out of the aid sector by improving data sharing on perpetrators and strengthening background checks. Funded by the UK Foreign, Commonwealth & Development Office (FCDO), the initiative is set to run until May 2026. More than 20 major aid organisations, including Oxfam, Save the Children, and the International Federation of Red Cross and Red Crescent Societies, support the project (INTERPOL, 2021). However, challenges persist in implementation, particularly concerning data-sharing regulations across jurisdictions (see also Chapter 10).

UN and IASC safeguarding measures

The United Nations has reinforced its zero-tolerance policy on SEAH. The Inter-Agency Standing Committee has sent Protection from Sexual Exploitation and Abuse (PSEA) coordinators to 40 high-risk zones (IASC, 2025). Nonetheless, critics argue that these efforts often focus more on institutional responses rather than addressing the root causes of gendered power imbalances (Daigle, 2022).

Humanitarian organisations' internal reforms

Oxfam, Save the Children, and other aid organisations have strengthened vetting, safeguarding policies, and staff training (Clarke, 2021). A key tool in this effort is the Protection from Sexual Exploitation, Abuse and Harassment (PSEAH) Index. The index describes 18 protection requirements that help organisations assess their policies (CHS Alliance, 2020). Since 2019, the CHS Alliance has run an international reporting platform where organisations can report perpetrators and screen new hires.

As of January 2025, over 300 organisations use the system that conducted more than 137,000 background checks, which led to the rejection of 385 applicants during recruitment (CHS Alliance, 2022).

Legal and jurisdictional efforts

Some governments are pushing for extraterritorial jurisdiction to prosecute aid workers accused of SEAH abroad, with the UK leading the effort. The UK Sexual Offences Act allows prosecution of UK nationals for sexual crimes overseas, but no aid workers have been prosecuted yet (Hear Their Cries, 2025). Donor agencies now tie funding to strict safeguarding compliance, pressuring organisations to strengthen accountability. After SEAH allegations against WHO workers during the Ebola outbreak in the DRC, the UK pushed for major reforms in how the WHO handles such cases (House of Commons, 2021).

Challenges and the way forward

The UK government leads efforts to combat SEAH in the aid sector. The FCDO has taken a leading role in shaping safeguarding policies, funding Project Soteria, and pushing for stronger accountability within international institutions.

Other European governments, especially those hosting major humanitarian headquarters, could do more. Switzerland, home to the International Committee of the Red Cross (ICRC), Médecins Sans Frontières (MSF), the United Nations humanitarian agencies, and various international NGOs, could enforce extraterritorial jurisdiction for SEAH cases. Likewise, France, Germany, and the EU should move beyond voluntary codes and adopt binding regulations.

Most safeguarding policies focus on preventing SEAH against local populations, yet SEAH within aid organisations remains overlooked. Furthermore, current policies on SEAH largely focus on either victims or perpetrators, but they ignore the role of organisations and the permissive environments they create. Many safeguarding measures emphasise supporting survivors or removing offenders, yet they fail to address the structural conditions within aid agencies that enable abuse to persist. Hierarchical cultures, weak oversight, and a reluctance to hold leadership accountable contribute to a climate of impunity. By framing SEAH as an individual issue rather than an institutional one, organisations evade responsibility, shifting focus away from their own failures in preventing abuse and fostering a culture of silence and complicity.

A systemic overhaul is needed. Intersectional feminist approaches emphasise dismantling hierarchical power dynamics in humanitarian work by amplifying local voices, diversifying leadership, and embedding safeguarding across all operations. True progress requires legal clarity, improved justice access, and accountability at all levels – targeting perpetrators, survivors, and permissive environments alike.

Summary points

- Sexual violence within the humanitarian sector is shaped by organisational, structural, and cultural dynamics, not just individual deviance.
- Precarity, hierarchy, and gendered power imbalances form a "perfect storm" enabling abuse.
- Many survivors are forced into silence due to fear of retaliation, career harm, or lack of effective reporting mechanisms.
- Addressing this issue requires structural change, including stronger accountability frameworks, survivor-centred support, and cultural transformation within aid organisations.

Further reading

- Mazurana, D., Donnelly, P. 2017. *STOP the Sexual Assault against Humanitarian and Development Aid Workers*. Somerville, MA: Feinstein International Center.
- Nobert, M., Williamson. C. 2017. *"Duty of Care: Protection of Humanitarian aid Workers from Sexual Violence."* Report the Abuse.
- Riley, C. L. 2020. "Powerful Men, Failing Upwards: The Aid Industry and the 'Me Too' Movement." *Journal of Humanitarian Affairs*, 2(3), 49–55. Retrieved Apr 6, 2025, from https://doi.org/10.7227/JHA.052
- Sauter, Melanie. 2024. "#AidToo, or When Situation Permits Rape: Sexual Violence among Humanitarian Aid Workers." *Journal of International Humanitarian Action* 9(1): 1. https://doi.org/10.1186/s41018-023-00146-1

References

Amnesty International. 2019. "South Sudan's Terrain Hotel Case File Goes Missing in Office of the President." *Amnesty International.* www.amnesty.org/en/latest/press-release/2019/09/south-sudan-missing-file-blocks-justice-for-terrain-hotel-rapes-murder/ (January 30, 2025).

Bian, Junru. 2022. "The Racialization of Expertise and Professional Non-Equivalence in the Humanitarian Workplace." *Journal of International Humanitarian Action* 7(1): 3. https://doi.org/10.1186/s41018-021-00112-9

Bradley, Miriam. 2019. "All Lives Are Equal but Some Lives Are More Equal than Others: Staff Security and Civilian Protection in the Humanitarian Sector." *Journal of Humanitarian Affairs* 1(2): 13–22. https://doi.org/10.7227/JHA.013

Buchanan, Cate, and Robert Muggah. 2005. *No Relief: Surveying the Effects of Gun Violence on Humanitarian and Development Personnel.* Geneva, Switzerland: Centre for Humanitarian Dialogue.

Bunch, Jesse. 2023. (United States District Court, District of Columbia) *JESSE BUNCH, et al., Plaintiffs, v. REPUBLIC OF SOUTH SUDAN, et Al.*

CHS Alliance. 2020. "PSEAH Index – English." *CHS Alliance.* www.chsalliance.org/get-support/resource/pseah-index/ (January 30, 2025).

CHS Alliance. 2022. "The Misconduct Disclosure Scheme." *The Misconduct Disclosure Scheme.* https://misconduct-disclosure-scheme.org (January 30, 2025).

Clarke, Gerard. 2021. "The Credibility of International Non-Governmental Organizations (INGOs) and the Oxfam Scandal of 2018." *Journal of Civil Society* 17(3–4): 219–37. https://doi.org/10.1080/17448689.2021.1994200

Daigle, Megan. 2022. *Gender, Power and Principles in Humanitarian Action.* London: ODI. HPG Report.

Daigle, Megan, Sarah Martin, and Henri Myrttinen. 2020. "'Stranger Danger' and the Gendered/Racialised Construction of Threats in Humanitarianism." *Journal of Humanitarian Affairs* 2(3): 4–13. https://doi.org/10.7227/JHA.047

Fast, Larissa. 2014. *Aid in Danger: The Perils and Promise of Humanitarianism.* Philadelphia, PA: University of Pennsylvania Press.

Fitzgerald, Louise F., Suzanne Swan, and Karla Fischer. 1995. "Why Didn't She Just Report Him? The Psychological and Legal Implications of Women's Responses to Sexual Harassment." *Journal of Social Issues* 51(1): 117–38. doi:10.1111/j.1540-4560.1995.tb01312.x.

Fleck, Dieter. 2013. "The Legal Status of Personnel Involved in United Nations Peace Operations." *International Review of the Red Cross* 95(891–92): 613–36.

Gaggioli, Gloria. 2014. "Sexual Violence in Armed Conflicts: A Violation of International Humanitarian Law and Human Rights Law." *International Review of the Red Cross* 96(894): 503–38.

Gardam, Judith, and Michelle Jarvis. 2000. "Women and Armed Conflict: The International Response to the Beijing Platform for Action." *Columbia Human Rights Law Review* 32: 1.

Gillespie, Elizabeth M., Roseanne M. Mirabella, and Angela M. Eikenberry. 2019. "#Metoo/#Aidtoo and Creating an Intersectional Feminist NPO/NGO Sector." *Nonprofit Policy Forum* 10(4). https://doi.org/10.1515/npf-2019-0019.

Hear Their Cries. 2025. "Hear Their Cries." www.heartheircries.org/ (January 30, 2025).

Heintze, Hans-Joachim. 2011. "Convergence Between Human Rights Law and International Humanitarian Law and the Consequences for the Implementation." In *International Law and Humanitarian Assistance*. Springer, Berlin: Heidelberg, 83–101. https://link.springer.com/chapter/10.1007/978-3-642-16455-2_6 (January 5, 2018).

House of Commons. 2021. *Progress on Tackling the Sexual Exploitation and Abuse of Aid Beneficiaries: Government Response to the Seventh Report of the Committee, Session 2019–21.* House of Commons. Special Report of Session 2019–21.

IASC. 2025. "Global Map PSEA Coordinators." https://app.powerbi.com/view?r=eyJrIjoiODIyMmM3NmUtYWI1Ny00MDI2LWJiNTQtODRkZjM0YzM0YmFlIiwidCI6Ijc3NDEwMTk1LTE0ZTEtNGZiOC05MDRiLWFiMTg5MjAyMzY2NyIsImMiOjh9 (January 30, 2025).

Ingber, Sasha. 2018. "South Sudan Soldiers Convicted Of Raping Aid Workers And Killing A Journalist." *NPR*. www.npr.org/2018/09/06/645215324/south-sudan-soldiers-convicted-of-raping-aid-workers-and-killing-a-journalist (January 30, 2025).

INTERPOL. 2021. "Project Soteria." www.interpol.int/en/How-we-work/Capacity-building/Capacity-building-projects/Project-Soteria (January 30, 2025).

Kemp, Edward, and Maarten Merkelbach. 2016. "Duty of Care: A Review of the Dennis v Norwegian Refugee Council Ruling and Its Implications." European Interagency Security Forum (EISF).

Kreft, Anne-Kathrin. 2020. "Civil Society Perspectives on Sexual Violence in Conflict: Patriarchy and War Strategy in Colombia." *International Affairs* 96(2): 457–78.

Lake, Milli. 2014. "Organizing Hypocrisy: Providing Legal Accountability for Human Rights Violations in Areas of Limited Statehood." *International Studies Quarterly* 58(3): 515–26.

Moser, Caroline, and Annalise Moser. 2005. "Gender Mainstreaming since Beijing: A Review of Success and Limitations in International Institutions." *Gender & Development* 13(2): 11–22.

Nobert, Megan. 2016. "*Prevention, Policy and Procedure Checklist: Responding to Sexual Violence in in Humanitarian and Development Settings.*", Report the Abuse, August 2016, page 138. www.gisf.ngo/wp-content/uploads/2017/08/2190-Report-the-Abuse-2017-Humanitarian-Workplaces-Free-from-Sexual-Violence-The-First-Steps-and-a-Call-to-Action.pdf accessed 25 August 2025.

Nobert, Megan. 2017. *Humanitarian Experiences with Sexual Violence: Compilation of Two Years of Report the Abuse Data Collection.* Report the Abuse, August 2017, pages 1–28. www.gisf.ngo/wp-content/uploads/2017/08/2190-Report-the-Abuse-2017-Humanitarian-Workplaces-Free-from-Sexual-Violence-The-First-Steps-and-a-Call-to-Action.pdf accessed 25 August 2025.

Nobert, Megan, and Christine Williamson. 2017. "Duty of Care: Protection of Humanitarian Aid Workers from Sexual Violence." In Report the Abuse, August 2017, pages 1–8. www.gisf.ngo/wp-content/uploads/2017/08/2190-Report-the-Abuse-2017-Humanitarian-Workplaces-Free-from-Sexual-Violence-The-First-Steps-and-a-Call-to-Action.pdf accessed 25 August 2025.

Reike, Ruben, Serena K. Sharma, and Jennifer M. Welsh. 2015. "Conceptualizing the Responsibility to Prevent." In *The Responsibility to Prevent: Overcoming the Challenges of Atrocity Prevention*, eds. Serena K. Sharma and Jennifer M. Welsh. Oxford, UK: Oxford University Press.

Reinisch, August. 2008. "The Immunity of International Organizations and the Jurisdiction of Their Administrative Tribunals." *Chinese Journal of International Law* 7(2): 285–306.

Sauter, Melanie. 2024a. "#AidToo, or When Situation Permits Rape: Sexual Violence among Humanitarian Aid Workers." *Journal of International Humanitarian Action* 9(1): 1. https://doi.org/10.1186/s41018-023-00146-1.

Sauter, Melanie. 2024b. "Politicized Health Emergencies and Violent Resistance against Healthcare Responders." *Journal of Peace Research* 61(4): 513–28. https://doi.org/10.1177/00223433231158144.

Seelinger, Kim Thuy. 2014. "Domestic Accountability for Sexual Violence: The Potential of Specialized Units in Kenya, Liberia, Sierra Leone and Uganda." *International Review of the Red Cross* 96(894): 539–64.

Shaw, Elyse, Ariane Hegewisch, and Cynthia Hess. 2018. "Sexual Harassment and Assault at Work: Understanding the Costs." *Institute for Women's Policy Research Publication, IWPR B* 376, 1–12.

Stoddard, Abby, Adele Harmer, and Victoria DiDomenico. 2009. *Providing Aid in Insecure Environments: Trends in Violence against Aid Workers and the Operational Response*. London: Overseas Development Institute. Aid Worker Security Report. www.odi.org/publications/3250-violence-aid-workers-operational-response-2009 (February 8, 2016).

Wood, Elisabeth Jean. 2014. "Conflict-Related Sexual Violence and the Policy Implications of Recent Research." *International Review of the Red Cross* 96(894): 457–78. https://doi.org/10.1017/S1816383115000077.

Zippel, Kathrin S. 2006. *The Politics of Sexual Harassment: A Comparative Study of the United States, the European Union, and Germany*. Cambridge, UK: Cambridge University Press.

Chapter 10

The global policing challenge

Protecting vulnerable populations in humanitarian crises

Paul Stanfield

By the end of this chapter, you will:

- Understanding the scope of exploitation in humanitarian crises, including how aid workers and officials exploit vulnerable populations.
- Challenges in detecting and responding to abuse in crisis zones, including legal loopholes, lack of data, and corruption in law enforcement.
- Insights into global initiatives, such as Project Soteria and the Childlight Global Child Safety Institute, and how they aim to address exploitation through better data collection and preventive measures.
- The importance of a data-driven approach, modelled on public health responses to crises like HIV/AIDS, to combat abuse effectively in humanitarian settings.
- Practical strategies for improving global responses to exploitation, including improved vetting processes, enhanced law enforcement collaboration, and fostering transparency and accountability within aid organisations.

Humanitarian crises, whether caused by war, natural disasters, or pandemics, exacerbate the vulnerability of already at-risk populations. These events create chaos, leaving children and displaced adults particularly exposed to exploitation and abuse.

Childlight Global Child Safety Institute, a research-based organisation using data to protect children globally, is investigating how child sexual abuse material (CSAM) circulates during crises, where legal and social disruptions can increase exploitation. For instance, the Ukraine conflict has raised concerns about traffickers targeting refugees (OSCE, 2023) amid heightened searches for sexualised content (Kingsley, 2022). This research aims to guide preventive measures to protect vulnerable populations.

However, there is an equally sinister dimension that demands urgent action. While aid workers are dispatched to provide support and protection, as noted elsewhere in this book, a troubling number of these helpers have used their positions to exploit the very people they are supposed to serve.

From past experience, we know that the international community has made efforts to address this issue. Yet, despite protocols and policies intended to safeguard vulnerable populations, exploitation remains too persistent a problem. The disturbing truth is that the international community still lacks a comprehensive, data-driven approach to understanding, let alone combating, abuse in humanitarian contexts.

This chapter explores the ongoing challenges of policing and responding to exploitation during humanitarian crises. It draws on insights from Childlight, the Global Child Safety research Institute, and INTERPOL's Project Soteria, a global initiative aimed at tackling abuse in the humanitarian sector.

The persistent issue of exploitation in humanitarian crises

Despite reforms in the humanitarian sector, exploitation continues to occur in crisis situations. Data is sparse, but the evidence we do have shows that aid workers and officials entrusted with the care of vulnerable populations have, in some instances, used their positions to exploit children and vulnerable adults. The author's experience as former Director of Organised and Emerging Crime at INTERPOL underscores this point: the information on these abuses is scattered, anecdotal and insufficient to drive meaningful reform.

The problem is compounded by the environments in which these abuses occur. In conflict zones and areas hit by natural disasters, law enforcement can be either non-existent or overwhelmed by other priorities.

Local police forces in these regions often lack both the resources and the political will to tackle the problem. In some cases, corruption further prevents any meaningful investigation into these crimes. Worse still, the perpetrators are sometimes protected by legal frameworks, such as diplomatic immunity, making prosecution difficult or impossible.

Challenges of detection and response

There are multiple reasons why exploitation persists in humanitarian settings. One of the most significant challenges is the lack of a robust evidence base. The response to public health crises, such as HIV/AIDS and COVID-19, has shown that understanding the scale and nature of a problem is essential for crafting effective responses. Unfortunately, when it comes to exploitation and abuse in humanitarian contexts, much of what we know is based on anecdotal evidence, which is far from sufficient.

This is the gap that Childlight, founded by the Human Dignity Foundation and hosted by the University of Edinburgh, seeks to address in the context of child sexual exploitation and abuse (CSEA). Childlight takes a health-focused, data-driven approach to understanding and tackling CSEA, highlighting the scale, nature, and risk and protective factors to inform the interventions that can best prevent it. In its recent *Into the Light* report (Childlight, 2024), Childlight produced the world's first global estimate of the prevalence of online child sexual exploitation, revealing that over 300 million children are affected annually. This figure provides a critical baseline for understanding the scale of the problem and to act as a catalyst for change.

This approach must now be extended to address the problem of exploitation in humanitarian settings. Sadly, not only does the humanitarian sector lack similar comprehensive data, but in some cases, there appears to have been a temptation not to turn over a rock and expose something that NGOs already know or at least suspect, and that has been identified for many years (Save The Children, 2008). Aid organisations and law enforcement must work together to build a reliable evidence base if we are to prevent future abuses. We owe it to vulnerable children and adults not to simply hope for the best as we wait for the next atrocity.

The role of project soteria

Following the scandals that highlighted the vulnerabilities within the aid sector (see Appendix 1), Project Soteria was launched by INTERPOL in 2018 with the support of the UK Foreign, Commonwealth & Development Office (FCDO) among others. It seeks to tackle sexual exploitation and abuse in humanitarian contexts by improving the vetting processes for aid workers and enhancing the capacity of law enforcement to respond to such incidents.

The project emphasises prevention, aiming to reduce the risk of offenders entering the aid sector in the first place. It also seeks to foster collaboration between NGOs, law enforcement agencies, and international organisations, building stronger mechanisms for detecting, investigating, and reporting abuse.

Despite these noble intentions implementation has been slow, hindered in part by the COVID-19 pandemic. More critically, like other initiatives before it Project Soteria has struggled to drive the transformational change needed across the humanitarian sector. While evidence continues to link a number of NGO workers to CSEA material, inadequate steps are being taken by several NGOs to stamp it out (International Development Committee, 2018). The lack of comprehensive, reliable data on the scale of abuse remains a significant barrier. Without this evidence base, it is difficult to convince governments, organisations, and law enforcement agencies to invest the necessary resources to prevent exploitation.

Addressing the root causes of exploitation

The root causes of exploitation in humanitarian crises are complex. First, there is the issue of the environments in which these abuses occur. Conflict zones and areas devastated by natural disasters are often characterised by insecurity and weak governance. Local authorities may be either unwilling or unable to investigate allegations of abuse. Even when cases are reported, corruption or competing priorities can prevent them from being fully investigated.

Second, the very nature of international humanitarian work can shield perpetrators from accountability. Diplomatic immunity and other legal protections often apply to aid workers and officials, making it difficult to prosecute offenders. Moreover, the culture within some organisations can foster a reluctance to report colleagues for fear of damaging the organisation's reputation or jeopardising one's own career. This creates an environment in which abuse can thrive, as perpetrators know they are unlikely to face consequences (UK Parliament, 2021).

To address these root causes, there needs to be a fundamental shift in how we approach exploitation in humanitarian contexts. Much like the successful public health approaches used to combat HIV/AIDS and

COVID-19, the fight against abuse must be data-driven and coordinated across multiple sectors.

Steps to improve global responses to exploitation

In order to effectively address the exploitation of vulnerable populations in humanitarian settings, several key steps must be taken. These steps are not simply bureaucratic measures but essential actions that will help prevent abuse, improve detection, and ensure that perpetrators are held accountable:

1 **Develop a strong evidence base**
   The collection and analysis of data must be prioritised. Without comprehensive data, we cannot understand the scale or nature of the problem. Aid organisations, law enforcement, and international bodies must collaborate to gather and share information on incidents of abuse.
2 **Establish global standards for reporting and investigating abuse**
   A lack of standardised reporting mechanisms has hampered efforts to track and address abuse. We need a unified, global system for reporting, investigating, and prosecuting exploitation in humanitarian contexts.
3 **Strengthen vetting procedures for aid workers**
   Existing vetting procedures for aid workers must be improved. The International Child Protection Certificate (ICPC) is a good example of a system that could be expanded globally. This criminal records check is for individuals working with children overseas helps prevent offenders from gaining access to vulnerable populations.
4 **Ensure accountability and transparency**
   Aid organisations must commit to greater transparency in how they handle allegations of abuse. This includes regularly reporting cases and outcomes to relevant authorities and ensuring that incidents are not covered up to protect reputations.
5 **Support victims and witnesses**
   Fear of reprisal often prevents victims and witnesses from coming forward. More robust support mechanisms must be put in place to protect those who report abuse. This could include independent oversight of investigations and stronger legal protections for witnesses.

6 **Remove legal barriers to prosecution**
   Diplomatic immunity and other legal protections should not shield perpetrators of abuse. The global community must work to close legal loopholes that allow offenders to evade justice.
7 **Enhance collaboration between NGOs and law enforcement**
   NGOs need to work more closely with law enforcement agencies. This collaboration must be based on trust and a shared commitment to tackling abuse. Aid organisations should not hesitate to share data with INTERPOL and other law enforcement bodies when abuse is suspected.
8 **Invest in law enforcement capacity**
   Many countries lack the resources and expertise needed to investigate cases of abuse in humanitarian contexts. International aid should include support for building local law enforcement capacity to handle these complex cases.
9 **Promote a culture of zero tolerance**
   Aid organisations must foster a culture in which any form of exploitation is seen as unacceptable. Leadership plays a key role here: senior staff must demonstrate a commitment to tackling abuse, and whistleblowers should be protected and supported.
10 **Treat exploitation as a public health issue**
   Finally, exploitation should be seen as a global public health issue, similar to pandemics like HIV/AIDS. This framing allows for a coordinated, multi-sector response that includes law enforcement, NGOs, public health agencies, and international organisations.

Conclusion

The exploitation of vulnerable populations during humanitarian crises is a global issue that demands a coordinated, data-driven response. While projects like Project Soteria and initiatives by organisations like Childlight have made progress, much more needs to be done. Developing a comprehensive evidence base, improving accountability, and strengthening collaboration between aid organisations and law enforcement are all critical steps in ensuring that those most in need of protection are safeguarded from harm. Only through sustained global action can we hope to prevent future abuses and create a safer, more accountable humanitarian sector.

Additional reading

- Childlight Global Child Safety Institute – *Into the Light* report: Childlight | Into the Light Index Overview
- Project Soteria Overview: DevTracker Programme GB-GOV-1-300784.

References

Childlight – Global Child Safety Institute (2024) *Into the Light Index on Child Sexual Exploitation and Abuse Globally: 2024 Report*. Edinburgh: Childlight.

HAP International (2008) *To Complain or Not to Complain: Still the Question*. Geneva: Humanitarian Accountability Partnership. Available at: https://publications.parliament.uk/pa/cm201719/cmselect/cmintdev/840/84004.htm [Accessed 27 March 2025].

International Development Committee (2018) *Sexual Exploitation and Abuse in the Aid Sector: Eighth Report of Session 2017–19*. London: House of Commons. Available at: www.parliament.uk/business/committees/committees-a-z/commons-select/international-development-committee/news-parliament-2017/sexual-exploitation-and-abuse-report-publication-17-19/ [Accessed 27 March 2025].

Kingsley, T (2022) 'Online searches for 'Ukrainian refugee porn' and 'Ukrainian rape' surge 300% as Russian war rages', *The Independent*, 27 July. Available at www.independent.co.uk/news/world/europe/ukraine-refugee-porn-rape-search-b2132402.html [Accessed 27 March 2025].

OSCE (2023) *Strengthening Child Protection in the OSCE Region: A Comprehensive Approach to Addressing Child Sexual Exploitation and Abuse*. Available at www.osce.org/files/f/documents/b/a/535383_0.pdf [Accessed 27 March 2025].

Save the Children UK (2008) *No One to Turn To: The Under-reporting of Child Sexual Exploitation and Abuse by Aid Workers and Peacekeepers*. London: Save the Children UK. Available at https://resourcecentre.savethechildren.net/document/no-one-turn-under-reporting-child-sexual-exploitation-and-abuse-aid-workers-and-peacekeepers [Accessed 27 March 2025].

UK Parliament (2021) *Inquiry into Sexual Exploitation and Abuse in the Aid Sector*. Available at www.theguardian.com/global-development/2021/jan/14/aid-sector-is-last-safe-haven-for-abusers-uk-investigation-warns [Accessed 27 March 2025].

Chapter 11

When vulnerability meets power

Rethinking mandatory reporting in safeguarding

Mayumi Fuchi

Chapter objectives

By the end of this chapter, you will:

- Examine the rise of mandatory reporting in the aid sector and its link to donor-driven accountability and their intended goals in safeguarding against SEAH.
- Identify the risks these systems pose to survivors' safety, autonomy, and community trust.
- Understand how power dynamics shape safeguarding outcomes and local implementation.
- Advocate survivor-centred, context-sensitive approaches that prioritise local voices and informed consent.

Introduction

The international aid sector stands at a critical crossroads. While its mission is deeply rooted in compassion, equality, and empowerment, it now faces an array of complex challenges in the area of safeguarding—specifically, the prevention of sexual exploitation, abuse, and harassment (SEAH) within global aid delivery. Central to these challenges is the debate surrounding mandatory complaint/reporting systems, often championed by regulators and donor governments as essential for ensuring accountability. On the surface, this zero-tolerance approach seems to reflect a sector-wide commitment to holding perpetrators accountable while offering crucial support to survivors.

However, growing evidence and reflection on the implementation of mandatory reporting systems reveal unintended consequences that may be undermining the very objectives they seek to achieve. Rather than guaranteeing protection, these systems can inadvertently heighten risks to survivors and erode trust within affected communities. At its heart, this issue brings to light the complex dynamics of power within the aid sector, prompting essential, difficult questions: *Do donor-imposed safeguarding frameworks truly prioritise the safety and dignity of the people they aim to protect, or do they simply perpetuate existing structural inequalities and reinforce donor-centric control over safeguarding practices?*

This briefing seeks to explore the complex dynamics of debate surrounding mandatory reporting, critically examining its practical and ethical implications while shedding light on emerging perspectives that challenge the status quo. By looking beyond the surface, it aims to facilitate a deeper understanding of these issues for NGOs, policy-makers, and all those involved in safeguarding work within the aid sector.

The rise of mandatory reporting in safeguarding

The introduction of mandatory reporting systems has become a key response to the high-profile scandals that have troubled the aid sector in recent years. These systems, examined in greater detail throughout this book, have been widely adopted in response to public outcry and the demand for greater accountability (UK Department of International Development, 2019; Henck, 2023). The fundamental premise of mandatory reporting is simple: organisations are required to report allegations of SEAH to the relevant authorities, regardless of the survivor's consent. This approach, often framed as a necessary measure to ensure transparency and accountability, has been championed as one of the most effective ways to deal with a persistent problem (CHS Alliance, 2021).

For donors—particularly Western governments and multilateral agencies—mandatory reporting serves as a tool to demonstrate their commitment to upholding high standards of safeguarding in line with their domestic regulations and legal (Office of Internal Oversight Services, 2021). By requiring organisations to implement these systems, donors aim to ensure that their investments are not implicated in cases of abuse or exploitation. The mandatory reporting framework becomes a critical element of donor-driven accountability, providing a visible, enforceable mechanism to address safeguarding failures. This approach seeks to assure the public, taxpayers, and stakeholders that funds are being used responsibly and that any allegations of misconduct are taken seriously (Goncharenko, 2020). It allows donors to demonstrate a proactive stance in the fight against SEAH within the aid sector, aligning their international policies with the high expectations set in their home countries.

However, this emphasis on safeguarding as a prerequisite for funding has unintended consequences. It places a significant burden on recipient organisations—especially smaller, local NGOs—who are often required to comply with complex reporting systems and standards that may not align with the realities of their operating environments (CHS Alliance, 2021). For local organisations, the pressure to meet these donor-imposed standards can divert attention away from the culturally sensitive, contextualised approaches that are required in safeguarding vulnerable communities. This dynamic can result in a one-size-fits-all approach, where policies are enforced without full consideration of local contexts or the needs of the populations being served. As safeguarding becomes increasingly tied to funding, the balance of power shifts, with donors holding greater influence over operational decisions, which may unintentionally undermine the agency of local actors who are closest to the communities in need of protection.

Despite its apparent simplicity and its promise of accountability, mandatory reporting has met with significant resistance within the aid sector. Many organisations—both large international players and smaller local NGOs—have expressed concerns about the practicality and ethics of enforcing such policies across diverse operational contexts (Independent Commission for Aid Impact, 2022). Critics argue that this approach oversimplifies the complexities of supporting survivors of SEAH. By prioritising external requirements over survivor-centric care, mandatory reporting policies can inadvertently cause harm, neglecting the specific needs and vulnerabilities of survivors (CHS Alliance, 2021; Walker-Simpson, 2017; Gaboune et al., 2023). These concerns point to a deeper issue: the ways in which donor-driven policies and institutional priorities are often misaligned with the on-the-ground realities that aid organisations face in the communities they serve.

The risks and limitations of mandatory reporting

While mandatory reporting is intended to foster safer environments, its implementation often reveals significant limitations, particularly in how it impacts survivors. Individuals who experience SEAH are already dealing with complex trauma, stigma, and power imbalances (Barnett & Duvall, 2005). A rigid mandatory reporting framework can further undermine their autonomy by compelling organisations to report allegations without taking into account the survivor's wishes (CHS Alliance, 2021). In tight-knit communities, the disclosure of abuse can expose survivors to further harm, such as retaliation and increased vulnerability. Fear of exposure may prevent survivors from seeking help in the first place, as they doubt that their confidentiality can be maintained (Fuchi, 2024).

Furthermore, in some cases, local laws or cultural norms may criminalise the behaviour or relationships that survivors wish to report, putting them at risk of legal consequences rather than providing protection (Aubone & Hernandez, 2013; Hossain et al., 2018; Muuo et al., 2020). This highlights the unintended consequences of mandatory reporting systems, where the aim of safeguarding is undermined by legal or cultural conflicts (Philips, 2020). In these settings, survivors may face considerable pressure from their communities, which could further silence them and increase the risk of further victimisation (Westendorf and Searle, 2017).

For NGOs, the pressure to comply with donor-mandated reporting systems can lead to unintended organisational behaviours that ultimately diminish the effectiveness of safeguarding efforts (Goncharenko, 2020). Fearing reputational damage or the loss of funding, some organisations may underreport incidents, fail to document cases properly, or engage in practices that obscure the true scale of SEAH within their operations. For smaller NGOs—especially local partners that often lack the resources to navigate the complex reporting requirements—this can create a significant burden. These organisations may struggle to balance compliance with donor expectations with their local knowledge and the unique needs of their communities, leading to uneven enforcement and diminished trust between local and international actors. Over time, safeguarding efforts may turn into box-ticking exercises, diverting attention from more substantive efforts to create safer environments for everyone involved (CHS Alliance, 2021).

Power asymmetries

Mandatory reporting policies are often shaped by the priorities of donor governments and institutions, with little input from the affected communities or the organisations that are directly implementing the policies (see Chapter 6). Donors, with their considerable financial influence, often set the agenda, imposing policies that may not be appropriate for the local contexts in which these policies are implemented (Clarke, 2021). This dynamic leaves local actors feeling disempowered, as they are pressured to adopt standards that are often disconnected from the realities on the ground (Daoust and Dyvik, 2021; Fuchi, 2024). By prioritising donor-driven priorities, safeguarding frameworks fail to address local needs effectively, reinforcing existing power asymmetries (Smith, 2017). This imbalance reinforces power asymmetries, leaving local actors disempowered in the shaping of safeguarding frameworks.

The gendered nature of SEAH exacerbates these power imbalances. As discussed in Chapter 9, women and girls are disproportionately affected by SEA, and their specific needs and vulnerabilities must be considered in the design and implementation of safeguarding frameworks (Freedman, 2018; Stern, 2021). In many contexts, the risks associated with mandatory reporting are heightened for women, who may face further such as retaliation or violence (Walker-Simpson, 2017; Harrington, 2022). A rigid, donor-driven reporting system that does not account for these gender-specific risks can further silence survivors and prevent them from seeking justice. For many women, the fear of retribution and the loss of privacy may outweigh the perceived benefits of reporting an incident (Ground Truth Solutions, 2023).

Therefore, safeguarding policies must take into account both the power dynamics at play and the gendered risks faced by survivors. It is crucial that policies allow survivors—particularly women—to retain agency in the process, ensuring they have control over how their cases are handled (CHS Alliance, 2021). This includes ensuring that survivors are fully informed of their options and understand the potential consequences of their decisions (Safeguarding Resource and Support Hub, 2021). The role of donors in shaping these policies must also be critically examined, as their priorities often shape the systems in ways that may not align with the needs of the communities most affected by SEAH.

Lessons from practice

As the aid sector grapples with the limitations of mandatory reporting, emerging practices suggest that a survivor-centred approach is essential, one that ensures survivors have control over how their cases are handled and are provided with tailored, culturally sensitive support. Ensuring that informed consent is sought before any reporting takes place is a critical aspect of this approach, as it allows survivors to make decisions based on their own experiences and needs.

Local actors often possess a deeper understanding of the cultural, social, and power dynamics at play within the communities they serve. By empowering these local organisations, aid agencies can create more effective and contextually relevant responses to SEAH. Policies should be co-designed with input from affected communities to ensure that they reflect local realities, rather than imposing external norms. Donors have an essential role to play in supporting these processes, but they must move beyond simply enforcing compliance. They should invest in strengthening the safeguarding capacities of local organisations and work collaboratively to develop flexible, context-sensitive safeguarding frameworks.

Conclusion

The international aid sector is at a pivotal moment in its approach to safeguarding. While mandatory reporting systems have brought attention to the issue of SEAH, their limitations are becoming increasingly clear. For NGOs, the challenge is not just about compliance with donor mandates but also about leading the way in shaping safeguarding practices that are genuinely effective, equitable, and centred on the rights and needs of survivors. This moment calls for bold leadership—leadership that is willing to challenge assumptions, confront power imbalances, and embrace complexity. By rethinking safeguarding through the lens of vulnerability and power, the sector can move closer to its mission of promoting dignity, justice, and safety for all.

Further reading

CHS Alliance. (2021). On the road to a survivor-centred approach: Learning from the implementation of safeguarding policies. www.chsalliance.org

Clarke, G. (2021). The Credibility of International Non-Governmental Organizations (INGOs) and the Oxfam Scandal of 2018. *Journal of Civil Society.* 17 (3–4), 219–237. https://doi.org/10.1080/17448 689.2021.1994200

Fuchi, M. (2024). NGO Accountability and Power Dynamics in Safeguarding: The Core Humanitarian Standard in Theory and Practice in Refugee Camps in Sudan. PhD Thesis. University of Birmingham.

Gaboune, A., Mohammed, A., and Naapi, J. (2023) Barriers to reporting misconduct: Understanding power, intersectionality and context. Oxfam International. Available at https://oxfamilibrary.openrepository.com/

bitstream/handle/10546/621533/cs-barriers-to-reporting-miscond uct-180823-en.pdf;jsessionid=94A0F0EF0114EF793F895FBA52E27 15A?sequence=1
Independent Commission for Aid Impact. (2022). The UK's approach to safeguarding in the humanitarian sector: A review. February 2022. Available at https://icai.independent.gov.uk/wp-content/uploads/01-AGU133_0 01_PSEA-Review-February-2022_100222_J-1.pdf

References

Aubone, A. and Hernandez, J. (2013). Assessing refugee camp characteristics and the occurrence of sexual violence: a preliminary analysis of the Dadaab complex. *Refugee Survey Quarterly*. 32 (4), 22–40.

Barnett, M. and Duvall, R. (2005). Power in International Politics. *International Organization*. 59 (1) (Winter, 2005), 39–75 (37 pages). Cambridge University Press.

CHS Alliance. (2021). On the road to a survivor-centred approach: Learning from the implementation of safeguarding policies. Available at www.chsa lliance.org

Clarke, G. (2021). The Credibility of International Non-Governmental Organizations (INGOs) and the Oxfam Scandal of 2018. *Journal of Civil Society*. 17 (3–4), 219–237. https://doi.org/10.1080/17448 689.2021.1994200

Daoust, G., and Dyvik, S. L. (2021). Reconceptualizing vulnerability and safeguarding in the humanitarian and development sector. *Social Politics: International Studies in Gender, State and Society*. 29 (1), 355–378.

Freedman, J. (2018). Sexual and gender-based violence against refugee women: A hidden aspect of the refugee "crisis". *Reproductive Health Matters*. 26 (52), 18–26. https://doi.org/10.1016/j.rhm.2016.05.003

Fuchi, M. (2024). NGO Accountability and Power Dynamics in Safeguarding: The Core Humanitarian Standard in Theory and Practice in Refugee Camps in Sudan. PhD Thesis. University of Birmingham.

Gaboune, A., Mohammed, A., and Naapi, J. (2023) Barriers to reporting misconduct: Understanding power, intersectionality and context. Oxfam International. Available at https://oxfamilibrary.openrepository.com/ bitstream/handle/10546/621533/cs-barriers-to-reporting-miscond uct-180823-en.pdf;jsessionid=94A0F0EF0114EF793F895FBA52E27 15A?sequence=1

Goncharenko, G. (2020). The multiplicity of logics, trust, and interdependence in donor-imposed reporting practices in the nonprofit sector. *Financial Accountability and Management*. 37 (2), 124–141.

Ground Truth Solutions. (2023). Against the odds: Strengthening accountability to women and girls in Afghanistan. Available at https://static1.squarespace. com/static/62e895bdf6085938506cc492/t/6411ad6f258b0d02a367b d2d/1678880115916/GTS_AFG_R1_March_2023.pdf

Harrington, C. (2022). Shifting the Scales: Transforming the Criminal Justice Response to Domestic Abuse. UK Home Office. Shifting the scales: Transforming the criminal justice response to domestic abuse. Available at www.gov.uk/government/publications/transforming-the-criminal-justice-response-to-domestic-abuse/shifting-the-scales-transforming-the-criminal-justice-response-to-domestic-abuse-accessible.

Henck, A. (2023). Safeguarding from Scrutiny: Toward a Critical Consciousness of Organizational Culture in Humanitarian NGOs. Dissertations. 987. University of San Diego. https://digital.sandiego.edu/dissertations/987

Hossain, M., Zimmerman, C., Kiss, L., Kone, D., Bakayoko-Topolska, M., Manan, D. K., Lehmann, H., and Watts, C. (2014). Men's and women's experiences of violence and traumatic events in rural Cote d'Ivoire before, during and after a period of armed conflict. *BMJ open*, 4 (2), e003644. https://doi.org/10.1136/bmjopen-2013-003644

Independent Commission for Aid Impact. (2022). The UK's approach to safeguarding in the humanitarian sector: A review. February 2022. Available at https://icai.independent.gov.uk/wp-content/uploads/01-AGU133_001_PSEA-Review-February-2022_100222_J-1.pdf

Muuo, S., Muthuri, S. K., Mutua, M. K., McAlpine, A., Bacchus, L. J., Ogego, H., ... and Izugbara, C. (2020). Barriers and facilitators to care-seeking among survivors of gender-based violence in the Dadaab refugee complex. *Sexual and reproductive health matters*, 28 (1), 1722404.

Office of Internal Oversight Services. (2021). Evaluation of the Prevention, Response and Victim Support Efforts Against Sexual Exploitation and Abuse by United Nations Secretariat Staff and Related Personnel. Inspection and Evaluation Division. 19 March 2021. Assignment No: IED 21-010.

Phillips, S. D. (2020, January). Putting humpty together again: How reputation regulation fails the charitable sector. *Nonprofit Policy Forum*, 10 (4), p. 20190032. De Gruyter.

Safeguarding Resource and Support Hub. (2021). Global evidence review of sexual exploitation and abuse and sexual harassment (SEAH) in the aid sector. Available at www.sddirect.org.uk/sites/default/files/2022-03/RSH_Global_Evidence_Review_Final_Design_V5.pdf

Smith, S. (2017). Accountability and sexual exploitation and abuse in peace operations. *Australian Journal of International Affairs*. 71 (4), 405–422.

Stern, J. (2021). Sexual violence and humanitarian aid: Gender, power and giving in international crises. Humanitarian Practice Network. https://odihpn.org

UK Department of International Development. (2019). Progress Report – One Year on from the October 2018 London Safeguarding Summit.

Walker-Simpson, K. (2017). The practical sense of protection: A discussion paper on the reporting of child abuse in Africa and whether international standards actually help keep children safe. Child Abuse Review. Special Issues: Comparing International Approaches to Safeguarding Children. 26 (4). https://doi.org/10.1002/car.2477

Westendorf, J. and Searle, L. (2017). Sexual exploitation and abuse in peace operations: Trends, policy responses and future directions. *International Affairs* (London). 93 (2), 365–387.

Chapter 12

Whistleblowing

The personal cost of speaking out and the human benefit of whistleblowers' courage

Leigh Heale

This briefing considers the role and experience of whistleblowers in the aid sector, highlighting the personal cost of speaking out and the human benefit of whistleblowers.

By the end of this chapter, you will:

- Understand what it means to 'blow the whistle' in the Aid sector, and the cost to individuals and organisations when it happens.
- Have explored the cultural pitfalls of organisations which have been subject to public whistleblowing scandals.
- Understand how to contribute successfully as a leader to an organisational speak up culture.

What does it mean to 'blow' the whistle?

Whistleblowing can be a loaded term, particular in the International Aid and Development sector. To 'blow the whistle' in its simplest form means for an employee to report suspected past, present or imminent wrongdoing, or an attempt to conceal wrongdoing, *which is in the 'public interest'* (43B (1), Public Interest Disclosure Act, 1998).

Whistleblowers can use a variety of reporting channels to disclose wrongdoing internally, for example to inform a line manager or a Board of Trustees in the Charity sector. Whistleblowers can also 'blow the whistle' externally and bring allegations of wrongdoing into the public domain for example through the media, regulatory bodies or government (Chalouat et al., 2019). This external form of whistleblowing has rocked the International and Development sectors as far back as the 2001 United Nations Sex-for-Food scandal in West Africa Refugee Camps (Ni Chonghaile, 2002), or the sexual abuse and exploitation of children by UN Peace Keepers in the Democratic Republic of the Congo in 2014 (UN News, 2016), and more recently the #AidToo 2018 scandal driven by the exploitation by Oxfam GB staff in Hati in 2011 (Chairty Commission, 2019), discussed in Appendix 1.

In many countries, legislation affords and protects those who whistleblow in certain circumstances, often regarding incidences which are in the public interest, from repercussions from their employers. However, how effective are these protections practically? And what happens in situations where such legal protection does not exist, as is the case of many locations where international Non-Governmental Organisations (INGOs) operate? Retaliation by employers such as termination, suspension, demotion, wage stagnation, and/or harsh mistreatment by other employees occurs. A report by the Ethics and Compliance Initiative (ECI) in 2023, post-COVID pandemic, found that globally 61% of whistleblowers had experienced retaliation in some form (ECI, 2023). There is a very real and valid perception within many sectors, both public and private, that blowing the whistle is simply not worth the personal cost.

Should blowing the whistle be courageous or should it be the sign of organisation failure?

An organisation with a healthy speak up culture, which actively encourages staff and representatives to voice concerns and suspected wrongdoing at all levels surely does not require their staff to be courageous in speaking up? After all, it should be considered normal. Staff should know that by raising a concern they will be listened to, respected, and treated in a just manner. This is the sign of a positive, accountable organisational culture. When a whistleblower must be courageous and suffer personal consequences, be that in their career, a decline in their mental health and wellbeing or financial losses, that is a sign of organisational failure beyond whatever the alleged wrongdoing is. The fact a staff member has not been able to feel valued and heard internally is a major indicator of a culture which is potentially dismissive of more extensive wrongdoing and could be a sign of a culture of fear of challenging power equating to a lack of accountability. In such situations, whistleblowers are indeed courageous and the organisation has failed, and therefore, whistleblowing is both an act of courage and a sign of failure on the part of their organisation.

There is irony in a sector which exists in its purest form to do good and yet has a reputation of managing whistleblowing so badly. Why is this? Some might say that when the idea that anything which could disrupt the organisation's mission, coupled with a cultural tolerance of behaviour in which the ends justify the means, whistleblowers are seen as disrupters and troublemakers, preventing the organisation from doing good.

When the whistle is blown organisations are often on the back foot, they have already potentially missed warning signs, or even worse actively ignored or discouraged them. Helen Evans, Global Head of Safeguarding at Oxfam GB 2012–2015 who blew the whistle in 2018 recalls that she attempted to speak with senior leadership team to discuss the issue of sexual exploitation being committed by Oxfam representatives both abroad and in the UK shops on multiple occasions, but was not given the time or space. Additionally, she repeatedly raised the issue of inadequate resourcing of safeguarding functions to manage and investigate allegations (Newman, 2018). Had she been given the space to raise concerns and actions taken by senior leaders the necessity to blow the whistle and expose the behaviour across the sector may never have occurred. Helen raised the issue repeatedly in 2015 and 2017, while the UK regulator, the Charity Commission also did not act appropriately by investigating all her claims until the allegations became public knowledge in 2018, sparking a scandal across the UK International Aid and Development sectors (see Appendix 1). Ultimately, this resulted in renewed initiatives and commitments by organisations to do better to protect their staff and representatives while importantly protecting those whom they seek to help, as discussed in Chapter 1.

Organisations have a choice, when on the back foot they can either take progressive action and focus in on the alleged wrongdoing and manage it well, which is the correct response. All too often however, organisations focus in on who is blowing the whistle, not the why. This creates a distraction for the organisation's effective handling and likely results in the whistleblower experiencing negative outcomes such as performance being questioned when it has never been before or putting them under undue pressure and scrutiny.

The identity of the whistleblower should not be the used to judge the validity of the alleged wrongdoing, but this happens all too often in the Aid sector, in some cases leading to staff being blacklisted from future employment. The case of Caroline Hunt-Matthes, former Senior Investigator at the United Nations High Commissioner for Refugees (UNHCR) (Government Accountability Project, 2018), is the longest-running UN retaliation whistle blowing case, taking 14 years to be settled in the UN's internal justice system in court in Geneva. Following the investigation of alleged sexual exploitation and rape case involving a local UNHCR staff member in 2003, Caroline raised several concerns regarding how the case had been managed including institutional obstruction during the investigation and conduct of senior officials. The response from the UNHRC was to terminate Caroline's fixed term contract. In 2013, this was determined by the United Nations Dispute Tribunal (UNDT) to have been an act of retaliation against her for questioning the investigation methods of the Inspector General's Office. The Judge also found that proper HR regulations and policies had been flouted and that Caroline had been subject to mischaracterisation by UNHCR. She was the only trained Investigator in the UNHCR at the time. The case was finally settled in 2018, following an appeal by the UNHRC into the 2013 ruling. This case demonstrates how the original wrongdoing – in this case the rape of female by a local UNHRC staff member, and the potential learning from that case, was vastly overshadowed by the retaliatory culture towards the whistleblower.

Time and again cases show that staff are vulnerable, regardless of legislation and non-retaliation policies which organisations have in place to protect them. Some would say that the systems in place are not designed to withstand the threat of potential disruption of the 'mission' and whistleblowers are all too often left crushed by the very systems designed to keep people safe.

It could be argued that organisations respond in this defensive way due to the potential risk of harm whistleblowing in the public domain can have upon the organisations ability to achieve their missions. For example, many face sanctions by regulators such as The Charity Commission, or by large donors, receive negative media coverage affecting public reputation and funding opportunities, ultimately affecting their ability to operate. Therefore, deflecting attention away from the 'why' and onto the 'who' can appear logical when faced with a crisis. This is a short-sighted approach and can cause longer term harm than facing the realities of the 'why' and learning appropriately, which in turns limits the chances of the wrongdoing occurring again, and seeks to build accountability and trust.

So how do leaders encourage speaking up within their staff and representatives?

In the #AidToo movement in 2018 the people who became public advocates for change were not unknown to the sector. They were highly respected individuals, so how were they not listened to by their respective organisations, and importantly what can we learn?

The Charity Commission's inquiry into the Children UK (2019b), which examined the handling of staff complaints of harassment, identified weaknesses in workplace culture and practices. Similarly, the Charity Commission's inquiries into Oxfam (Charity Commission, 2019a) found that a 'poor culture of behaviour' and 'poor accountability by staff' allowed individuals to behave badly.

Both organisations had safeguarding policies, and clear reporting procedures, yet they were not effective. Policies and procedures on whistleblowing, having a dedicated anonymous hotline in place for staff to report concerns, do not protect people and organisations. They are necessary, but not sufficient. Both Save the Children UK and Oxfam GB are cautionary tales for Boards and senior leadership teams who feel 'this couldn't happen here' simply because these tools exist. Tools need to be many things to be successful and used. So, for example, ask yourself are your whistleblowing policies contextually relevant, do they use accessible language, are they accessible to all parts of the organisation? How are they socialised beyond a physical presence of being on a poster in an office or covered in an introduction learning module? As leaders we have a responsibility to champion these policies and procedures, to be inquisitive and ask questions of our staff teams which explore their understanding and likelihood of tools to be used.

Great senior leadership teams make time to listen to staff engagement survey findings and make changes based on them. They take responsibility for asking the difficult questions and to having the courageous conversations, they do not delegate these things to others, and they role model active listening and respond well when colleagues do speak up. They should ensure that functions such as safeguarding and wellbeing teams are adequately funded and staffed by professionals, who can support leadership teams in creating open and safe cultures, who respond with pace and professionalism when concerns and reports are made. Often these functions act as an organisation's conscience, and senior leaders do well to listen to them, but also challenge when needed. An organisation which can challenge supportively within itself often demonstrates a strong speak up culture, where people are truly heard.

Creating a safe and open culture for all staff and representatives to speak up should not be left to chance or to a few individuals, nor to be reliant on policies and procedures, it takes active, informed and engaged leaders to do so. Reitz and Higgins (2019) found that often '*Getting people to speak up is often less about the less powerful having a voice and more about the more powerful really wanting to listen*' a reminder to all of us in leadership of the direct link between power and whistleblowing.

So, if or when the whistle is blown, remember to focus on the 'what' and not the 'who'. Examine the 'why' and focus on responding proactively through a listening learning lens. Organisations which respond appropriately and openly to challenges are more likely to remain relevant and go on achieving their missions, compared to those who lack accountability and ultimately relevance, harming their mission and those whom they often seek to help. That mindful, positive approach is more likely to help maintain a positive organisational culture, will help retain a motivated and productive workforce and above all maximise the probability that services are as effective as they can be – surely the ultimate goal of all our organisations, large and small.

References

Chalouat, I., Carrión-Crespo, C. & Licata, M., 2019, Law and Practice on Protecting Whistle-blowers in the Public and Financial Services Sectors. International Labour Office, Geneva.

Charity Commission, 2019a, Inquiry Report: Summary Findings and Conclusions Oxfam https://assets.publishing.service.gov.uk/media/5cff7fabed915d09a33c2142/Inquiry_Report_summary_findings_and_conclusions_Oxfam.pdf accessed 28th April 2025.

Charity Commission, 2019b, Statement of the Results of an Inquiry The Save the Children Fund (Save the Children UK) https://assets.publishing.service.gov.uk/media/5e5fd9b8e90e077e385b3a72/The_Save_the_Children_Fund__Save_the_Children_UK__Inquiry_report.pdf accessed 28th April 2025.

Ethics & Compliance Initiative, 2023, 2023 Global Business Ethics Survey: The state of ethics & compliance in the workplace. Arlington.

Government Accountability Project, 2018, Longest-running UN Whistleblower Case Ends with Settlement and UNHCR Statement of Regret https://whistleblower.org/press/longest-running-un-whistleblower-case-ends-settlement-and-unhcr-statement-regret/ accessed 28th April 2025.

Newman, 2018, Oxfam Whistleblower: Allegations of Rape and Sex in Exchange for Aid – Channel 4 News www.channel4.com/news/oxfam-whistleblower-allegations-of-rape-and-sex-in-exchange-for-aid accessed 28th April 2025.

Ni Chonghaile, Clar, 2002, Sex-for-food scandal in West African refugee camps, The Lancet, Volume 359, Issue 9309, 860–861.

Public Interest Disclosure Act, 1998, www.legislation.gov.uk/ukpga/1998/23/section/1 accessed 28th April 2025.

Reitz, M. & Higgins, J., 2019, Introduction; Speaking the truth in a world of power. In: Speak Up, Pearson Education Limited.

UN News, 2016, UN Sexual Misconduct Investigation in DR Congo Finds Violations and Cases of Abuse. https://news.un.org/en/story/2016/04/525982 (accessed 28 April 2025).

Chapter 13

Strengthening safeguarding and accountability through an international aid ombuds for children

Ma-Luschka Jean-Louis and Kirsten Pontalti

Chapter objectives

By the end of this chapter, you will:

- understand the history and debate surrounding a global aid ombuds system for children;
- learn the role and principles of an organisational Ombudsperson ('Ombuds') for children;
- explore how an ombuds system can strengthen safeguarding, children's rights, and accountability, drawing on the SOS Children's Villages Ombuds Office case study; and
- assess the feasibility of a global aid ombuds system operating across borders and compelling action by governments and aid agencies.

Introduction

Despite efforts to improve safeguarding practices, the international development and humanitarian aid sector continues to grapple with persistent failures in protecting vulnerable populations, particularly children. While safeguarding measures have become more standardised with established norms and benchmarks, accountability and protection for vulnerable populations remain inadequate. SOS Children's Villages' experience establishing a global Ombuds Office for children illustrates how an international aid ombudsperson (Ombuds) system for children could enhance safeguarding, participation, and accountability for children and ensure they realise their rights to protection and participation in matters that affect them.

Background

Government ombuds in many countries promote accountability by addressing formal disputes in governmental and corporate sectors. They investigate complaints and ensure decisions are lawful and fair. An organisational ombuds, by contrast, provides an informal space to resolve concerns and highlight systemic issues to leadership (International Ombuds Association, 2024). In the aid sector, organisational ombuds focus on improving accountability to beneficiaries—those with no recourse—rather than citizens or personnel. They follow four principles: independence, impartiality, confidentiality, and informality. These principles enable them to mediate impartially, support solutions without bias, and offer a safe, confidential space to raise concerns without fear of retribution (Figure 13.1).

The idea for an independent ombuds system in the aid sector first emerged after the 1996 Joint Evaluation of Emergency Assistance to Rwanda (JEEAR, 1996), which recommended creating a humanitarian ombudsperson role. This led to the Humanitarian Accountability Partnership (HAP) in 2001, which evolved into the Core Humanitarian Standard (CHS) in 2015 (CHS, 2024). Allegations of exploitation and abuse by Oxfam personnel in 2018, among others, reignited calls for stronger accountability systems (Oxfam International, 2018). The CHS Alliance advocated for an ombuds system to strengthen safeguarding and accountability in the aid sector (CHS Alliance, 2018). In response, an Ad Hoc Donor Technical Group on Safeguarding formed to assess the need for an ombuds system and how it might fit with existing governance structures (Hilhorst et al., 2018). Recognising the sector's utter failure at self-regulation, the Dutch and UK governments supported establishing

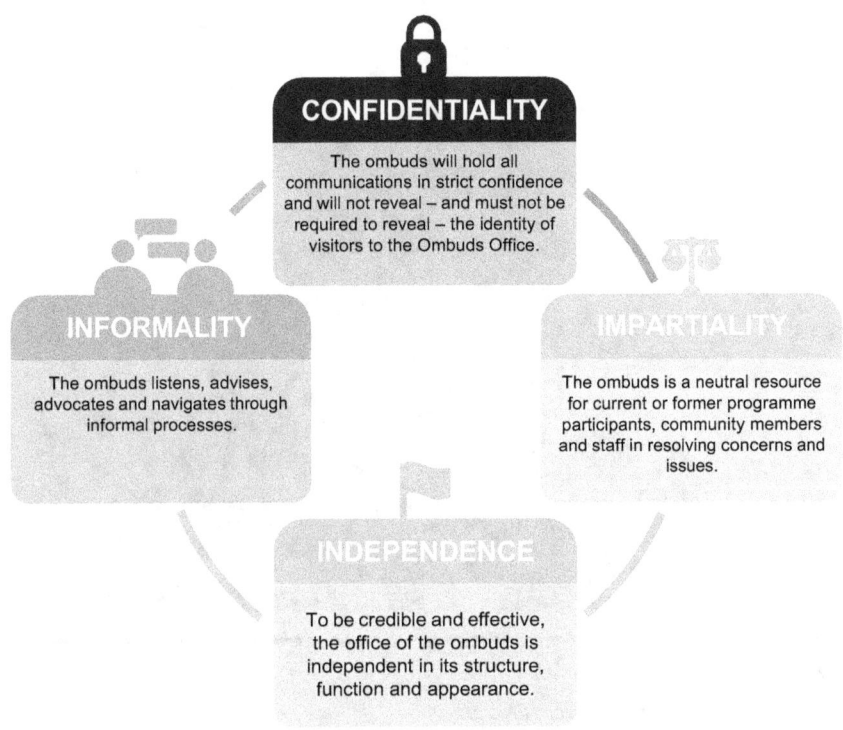

Figure 13.1 Ombuds' Principles.
Source: The Ombuds Office for SOS Children's Villages (2022).

an International Ombuds for Humanitarian and Development Aid (IOHDA) (Carolei, 2022). However, despite consensus, no organisations have implemented such a system for beneficiaries, although most UN agencies have an Ombuds for staff and GAVI and the Global Fund have recently set up a joint Ombuds for staff.

A pioneering moment occurred in 2021 when SOS Children's Villages, the world's largest organisation focused on children without parental care or at risk of losing it, faced a child safeguarding crisis of its own. The crisis exposed systemic gaps in protection across the federation's 130+ national member associations. The federation took immediate action, embedding an ombuds system in its 2021 Safeguarding Action Plan. This made the federation the first international NGO to create a global ombuds system dedicated to ensuring the rights and well-being of its participants and beneficiaries – children and young people (SOS CV, 2023).

The Ombuds Office for SOS Children's Villages (the Ombuds Office) listens to anyone with a concern about a child or young person in

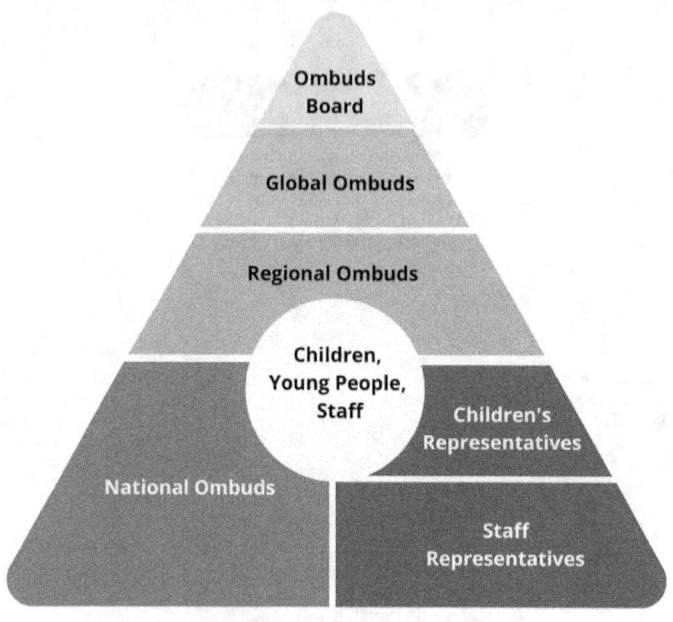

Figure 13.2 **Ombuds Model.**
Source: Azzopardi and Fairholm (2022).

federation programmes, past or present, and supports them to navigate and find solutions within the organisation or externally, as appropriate. SOS Children's Villages has committed to ensuring that all children and young people within its programmes and services, past and present, have access to an independent organisational ombuds or equivalent.

The Ombuds Office maintains its independence while collaborating with safeguarding and other departments to create safe environments without duplicating their formal roles and responsibilities. Ombuds are supported by their senior Ombuds supervisor/mentor and dialogue with their advisory group quarterly. Advisory groups are comprised of National/Regional Directors, Safeguarding, Programmes, Human Resources, and Youth Participation members appointed to be responsible for implementing and supporting the Ombuds.

An Ombuds Board of external experts provides governance and advice to the Ombuds Office and has direct access to the federation's executives (see Figure 13.2). The Ombuds Office consults internal funding partners at its discretion.

The following case study of the Ombuds Office illustrates how a global ombuds system could strengthen safeguarding and accountability, ensuring children's rights to protection, voice, and participation are upheld.

Case study: The Ombuds office for SOS children's villages

Introduction

The Ombuds Office for SOS Children's Villages was created to address grievances by reducing power inequalities and increasing accountability. It aimed to provide a safe space for anyone with concerns about a child in SOS programmes to consult an Ombuds and find solutions (O'Kane and Pontalti, 2024a). To determine the need and feasibility of this support, SOS Children's Villages consulted 315 children and young people in Benin, Sierra Leone, and Uruguay, supported by experts in child protection and participation from Proteknôn Foundation (www.proteknon.net/). Proteknôn also consulted stakeholders and experts in safeguarding and ombuds work and conducted desk reviews.

Through activities like body mapping and interactive games, children highlighted traits an Ombuds should embody. They emphasised an Ombuds should:

- be independent, trustworthy, confidential, impartial, and supportive – people who can help without fear of repercussion, boosting confidence to report concerns.
- act as an independent intermediary who takes prompt action to mediate and resolve issues.

By mid-2024, consultations had expanded to include 1,550 children and young people in 30 countries. Feedback revealed significant barriers to reporting concerns, such as lack of trust in staff and inadequate safeguarding systems (O'Kane and Pontalti, 2024b), affirming the need for a global Ombuds Office based in every national association.

> Having an Ombuds is a good idea because it will solve the problem of confidentiality. They will be the direct intermediary in contact with the children to protect the children.
> (Adolescent in SOS Children's Villages Benin consultations, translated from French)

Consultations with safeguarding and ombuds experts highlighted additional benefits: Independent Ombuds can identify risks, themes, and gaps, and dialogue with management to enhance safety and well-being. By fostering a *speak-up* culture, Ombuds promote open communication, reducing exploitation, abuse, neglect, silence, and conflicts of interest. Their presence signals SOS Children's Villages' commitment to addressing grievances and preventing harm and helps shift the organisation's culture to be more child rights and child-centred, participatory, and accountable – an organisation that listens and responds to children and young people.

Piloting and scaling up the Ombuds approach

SOS Children's Villages faced internal and external pressure to quickly implement a central global Ombuds Office to help address historical and current safeguarding concerns. However, consultations showed that a top-down approach would be ineffective. Children emphasised the need for frequent, personal interaction to build trust. The Proteknôn team proposed a *child-centred, ground-up approach* that adapts the model to each local context and seeks local solutions to local challenges, implemented through meaningful child participation.

In 2022, the interim global Ombuds Office piloted this approach in Benin, Sierra Leone, and Uruguay. Ombuds advisory groups, comprised of National/Regional Directors, Safeguarding, Programmes, Human Resources, and Youth Participation members appointed to be responsible for implementing and supporting the Ombuds, trained children and young people in recruitment processes (O'Kane and Pontalti, 2024c). Children's panels interviewed and shortlisted candidates for National Ombuds roles, with some participating in selecting Regional and Global Ombuds. The young people proved adept judges of character, uniquely positioned to identify candidates committed to listen and respond to children. This process empowered children to shape the leadership of the system tasked with their protection. Participants said they felt valued because they saw their priorities from the consultations reflected in job descriptions and the hiring of Ombuds they selected.

After helping to appoint National Ombuds, children chose peers and staff to serve as Children's Representatives and Staff Representatives. In most countries, Children's Representatives were appointed from existing participation structures. These young leaders raise awareness of the Ombuds Office, act as liaisons, and provide feedback to improve effectiveness. This adds accountability, signalling that Ombuds are answerable to the young people they serve.

In October 2022, the first National Ombuds began work in Benin, followed shortly thereafter by Sierra Leone and Uruguay. Meanwhile, preparations for scaling up were underway. By 2027, the goal is for every national association to have an organisational Ombuds or a local equivalent.

Progress, impact, and challenges

The Ombuds Office is now expanding globally. As of May 2025, it has:

- a Global Ombuds, five Regional Ombuds, and support staff;
- an Ombuds Board comprised of experts in Ombuds work, child rights, and child protection, including safeguarding;
- 23 national associations with National Ombuds;
- 11 national associations working with an approved local ombuds alternative; and
- over 45 national associations in the process of establishing a National Ombuds.

Additionally, the Ombuds Office has now been embedded within federation statutes. Two years into its operation, the Ombuds Office is beginning to demonstrate impact:

- Children are participating in the Ombuds Office and their own protection.
- Ombuds are successfully resolving inquiries and demand for services is growing.
- National associations are consistently addressing risks and gaps identified by their Ombuds.
- Management and staff with an Ombuds have an independent resource for consultation and capacity building, enhancing their ability to safeguard children.

Alongside these successes, the Ombuds Office faces several challenges:

- Safeguarding its independence to maintain effectiveness.
- Addressing internal resistance through open communication and dialogue.
- Providing ongoing coaching for Ombuds to navigate complex contexts.
- Securing sustainable funding to ensure long-term operations.

Moving forward, the Ombuds Office must pace its rollout carefully, prioritising quality over speed. Adapting the ombuds model to ensure long-term sustainability is crucial to reaching and serving all children across the federation.

Discussion

Child protection and safeguarding experts must evaluate whether a global aid Ombuds for children is needed and feasible in the international aid sector.

In any context, but especially when working with vulnerable children in development and humanitarian contexts, it is critical to have well-functioning child safeguarding systems. The UN CRC, the Grand Bargain's 'Participation Revolution' (Grand Bargain, 2016), and the Core Humanitarian Standard (CHS, 2018) all commit to give children access to an independent, responsive complaint mechanisms (CHS Commitment 5) and the opportunity to participate in decisions that affect them. Independent Commissions, such as those for Oxfam (Independent Commission, 2019, pp 13–15) and SOS Children's Villages (Independent Special Commission, 2023), emphasise that a safeguarding system will never be complete without an external, independent, child-friendly complaint and accountability system for children.

Key messages

Learning from the first global organisational ombuds system for children offers valuable insights. The Ombuds Office case study shows that:

- Children who depend on aid programmes for direct care and their basic needs are especially vulnerable and face barriers to voicing concerns. They need an independent, child-friendly, confidential, and impartial person to listen and help navigate options while preserving their agency.
- Meeting the Ombuds in person is essential to building trust.
- Children and young people must participate in selecting the Ombuds.
- An Ombuds Office is not a formal *check and balance* on safeguarding, but acts as an impartial ally who speaks truth to power.
- Ombuds and safeguarding teams have distinct, complementary roles. Ombuds share insights and collaborate to address risks and gaps without duplicating safeguarding functions; they are a second-tier complaint mechanism.
- Ombuds rely on reasonably mature safeguarding systems to ensure they refer cases appropriately, rather than filling capacity gaps.
- Building trust, embedding the Ombuds mandate, and achieving organisational integration takes time and persistence.
- A *ground-up approach* is vital. The ombuds model must be adapted to the local context to be relevant and find local solutions for local challenges.

- The *ombuds principles* of independence, confidentiality, impartiality, and informality are key to building trust, reducing power imbalances, and addressing accountability gaps.

For an Ombuds Office to succeed, it requires leadership committed to dismantling hierarchical and patriarchal systems while promoting equality, justice, and social change. Ombuds shift organisational culture by empowering children, challenging power imbalances, and holding decision-makers accountable, which threatens those resistant to change. Strong executive support is essential to:

- safeguard the Ombuds' independence within the organisation;
- institutionalise the Ombuds Office so it is legally anchored within existing structures;
- prioritise and stabilise resources for external accountability systems for children, akin to external financial audits; and
- support Ombuds in navigating complex power dynamics:

Conclusion

In the absence of effective, independent accountability mechanisms that ensure the aid sector consistently upholds the rights of all children to be heard, protected, and participate in matters that affect them, a global aid ombuds for children is an essential addition to the safeguarding toolkit. A joint inter-agency and donor committee should be created to develop a comprehensive proposal for the aid sector that draws on learning from the Ombuds Office. The proposal's implementation would require tremendous perseverance and flexibility, but it could provide part of the solution to strengthening safeguarding and accountability to children. It is now time for the aid sector to embrace an independent accountability system granting a voice and power to the most vulnerable.

Further reading

- The Ombuds Office for SOS Children's Villages website showcases a global ombuds system for children, featuring briefing papers, reports, and FAQs (Ombuds Office, 2024).
- Key documents on the need for and debate around an international aid ombuds include:
  - 'The International Ombuds for Humanitarian and Development Aid Scoping Study' (Hilhorst et al., 2018).

- 'The unfinished accountability revolution' analyses progress from the Rwandan genocide to 2014 (Sphere, 2014).
- 'Aid agencies can't police themselves. It's time for a change' and its response, 'Opinion: how donors can address aid agency oversight' (Hilhorst, 2018; Gottlieb, 2018).
- 'A humanitarian ombudsman revisited' discusses challenges and advocates for a pilot implementation (Mitchell and Christoplos, 2028).
- For insights into organisational ombuds (with a US focus), see the International Ombuds Association website (IOA, 2024).

References

Azzopardi, A. and Fairholm, J. (2022) *Pilot Ombuds Master Charter*. Vienna: The Ombuds Office for SOS Children's Villages, SOS Children's Villages International.

Carolei, D. (2022) 'An International Ombudsman to make non-governmental organizations more accountable? Too good to be true ...', *Leiden Journal of International Law*, 35, pp. 867–886.

CHS Alliance (2018) *Core Humanitarian Standard on Quality and Accountability*. [Online]. Available at: www.chsalliance.org (Accessed: 8 December 2024).

Core Humanitarian Standard (CHS) 2024 version (2015 version not available). [Online]. Available at: www.corehumanitarianstandard.org/the-standard (Accessed: 8 December 2024).

Hilhorst, D. (2018) 'Aid agencies can't police themselves. It's time for a change', *The New Humanitarian*, 22 February. [Online]. Available at: www.thenewhumanitarian.org/opinion/2018/02/22/aid-agencies-can-t-police-themselves-it-s-time-change (Accessed: 8 December 2024).

Hilhorst, D., Naik, A. and Cunningham, A. (2018) *International Ombuds for Humanitarian and Development Aid Scoping Study*. Erasmus University Rotterdam. [Online]. Available at: www.iss.nl/sites/corporate/files/2018-10/2018%20International%20Ombuds.pdf (Accessed: 8 December 2024).

Independent Commission on Sexual Misconduct, Accountability and Culture (2019) *Committing to Change—How Oxfam Can Become Accountable and Protect the People It Serves: Final Report*. [Online]. Available at: www-cdn.oxfam.org/s3fs-public/oxfam_ic_finalreport-en.pdf (Accessed: 8 December 2024).

Independent Special Commission (2023) *Investigating Allegations Arising from the Work of SOS Children's Villages: Final Report, Part 1*. [Online]. Available at: www.sos-childrensvillages.org/getmedia/35ceea40-a0fb-469b-a3c9-5500e23fa88c/ISC-Final-Report.pdf (Accessed: 8 December 2024).

International Ombuds Association (no date) *What is an Ombuds?* [Online]. Available at: www.ombudsassociation.org/what-is-an-ombuds- (Accessed: 8 December 2024).

Mitchell, J. and Christoplos, I. (2018) 'A humanitarian ombudsman revisited', *ALNAP Blog*, 15 March. [Online]. Available at: www.kuno-platform.nl/knowledge_base/a-humanitarian-ombudsman-revisited (Accessed: 25 August 2025).

O'Kane, C. and Pontalti, K. (2024a) *Story 1: Children and people's participation in the design and implementation of the Ombuds Office*. Vienna: The Ombuds Office for SOS Children's Villages, SOS Children's Villages International. [Online]. Available at: www.ombuds-sos-childrensvillages.org/getmedia/d1a46163-37db-498f-9968-227b9b0a93b9/Story-1_Child-participation.pdf (Accessed: 8 December 2024).

O'Kane, C. and Pontalti, K. (2024b) *Story 2: Learning from Children and Young People about Barriers and Enablers to Sharing Concerns*. Vienna: The Ombuds Office for SOS Children's Villages, SOS Children's Villages International. [Online]. Available at: www.ombuds-sos-childrensvillages.org/getmedia/58b1e1b8-2b6b-478c-92c2-24cc2481acb4/Story-2_Barriers-and-Enablers.pdf (Accessed: 8 December 2024).

O'Kane, C. and Pontalti, K. (2024c) *Story 3. Children and Young People's Participation in Recruitment for the Ombuds Office*. Vienna: The Ombuds Office for SOS Children's Villages, SOS Children's Villages International. [Online]. Available at: www.ombuds-sos-childrensvillages.org/getmedia/2b752e38-592e-4b09-bbfb-93fa73dd9c35/Story-3_Child-participation-in-recruitment.pdf (Accessed: 8 December 2024).

Ombuds Office for SOS Children's Villages (2022) *Ombuds Implementation Toolkit: A brief guide for implementing a National or Regional Ombuds*. Vienna: SOS Children's Villages.

Overseas Development Institute (1996) *Network Paper 16, The Joint Evaluation of Emergency Assistance to Rwanda: Study III Principal Findings and Recommendations*. Relief and Rehabilitation Network, Overseas Development Institute. ISSN: 1353-8691. [Online]. Available at: https://odihpn.org/wp-content/uploads/1996/06/networkpaper016.pdf (Accessed: 8 December 2024).

Oxfam International (2018) *Oxfam Scandal and Sector Response*. [Online]. Available at: www.oxfam.org (Accessed: 8 December 2024).

Proteknôn Foundation for Innovation and Learning (no date). [Online]. Available at: https://www.proteknon.net/ (Accessed: 8 December 2024).

SOS Children's Villages (SOS CV) (2023) *A Global Ombuds Office Strengthens Safeguarding at SOS Children's Villages*, 16 June. [Online]. Available at: https://www.sos-childrensvillages.org/news/global-ombuds-office (Accessed: 8 December 2024).

SOS Children's Villages (no date). [Online]. Available at: https://www.sos-childrensvillages.org/news/global-ombuds-office/ (Accessed: 8 December 2024).

Sphere (2014) *20 Years After the Rwandan Genocide: The Unfinished Accountability Revolution. An Interview with John Borton*. 20 March. [Online]. Available at: https://spherestandards.org/20-years-after-rwandan-genocide/ (Accessed: 8 December 2024).

The Grand Bargain (2016) *A Participation Revolution: Include People Receiving Aid in Making the Decisions Which Affect Their Lives*. [Online]. Available at: https://interagencystandingcommittee.org/a-participation-revolution-incl

ude-people-receiving-aid-in-making-the-decisions-which-affect-their-lives (Accessed: 25 August 2025).

The Ombuds Office for SOS Children's Villages website (no date). [Online]. Available at: www.ombuds-sos-childrensvillages.org/ (Accessed: 8 December 2024).

Chapter 14

Shaping the future of safeguarding in the international aid and development sector

Steve Reeves and Marcus Erooga

Chapter objectives

By the end of this chapter, you will:

- Appreciate the political and economic context in which the IAD sector is operating.
- Understand the collective observations and recommendations for change made by a select number of specialists, including some of the authors of this book.
- Explore the importance of community ownership of safeguarding measures and the power, leadership, and ethical challenges which may affect this being realised.

Introduction

The final chapter of this book consolidates the insights shared during a roundtable discussion involving authors of this book and some of their trusted colleagues, all safeguarding professionals, researchers, policymakers, and senior leaders. This dialogue aimed to address the fundamental tensions, operational challenges, and ethical dilemmas that persist in the safeguarding practices of the sector. It also sought to offer forward-looking recommendations that can inform the development of more effective, culturally sensitive, and survivor-centred safeguarding frameworks.

The roundtable drew on the in-depth perspectives and thinking of the authors, drawing on their professional experience and research. If concepts or approaches trigger the interest of the reader, there is an opportunity to learn more in the chapters written by the participants and by following up the recommended reading provided in each chapter.

At the time of writing, the political landscape in which the International Aid and Development (IAD) sector operates is disrupted. While Non-Governmental Organisations (NGOs) have long argued that the institutional funding for aid and development is insufficient, there has been a consensus that those with access to greatest financial resources, most particularly governments of industrialised Western democracies, would be a relatively consistent and reliable source of funding and support for tackling the systemic issues that affect the world's poorest and most marginalised people.

The roundtable took place in early 2025, which was shortly after the Trump administration announced a 90-day pause and review on all United States federal overseas aid spending in January 2025. This also included a commitment to review the United States Agency for International Development (USAID) and programmes to the value of $54 billion were ended (Briefing 10196, House of Commons, 2025).

The United Kingdom's commitment to align with the United Nations (UN) target of spending 0.7% of Gross National Income (GNI) on aid was achieved in 2013, but that commitment to spending has reduced twice in the period since, with the UK government elected in 2024 using previously earmarked ODA money to pay for increased defence and military spending, leaving the current UK commitment at 0.3% of GNI from 2027. In 2020, a previous UK government had already amalgamated the Department for International Development (DFID) into a new Foreign, Commonwealth and Development Office (FCDO). While notable, these examples are not the only ones to adversely affect global ODA spending in the recent past (Briefing 10196, House of Commons, 2025).

Whether or not individual governments restore or increase their ODA spending, which is always a possibility, the notion of reliable ODA spending, administered by specialist government agencies such as DFID and USAID, appears to be something on which the world's poorest and the IAD sector can no longer rely.

Just as the sector itself is at a critical juncture, so too is its response to the safeguarding challenges central to its work. Safeguarding in the international aid and development sector has evolved significantly, yet its fundamental challenges remain. Despite numerous policies, frameworks, and initiatives aimed at curbing abuse and exploitation, the sector continues to struggle with systemic failures that undermine its effectiveness.

Safeguarding remains a deeply complex and evolving field. While there is broad consensus on the need to protect people from harm, the implementation of safeguarding measures often reveals deep-seated challenges related to power dynamics, cultural differences, and competing priorities. The roundtable discussion highlighted that much of the existing safeguarding infrastructure remains heavily influenced by institutions in the Global North and their funding mechanisms. As a result, frameworks designed to ensure accountability and prevent harm are often implemented in the Global South without adequate consultation with communities or adaptation to local circumstances.

A recurring theme throughout the discussion was this tension between universal safeguarding standards and contextual realities. This tension becomes most apparent when organisations attempt to apply standardised frameworks across diverse cultural, social, and legal environments. The mismatch between externally devised safeguarding policies and the realities of local contexts can undermine trust, diminish effectiveness, and even cause harm to the very people those policies are intended to protect, a theme elaborated on in earlier chapters.

The discussion underscored the shortcomings of a compliance-driven approach to safeguarding. While adherence to some form of common policy is essential, participants emphasised that more effective safeguarding requires a nuanced, context-sensitive approach that acknowledges cultural differences, incorporates local knowledge systems, and prioritises the well-being of survivors. Such an approach needs the development of locally appropriate accountability mechanisms, leadership models that actively promote learning and adaptation, and funding frameworks that prioritise effectiveness over mere compliance.

The roundtable discussion also raised critical questions about the role of donors and how their expectations shape safeguarding practices. Too often, organisations prioritise the appearance of compliance over genuine engagement with the communities they serve. The disconnect between donor expectations, or the perception of them, and local realities creates significant barriers to implementing effective safeguarding practices.

The remainder of this chapter addresses these themes, presenting key discussions and recommendations aimed at enhancing safeguarding practices within the sector. Given the nature of the issue, there was considerable overlap in the various emerging themes. The discussion divided into:

- Reframing the Starting Point
- The Intersection of Safeguarding, Leadership and Culture
- Operational and Ethical Complexities
- Donor Influence and Power Dynamics

Each section concludes with practical recommendations designed to promote safeguarding systems that are both responsive to local realities and consistent with global safeguarding principles.

Key themes

Reframing the starting point

One of the recurring challenges is the tension between the need for global safeguarding standards and the importance of contextualising policies to reflect local realities. While standardisation ensures elements of consistency and accountability across international organisations, rigid adherence to external frameworks often results in culturally inappropriate safeguarding mechanisms that fail to resonate with local communities.

The lack of resonance with community custom, practice, and preference can result in a tendency to see safeguarding as a compliance, externally imposed, obligation, rather than an approach which maintains the rights of communities, ensures that members of those communities are safe, and maximises the effectiveness of community interventions.

The roundtable, drawing on the insights from the 'Donor power and safeguarding: enforcing compliance or enabling organisational safety?' and 'The challenge of a standards-based approach to safeguarding' chapters of this book, considered the more nuanced approach of 'indigenisation', in which safeguarding frameworks are informed by existing local practices and are clearly under the influence and control of the communities in which they operate. This contrasts with merely the adaptation of models largely shaped in other places, most usually the head offices of large NGOs, umbrella organisations, or donors.

There is a wealth of community-based knowledge on keeping people safe, but it is often overlooked in favour of pre-established compliance requirements, which allow large NGOs a perceived ease of operation, regulatory comfort, and a semblance of consistency. The disconnect can foster resistance and, at times, limits the effectiveness of safeguarding efforts. The future of safeguarding should prioritise partnerships with local actors, ensuring that global policies complement, rather than override, local protective measures.

The discussion revealed that risk management strategies may be dictated by donor requirements rather than genuine safeguarding concerns. In some cases, organisations feel pressured to demonstrate compliance even when the mechanisms being implemented are not suitable for the local context. This misalignment can create inefficiencies and even potential harm, particularly when organisations adopt superficial measures designed to meet external expectations rather than address the actual safeguarding needs of the communities they serve.

The significance of regulatory or donor compliance is not irrational on the part of organisational leadership and can be explained by a variety of factors, including the steps taken by regulators and government in the UK. If the consequence of a failure (or perceived failure) to adopt an externally justifiable and comprehensible approach is the possibility of an inquiry by a regulator and restricted access to extensive funding, it is unsurprising that compliance with a set of standards, congruent with narrow regulator and donor expectations is seen as a rational governance position. This approach, however, often fails to address the specific risks in different environments; both the latent risks and those caused or exacerbated by the circumstances which may have triggered the involvement of NGOs.

A shift is needed towards risk-informed safeguarding, where organisations work closely with communities to begin to identify the most pressing safeguarding threats and developing appropriate responses. The obligation of NGOs to ensure the appropriate behaviour of their staff and representatives remains unchanged, but the priorities for further harm reduction and prevention rest in a broader view of the specific risks in diverse locations. Successful safeguarding may, or rather should, look different everywhere, but have a common thread of consistency in objectives.

Another key theme was the need for organisations to rethink how power dynamics influence safeguarding practices. The tendency for safeguarding frameworks to be designed and implemented by actors from the Global North, with little input from the communities they are intended to protect, reinforces existing power imbalances. Participants called for a more inclusive approach that recognises the legitimacy of local knowledge systems and involves local actors as equal partners in the safeguarding process.

This paradigm shift challenges the idea that compliance equals safety. While compliance is necessary for governance and accountability, effective safeguarding requires a flexible, risk-based approach that adapts to evolving threats. Organisations, and those who create standards and obligations for them, must be willing to prioritise impact over bureaucracy, ensuring that safeguarding measures directly address real-world challenges rather than being an exercise in box-ticking.

The intersection of safeguarding, leadership, and culture

A major theme was the tendency for organisational leadership to prioritise compliance over meaningful community engagement. Leaders who would consider themselves sensitive to the needs of communities can easily be distracted by other pressures and become preoccupied with meeting donor expectations or avoiding reputational damage. This emphasis on compliance can stifle creativity and discourage staff from raising concerns or proposing innovative solutions.

Leadership and organisational culture are critical components of effective safeguarding. While compliance frameworks provide necessary guidelines, their implementation depends largely on the attitudes and behaviours of those in leadership positions. Effective leadership requires more than enforcing policies; it demands a commitment to fostering a culture of learning, inclusivity, and continuous improvement.

The discussion, benefiting from the Leadership and Culture: What do we mean and why are they so fundamental? chapter, highlighted the importance of constructive challenge within organisations. Leaders must create an environment where members of teams feel empowered to question established protocols and propose alternative approaches without fear of criticism or reprisal. Promoting a culture of openness where mistakes are treated as opportunities for learning rather than grounds for punishment is an essential element of the culture needed in organisations with successful safeguarding approaches.

The discussion recognised the importance of promoting local leadership and shifting practice in the many international agencies which rely heavily on expatriate leadership, which can undermine the ownership of safeguarding practices. This requires organisations to recognise existing skills in local leaders and actively invest in training and empowering staff working in the countries of which they are nationals to develop safeguarding frameworks that are relevant to the context.

The roundtable stressed the importance of collaborative leadership models. Safeguarding cannot be achieved by organisations acting alone; it requires partnerships that promote shared learning and resource-sharing. Leaders must be willing to engage in meaningful collaboration with local actors, promoting inclusive decision-making processes that prioritise community input.

Participants also highlighted the need for organisations to adopt trauma-informed leadership practices. Leaders at all levels of organisations must be equipped to respond empathetically and effectively to the needs of survivors, prioritising their wellbeing over organisational reputation or compliance requirements.

One of the most uncomfortable truths of leadership in the sector is that too few people with power and authority are willing to give it up and make way for others. For leadership and authority to be effectively exercised as close to community level as possible, someone needs to cede power elsewhere.

This shift can take many forms, but a particularly resonant example shared was from a humanitarian organisation operating in East Africa. The regional team, composed largely of local staff, had successfully developed relationships with community leaders and was managing safeguarding referrals in culturally sensitive and effective ways. However, all external communication—particularly with donors—was still routed through a head office team based in Europe. This led to delays, diluted messaging, and occasional misrepresentation of local realities. The question raised was: why should those most familiar with the context be silenced in favour of distant actors? At what point are those with power and authority willing to step aside and let those with proximity, trust, and capability lead the conversation?

To create meaningful change, safeguarding must be embedded into everyday organisational culture, from leadership engagement to those in routine contact with communities. This requires investment in regular training, transparent leadership, and a commitment to ongoing reflection and adaptation. A strong safeguarding culture is not dictated by policy alone but is cultivated through ethical leadership and open dialogue at all levels.

Operational and ethical complexities

Implementing safeguarding frameworks across multiple jurisdictions introduces complex ethical and operational challenges. One of the most persistent difficulties is navigating local legal frameworks, particularly in regions where labour laws, law enforcement capacity, and cultural practices vary significantly.

The issue of accountability emerged as one of the most complex themes during the roundtable discussion. The challenge of ensuring accountability while respecting cultural, social, and legal differences was a recurring point of debate. Organisations operating within the international aid and development sector often find themselves caught between competing demands: adhering to donor requirements, respecting local customs, and ensuring the safety and wellbeing of vulnerable people.

For example, employment law constraints in some countries may prevent organisations from dismissing staff for safeguarding violations if such actions do not constitute legal misconduct under local regulations. This raises difficult questions about how global organisations can uphold safeguarding principles while respecting national labour laws. A balance must be struck between ensuring accountability and navigating legal constraints, often requiring case-by-case ethical decision-making.

Many organisations will find themselves subject to multiple jurisdictions and varied labour laws in the places in which they work. Some of those jurisdictions will not clearly define the breach of an organisational safeguarding policy or abuse of some in receipt of services as gross misconduct. Good employers may perceive themselves to be a difficult position, wanting to uphold importance safeguarding principles, while also not wanting to breach employment laws. That does not, however, mean that no action can be taken, but it is reliant on management courage and risk management.

Conducting a disciplinary process and dismissing an employee for a safeguarding related misconduct can be done ethically and fairly, but the consequence may be that a Court finds that some form of compensation is payable to the individual. While distasteful, organisations with integrity and courage will usually consider that removing someone who has harmed others, and may still pose a risk of harm, is a far higher priority than avoiding having a compensation award made against it.

Safeguarding reporting obligations present a complex dilemma. In some contexts, law enforcement systems may be under-resourced, corrupt, or even hostile towards certain types of victims. In some cases, reporting safeguarding concerns to local authorities may do more harm than good and the pressure on organisations to understand and evaluate this risk is high. Standardised reporting requirements are often unworkable in countries where local law enforcement is either ineffective or complicit in abuse.

Further complicating matters, victims, or survivors may refuse to cooperate with authorities due to distrust or fear of retaliation. This raises profound ethical questions about how to balance the needs of survivors with the expectations of donors and regulators. Often organisations develop alternative safeguarding mechanisms, such as working with trusted local partners or establishing independent oversight mechanisms that prioritise survivor safety over legal formalities.

In some instances, there are alternatives to engaging local law enforcement agencies or criminal justice agencies. One of the most striking examples shared during the discussion was the Simon Harris case in Kenya. Harris ran a charity in Kenya and was accused of extensive sexual abuse of children engaged with its programmes. He was charged under the UK's Sexual Offences Act 2003, which allows British nationals to be held accountable for abuse committed abroad, the first time this law has been used for offences in Africa (BBC, 2015).

The UK's National Crime Agency (NCA) expended considerable resources to conduct an extra-territorial prosecution, in part due to inadequate local law enforcement structures. While this intervention succeeded in reducing the harm posed by a serious, internationally mobile, offender, and provided an element of justice, it underscored the unsustainability of relying on external enforcement mechanisms as a substitute for building local capacity. The levels of resources expending on an individual case could have a significant impact on local capacity, but the system in place at that time did not incentivise that type of investment, although following this investigation extensive law enforcement capacity building was undertaken in Kenya (PMO, 2018).

INTERPOL's Project Soteria was highlighted as an attempt to tackle some of the capacity issues in countries which are recipients of significant aid, but the work is difficult and needs to be focused on the places of greatest potential impact. Participants noted the consensus that most of those perpetrating abuse and exploitation are nationals of the countries in which they cause harm. While extra-territorial prosecutions may have their place they are rarely an option, and rather than empowering local systems to develop their own safeguarding mechanisms, external interventions can inadvertently undermine local ownership of safeguarding efforts.

The importance of trauma-informed practices also emerged as a central theme. Survivors of abuse frequently report dissatisfaction with how their complaints are handled, particularly when response procedures are invasive or re-traumatising. Organisations must be willing to adapt their practices to ensure that survivors feel safe, respected, and empowered throughout the reporting and subsequent investigation processes.

The discussion emphasised the need for organisations to establish context appropriate accountability mechanisms. This involves working collaboratively with local stakeholders to design systems that are both culturally relevant and practically effective. Organisations must also be transparent in their decision-making processes, documenting how safeguarding decisions are made and ensuring that survivors are involved in those processes whenever possible.

A truly effective safeguarding framework must be survivor-centred, ensuring that control over the reporting and response process by victims and survivors is maximised. However, many existing safeguarding mechanisms appear to prioritise organisational reputation and regulatory compliance over survivor needs. This may lead to processes, and consequences, that are more traumatic than the original abuse, deterring survivors from coming forward.

Trauma-informed safeguarding must become the norm, with policies designed to empower survivors rather than retraumatise them. This includes:

- Prioritising survivor choice and agency in safeguarding investigations.
- Avoiding rigid reporting structures that compel survivors to engage with systems that may not be in their best interest.
- Embedding psychosocial support into safeguarding responses.
- Encouraging organisations to be flexible in their approaches to justice and accountability, recognising that one-size-fits-all frameworks rarely serve survivors effectively.

To bridge the gaps, organisations must work closely with donors to develop systems that account for both global consistency and local relevance. This could include the establishment of localised ombudsperson models, the background to which is discussed in the Strengthening Safeguarding and Accountability Through an International Aid Ombuds for Children chapter.

Donor influence and power dynamics

A critical issue shaping safeguarding policy is the role of donors. Many organisations rely on donor funding, which often comes with prescriptive safeguarding requirements. While donors play a crucial role in driving accountability, their influence can sometimes limit safeguarding innovation, forcing organisations to adopt standardised approaches that are not always fit for purpose.

The power imbalance between donors and recipient organisations means that funding priorities often override the practical realities of safeguarding implementation. Organisations may feel compelled to accept funding conditions that do not align with local safeguarding needs, leading to policies that are ineffective or counterproductive.

An example was shared regarding a programme in Afghanistan where donors routinely demanded that the sexual orientation of survivors be recorded. This requirement clashed with the cultural and legal realities of the region, requiring the organisation to engage with the donor in a way that eliminated the risk of harm to vulnerable people, without giving the impression that its safeguarding or data gathering was substandard.

A fundamental issue raised during the conversation was the challenge of short-term, project-based funding, which undermines the potential for sustainable safeguarding systems. Organisations are frequently required to demonstrate compliance within narrow timeframes dictated by funding cycles, meaning that their efforts often focus on meeting donor expectations rather than developing robust, contextually appropriate safeguarding systems that can endure beyond the lifespan of individual projects.

For example, an organisation operating in the Democratic Republic of Congo reported being pressured to produce compliance reports and conduct training workshops to meet donor requirements. However, due to limited funding and lack of follow-up support, local actors were left without the tools necessary to implement safeguarding frameworks in a way that suited the context. Once the project funding ended, the safeguarding mechanisms collapsed, leaving communities without adequate protection.

Many donors aspire to fund innovative work, which can help develop solutions to complex challenges, but can also be responsible for endless attempts to refine solutions that work and should simply be scaled.

Donors were seen as always wanting to fund something innovative, so programmes of funding were limited to set periods, such as three years, without an option to extend because the work would no longer be 'innovative' at that point. This creates a funding starvation cycle. Projects and communities can find themselves subject to endless innovation, when simple programme delivery would be in their better interests.

Participants also spoke of innovation too frequently being seen as synonymous with technology, rather than new approaches; the result being an oversupply of smart phone applications and an underinvestment in the engagement with communities which would yield greater safeguarding returns.

For some at the heart of the issue rests the notion that too many donors operate in a way that implies that they consider projects they find to be taking place in a risk-free bubble. Current funding models focus primarily on expected results rather than the cost of mitigating risks. Organisations are often left under-resourced for essential safeguarding tasks that fall outside formal compliance frameworks.

In too many instances, people are approving funding bids that do not consider the risk of a safeguarding incident until it happens, too often what follows is the apportioning of blame to either organisations or individuals, when the fundamental problem lies in the programme design and lack of comprehensive funding for all that the delivery of it entails.

Participants repeatedly called for donors to adopt more flexible funding models that actively support risk mitigation, capacity building, and cultural competence. Rather than emphasising compliance as an objective, donors should provide funding that allows organisations to develop safeguarding frameworks that are adapted to local realities. This includes allowing organisations the freedom to experiment with innovative approaches and to learn from their mistakes without fear of losing funding.

The discussion underscored the need for collaborative partnerships between donors, local organisations, and international agencies. Safeguarding cannot be effectively addressed by any single actor; instead, it requires ongoing dialogue and cooperation between multiple stakeholders. Organisations must be willing to share knowledge, pool resources, and work together to develop safeguarding systems that are genuinely responsive to the needs of the communities they serve.

The roundtable highlighted the importance of prevention rather than reaction. Rather than relying solely on punitive measures, organisations should invest in capacity-building initiatives that empower local communities to identify and address safeguarding concerns before they escalate into serious harm. This preventative approach not only reduces the risk of abuse but also promotes resilience and sustainability within communities.

A more equitable safeguarding model requires:

- Shifting accountability to donors, ensuring they are also responsible for safeguarding outcomes rather than just compliance requirements.
- Creating more flexible funding mechanisms that allow recipient organisations to develop safeguarding approaches that are contextually relevant.
- Empowering organisations to push back against restrictive donor requirements when they undermine effective safeguarding practices.

Reflections and next steps

The challenges discussed in this chapter underscore that achieving meaningful safeguarding is far more complex than merely adhering to externally prescribed standards or ticking boxes for donor compliance. It demands a comprehensive re-evaluation of how safeguarding practices are conceptualised, developed, and implemented, prioritising responsiveness to local contexts and genuine survivor engagement.

Reflecting on the deeply troubling events and crises that bought safeguarding in the sector to a point of crisis described earlier the instinctive response of many to enforce greater uniformity and rigidity should not be the sector's primary response. Instead, organisations must respond by allowing more sensitive and contextual responses to safeguarding, ensuring they are attuned to local realities and the genuine needs of survivors.

A recurring theme has been the necessity of shifting safeguarding frameworks from a compliance-centric model towards approaches deeply rooted in local cultures, realities, and priorities. Organisations must commit to fostering genuine partnerships with local communities and leaders, harnessing and empowering local knowledge and expertise. This shift necessitates a critical assessment of organisational leadership and culture, ensuring leaders at all levels not only enforce safeguarding policies but model transparency, accountability, and empathy. Encouraging a culture of learning and reflection will enable teams to continuously evolve safeguarding practices in response to real-world challenges.

Addressing operational and ethical complexities requires courageous conversations about accountability. Organisations must strike a careful balance between adhering to global safeguarding principles and respecting local legal and cultural contexts. Prioritising survivor-centred and trauma-informed practices demands flexibility and adaptability, ensuring that safeguarding systems serve rather than retraumatise survivors.

Donors, whose influence permeates every aspect of safeguarding, hold significant responsibility for enabling or constraining effective practices. A fundamental reassessment of donor approaches is necessary, moving beyond rigid compliance frameworks towards flexible, adaptive funding models that allow organisations to experiment, innovate, and respond effectively to local safeguarding challenges. Donors must actively partner with organisations and communities, promoting sustainable capacity building rather than short-term interventions.

There are several critical next steps for stakeholders across the sector:

- Embed meaningful local consultation into every stage of safeguarding policy and programme development, ensuring that local knowledge and practices shape safeguarding frameworks.
- Promote leadership cultures committed to continuous improvement, transparency, and responsiveness, actively supporting staff to voice concerns and propose innovative safeguarding solutions.
- Develop flexible, risk-informed approaches that prioritise the specific safeguarding threats faced by communities, emphasising survivor wellbeing and choice.
- Encourage donor flexibility and collaboration, advocating for funding mechanisms that prioritise contextually relevant safeguarding

measures, capacity building, and local ownership over compliance-driven outcomes.

Safeguarding needs to evolve and become a genuinely ethical, culturally sensitive, and survivor-focused activity. This requires concerted action from all those engaged in the sector to create a system that is not only effective in preventing harm but also trusted, resilient, and empowering for those in need of safeguarding.

Further reading

- For a detailed insight into the safeguarding journey of a complex international organisation: A Case Study on SOS Children's Villages with Accountable Now (2025): <https://accountablenow.org/wp-content/uploads/2025/04/Safeguarding-Failures-and-Lessons.pdf> accessed 23rd April, 2025.
- For those interested in exploring more viewpoints and insights about some of these issues: Sexual Exploitation and Abuse in Peacekeeping and Aid, edited by Jasmine-Kim Westendorf and Elliot Dolan-Evans, Bristol University Press (2024)

References

BBC News, (26 February 2015) 'UK charity boss Simon Harris jailed for Kenya child sex abuse' <www.bbc.co.uk/news/uk-england-31599524> accessed 27th March, 2025.

Loft P, Brien P, (2025) 'US aid, the UK, and funding for multilateral aid bodies in 2025' (Briefing Paper Number 10196, House of Commons Library 18 March 2025) <https://researchbriefings.files.parliament.uk/documents/CBP-10196/CBP-10196.pdf> accessed 27th March, 2025.

Prime Minister's Office (PMO), (2018) 'New cyber unit to tackle child sex abuse in Kenya' <www.gov.uk/government/news/new-cyber-unit-to-tackle-child-sex-abuse-in-kenya> accessed 27th March, 2025.

Appendix 1

A brief timeline of events from 2011 to 2018 (based on BBC, 2018)

Marcus Erooga

2011

Allegations were raised orally in early July 2011 by a whistleblower with Oxfam GB's senior leadership during an International Programme Leadership team meeting held at Oxfam GB's HQ. These concerns were followed up in writing by the whistleblower on 12 July 2011.

An internal investigation commenced on 23 July with an investigation team dispatched to Haiti. The internal investigation started examining allegations against, and the conduct of, three members of staff. By the time it concluded it had extended to investigating 10 members of staff and reportedly involved over 40 witnesses.

The outcome of the investigations led to various individual disciplinary hearings. An overarching final investigation report for all cases was produced in August 2011. The final report also contained recommendations for wider action for Oxfam GB and identified learning for the future. This report was subsequently made public in 2018 (Oxfam 2011).

In September it was reported that Oxfam GB's country director in Haiti has resigned after an internal investigation found six members of staff guilty of misconduct, having "(been in ... breach of Oxfam GB's behavioural code of conduct, bringing Oxfam's name into disrepute, abuse of power and bullying with Oxfam." Oxfam stressed that none of the charges involved beneficiaries and were not related to fraud or misuse of donations (Civil Society, 2011).

2017

In October 2017 newspapers reported that the number of reports of sexual exploitation by Oxfam staff and partners had increased from 26 in 2014/15 to 87 in 2016/17 (*The Times*, 2017).

The Charity Commission opened an inquiry into Oxfam in November, and in December issued a case report which concluded further work was needed in respect of HR culture, overall governance and management of safeguarding (Charity Commission, 2017).

2018

In February 2018 *The Times* newspaper alleged Oxfam had covered up claims that senior staff working in Haiti in the wake of the 2010 earthquake used sex workers, some of whom may have been underage. Among the male staff accused of sexual misconduct is Oxfam's then director of operations in Haiti, who is alleged to have engaged in this conduct a villa rented for him by Oxfam.

Oxfam responded that it had uncovered the accusations in 2011 and immediately launched an internal investigation, which had been reported at the time, albeit without the nature of the allegations being made public. It also published a redacted version of the 2011 internal inquiry report (Oxfam, 2011).

According to this, four members of staff were dismissed and three, including the then director of operations in Haiti, were allowed to resign before the end of the investigation. It stated that claims of underage girls being involved were not proven. It also reveals that three of the men accused of sexual misconduct physically threatened witnesses during the charity's investigation.

It also announced *'a package of measures to strengthen the prevention and handling of sexual abuse cases'* in the wake of revelations published by *The Times* (Civil Society, 2018).

The Chief Executive of Save the Children UK, also announced that his organisation would be looking at strengthening its safeguarding procedures following the scandal, with a range of specific proposals they would consider (Save the Children, 2018). The following day the Oxfam Deputy Chief Executive, who had been a programme director at the time of the alleged incidents, resigned from her post.

Oxfam's former global head of safeguarding between 2012 and 2015 then accused Oxfam and the Charity Commission of not acting quickly enough after a report was compiled highlighting the scale of the problem. she stated that Oxfam's chief executive stopped her from presenting a report compiled from confidential internal surveys of the charity's international aid staff which highlighted further instances of sexual harassment, sex in exchange for aid handouts and rape. The CEO responded that he felt the issues were addressed in the 2011 internal inquiry report (Oxfam, 2011).

As a consequence of *The Times* story the UK Culture Secretary ordered Oxfam to hand over all the evidence to the Charity Commission. The Charity Commission then stated that Oxfam made a report to them in August 2011 about an ongoing internal investigation into allegations of misconduct by staff members involved in their Haiti programme. This explained that the misconduct related to inappropriate sexual behaviour, bullying, harassment and the intimidation of staff, but stated there had been no allegations, or evidence, of any abuse of beneficiaries. It also made no mention of any potential sexual crimes involving minors.

The Charity Commission indicated that their approach would have been different had the full details reported been disclosed at the time (Charity Commission, 2018a). A statutory inquiry, the most serious action the Commission can take, was then opened (Charity Commission, 2018b). That report was published in June 2019 (Charity Commission, 2019).

Political pressure ensued, with the president of Haiti, Jovenel Moïse, condemning Oxfam and a senior government source in Haiti confirming that an investigation would be launched into foreign aid agencies operating there (BBC, 2018b). UK Prime Minister Theresa May and International Development Secretary Penny Mordaunt both expressed support for an urgent Charity Commission investigation and the International Development Secretary indicated that funding for Oxfam could be ended if it could not account for the way it handled claims.

Oxfam agreed to withdraw from bidding for any new UK Government funding until the Department for International Development (DFID) was satisfied that they could meet the standards expected (DFID, 2018). The European Commission, which gave €1.7m to Oxfam's Haiti programme in 2011, threatened it was ready to *'cease funding any partner not living up to high ethical standards'*.

Oxfam also announced the establishment of an independent review of the charity's culture and safeguarding system.

The charity said the commission would look at all aspects of culture, policy and practices relating to safeguarding and the findings would be made public within 12 months. That report was published in 2019 (Oxfam, 2019).

Four months after the Times first reported the concerns, the Chief Executive of Oxfam said he would stand down at the end of the year.

In evidence to a subsequent hearing of the House of Commons International Development Committee, Save the Children chief executive Kevin Watkins described the Oxfam scandal as a *'wake up call'* for the sector. The Committee subsequently published two reports addressing relevant issues (IDC, 2018, HC2017-2019, HC840, and IDC, 2019, HC2019-2020, HC111).

References

BBC, 2018 *Oxfam Haiti allegations: How the scandal unfolded*, 18th February, https://www.bbc.com/news/uk-43112200 accessed July 12 2023

Charity Commission, 2019 *Statement of the Results of an Inquiry: Oxfam* https://assets.publishing.service.gov.uk/government/uploads/system/uploads/attachment_data/file/807945/Statement_of_the_Results_of_an_Inquiry_Oxfam.pdf accessed July 12 2023

Charity Commission, 2018a *Charity Commission statement on Oxfam*, https://www.gov.uk/government/news/charity-commission-statement-on-oxfam, accessed July 12 2023

Charity Commission, 2018b *Charity Commission opens statutory inquiry into Oxfam and sets out steps to improve safeguarding in the charity sector*, https://www.gov.uk/government/news/charity-commission-opens-statutory-inquiry-into-oxfam-and-sets-out-steps-to-improve-safeguarding-in-the-charity-sector, accessed July 12 2023

Charity Commission, 2017 *Oxfam: case report*, tps://www.gov.uk/government/publications/charity-case-report-oxfam/oxfam-case-report accessed July 12 2023

Civil Society, 2018 *Oxfam announces 'package of measures' amid fallout from Haiti scandal* https://www.civilsociety.co.uk/news/oxfam-chair-announces-package-of-measures-amid-fallout-from-haiti-scandal.html#sthash.WtZJEnGB.dpuf accessed July 12 2023

Civil Society, 2011 *Oxfam boss in Haiti stands down after staff misconduct* https://www.civilsociety.co.uk/news/oxfam-boss-in-haiti-stands-down-after-staff-misconduct.html accessed July 12 2023

International Development Committee, 2018 *Sexual exploitation and abuse in the aid sector, HC2017-2019, HC840* https://publications.parliament.uk/pa/cm201719/cmselect/cmintdev/840/840.pdf, accessed July 11 2023

International Development Committee, 2019 *Follow-up: Sexual exploitation and abuse in the aid sector, HC2019-2020, HC111* https://publications.parliament.uk/pa/cm201919/cmselect/cmintdev/111/111.pdf, accessed July 11 2023

O'Neill, S, 2017 *Oxfam workers claim bosses harassed them*, The Times, 28th October, https://www.thetimes.co.uk/article/oxfam-workers-claim-bosses-harassed-them-grtbmwssq, accessed July 12 2023

Oxfam, 2019 Independent Commission on Sexual Misconduct, Accountability and Culture *Committing to Change—How Oxfam Can Become Accountable and Protect the People It Serves: Final Report*, https://www-cdn.oxfam.org/s3fs-public/oxfam_ic_final_report-en.pdf, accessed July 11 2023

Oxfam, 2011 *Investigation Report FR N5 – Haiti* https://www.oxfam.org.uk/about-us/tackling-abuse-information-and-updates/haiti-investigation-report/ accessed July 10 2023

Save the Children, 2018 *Protecting children is the most important thing we do*, https://www.savethechildren.org.uk/blogs/2018/protecting-children-important-thing, accessed July 12 2023

Appendix 2
Understanding effective safeguarding culture

Bond

Appendix 2 ■ 199

bond

Understanding effective safeguarding culture

A tool to help organisations understand the indicators and behaviours associated with safeguarding culture.

Bond.org.uk

EFFECTIVE SAFEGUARDING CULTURE

Introduction

Organisational culture is the basis for safeguarding to be practiced well in an organisation: where people are and feel safe to engage and anyone in, or impacted by, an organisation is empowered to report concerns wherever they may arise.

Organisations often find it difficult to analyse or critique their own organisational culture.

This tool has been designed to help facilitate conversations within organisations, at all levels, to improve the collective understanding of what constitutes a positive safeguarding culture.

It describes behaviours that are often indicative of an organisational culture that is non-compliant with good safeguarding practice and progresses to behaviours that are more likely to be indicative of a culture where best safeguarding practice is genuinely valued and is part of the lived experience of those within, or impacted by, the organisation.

It can be used to introduce or support the safeguarding leadership tool, or as a standalone tool.

EFFECTIVE SAFEGUARDING CULTURE

Using the tool

When people try to describe behaviours that are indicative of a positive safeguarding culture within their organisation, they often describe behaviours that are more indicative of compliance. For example, the statement: "Everyone in our organisation completes a safeguarding induction course" is a statement about meeting a minimal standard of compliance, rather than one that describes the impact on behaviours that attending such a course should have.

An effective way in which this tool can be used is to:

> Gather participants in groups, either as mixed cross-organisational groups, separate teams or as a whole staff team in smaller organisations.

> Share the tool, either electronically or as handouts, but with the final column "Effective safeguarding culture" removed or covered.

> Ask participants in groups or pairs to complete this last column: What behaviours do they feel would indicate an effective safeguarding culture?

> Ask participants to reflect on the extent to which these behaviours are evident in their own organisation or team.

This information can then be used in to improve safeguarding engagement and practice.

Appendix 2

EFFECTIVE SAFEGUARDING CULTURE

Policies and procedures

Non-compliance >>	Minimal compliance >>	Effective safeguarding culture
Safeguarding policy for children and vulnerable adults either does not exist, is of poor quality, or is outdated.	An up to date safeguarding policy exists, but there is limited evidence that staff are **adhering** to the policy, or have been trained to do so.	A robust and effective policy exists, is a key part of induction and is **lived** day-to-day, with supporting processes in place which are used regularly.
Staff are **unaware** of the existence of the policy or know that it is in place but there is no requirement to adhere to it.	Staff feel uncertain about the policy, unclear about how to **access** it (where it is located), who "owns" it, and how to apply it.	Policy is well **integrated**: staff **proactively** refer and adhere to policy and processes, which **guide** behaviour and actions.
Safeguarding policy is not reflected in or connected to other relevant policies.	There is mention of safeguarding in some, though not all, related policies and there is no adequate process for checking implementation.	Relevant organisational policies have safeguarding as an integrated element and are actively considered by all those who have safeguarding integrated into their roles and functions.
Policy does not seek to address **power or gender** imbalances.	Some evidence that processes supporting the policy are attempting to be inclusive, however this is experienced as **tokenistic**.	Processes are sensitive to gender and power imbalances, **inclusive** and explicitly ensure that the perspectives of those most at risk are addressed. Staff are able and willing to challenge when that is not achieved.
Processes do not consider the unique needs of different at-risk groups.	Some senior leaders exhibit behaviour that is not consistent with the policy, which suggests that "the rules do not apply to them."	
Staff do not understand how they can influence the policy; there is a **lack of transparency** about policy development.	Rules are followed without an understanding of their reasoning – leading to **inconsistent or inappropriate implementation** in different contexts.	There is rigour amongst all staff in adhering to and upholding policies and processes.
Widespread belief that the rules in the policy are easily or often flouted or ignored.		There are demonstrable, contextualised and effective approaches to **embedding** core and consistent safeguarding standards.

Appendix 2

EFFECTIVE SAFEGUARDING CULTURE

2 Safer programming

Non-compliance >>>

Safeguarding is only considered when donors demand it (for example, in due diligence assessments), and never proactively.

Safeguarding capability and standards are compromised and not seen as an essential component to operational response teams (for example, safeguarding staff are not involved in programme discussions or decisions or not seen as part of the operational team).

Time pressures often result in safeguarding failures (for example, not completing criminal record checks or risk assessments of new programmes or activities).

Safeguarding issues are spoken about with disdain, frustration or are never mentioned at all.

There is no consistent and ongoing assessment of safeguarding risks in programmes, including within partnerships.

Minimal compliance >>>

Ad hoc consideration of safeguarding risks and response in programme design and implementation.

On occasion, senior leaders agree that, due to **time pressures**, safeguarding standards cannot be met.

If safeguarding risks and issues are raised about partners and programme activities, these are seen as a **frustration** to be overcome, not a legitimate concern to be addressed.

Staff do not feel supported to challenge poor practice, instead relying on **hierarchical structures** or gossip to express frustrations or share risks.

Risk assessments are ad hoc, done without guidance and commitment to consistent training, review and checks.

Effective safeguarding culture

Safeguarding is **integral** to all stages of the programme cycle. Managers actively check how safeguarding has been considered and addressed.

Consistent safeguarding standards are upheld and teams resist pressure to cut corners on safeguarding (for example, in rapidly moving emergency response).

Leadership will only approve new projects or initiatives if they are assured that safeguarding is properly embedded and risks are fully assessed.

All staff and volunteers are **empowered and supported** to challenge poor safeguarding practices, and their concerns are addressed.

There is a **consistent process** to assess partners and programme safeguarding processes, ensuring there is staff capacity, supported by ongoing mentoring and training.

EFFECTIVE SAFEGUARDING CULTURE

3 Survivor-centred approach

Non-compliance 	Minimal compliance 	Effective safeguarding culture 
A survivor-centred approach is not, or not seen to be, an organisational priority.	Senior leaders frequently ask about reputational impact before asking about the welfare of the survivor.	Leaders demonstrate doing the **right thing for survivors** by placing them at the heart of their response, even above the interests of the organisation (for example, risk to fundraising) and ensure there is a strong track record of support.
Reporting processes do not prioritise the welfare of the survivor. They may be **non-confidential** or even require survivors to report to the police.	Reporting processes are **confidential**, but there is still a lack of sense of safety, accessibility and uptake in reporting.	Organisational reporting processes **prioritise the wellbeing of survivors.**
Responding to cases does not take the needs and preferences of the survivor into account.	Survivors may be asked what s/he needs, but this is not consistently taken into account in the response.	Survivors are consulted and involved in determining the response to their concerns.
Reporting mechanisms do not enable **rapid response**, missing the 72-hour window to provide PEP to sexual assault survivors.	There is a lack of clarity and provision for 72-hour referral care. Staff running **investigations** may have received training, but not specifically for investigating safeguarding concerns.	Staff undertaking investigations receive **safeguarding specific training.**
Untrained, unsupervised staff run investigations; using inappropriate or even shaming language and questions.	Some limited funding may be available for survivor care, but there is a lack of clarity over how to access it.	Financial and other **resources** (for example, PEP or counseling) are allocated to survivor care and investigations are properly resourced.
No **funding** is allocated to survivor-care.	There is provision for confidentiality in knowledge of, storage and access to sensitive information, but it is not followed or monitored well.	Confidentiality in knowledge of, storage and access to sensitive information is routinely followed and monitored.
Confidential and sensitive data is not kept secure.		
Organisation has never considered that **survivors may be among their workforce.**	The organisation recognises that their workforce is likely to include survivors but takes no action in respect of that.	Survivors report that the organisation is a safe place for the employment of survivors.

EFFECTIVE SAFEGUARDING CULTURE

Awareness raising

Non-compliance >>>	Minimal compliance >>>	Effective safeguarding culture
Safeguarding is rarely, if ever, discussed until there is an incident.	Some limited communications materials on safeguarding are available but may not be in the correct languages, or may not be accessible to all (for example, due to illiteracy).	Regular open discussion and **ongoing dialogue** is evident, especially with communities.
A general lack of understanding of the organisation's legal Duty of Care to safeguard; and lack of understanding of the definitions of abuse and how to report it.	An awareness of duty to report but not a consistent understanding of, and approach to, safeguarding.	CEO and senior leadership lead from the front, talking about safeguarding and promoting corporate responsibility. They are visibly **engaged with safeguarding** learning opportunities.
Pervasive belief that abuse by a member of the organisation "couldn't happen here" or that abuse is "dreadful, but rare."	Attitude that abuse is "possible, but very unlikely to happen here".	The relevance of safeguarding training is clear to all. There is active discussion of vulnerability and a commitment to addressing it.
Senior leaders **avoid or decline** to attend safeguarding training and do not prioritise attending **mandatory training.**	Senior leadership does not champion safeguarding training or request shorter training for senior staff.	Leaders model **commitment to learning** and development about safeguarding.
There is a lack of resourcing, training and ongoing support for staff and organisational awareness.	There is an ad hoc approach to training. Investment in some training but lack of clarity on frequency and mandatory requirement.	Good quality and accessible information, training and learning opportunities are available for all staff. Regular checks on awareness and compliance.
Absence of clarity over what training is essential for all staff. Safeguarding is not mentioned by senior leaders in briefings or meetings.	Senior leaders do not openly discuss insights into safeguarding. Safeguarding may be on the agenda for key meetings, but issues are shared in a non-compelling or "dry" manner.	Senior leaders **regularly share insights** around safeguarding that bring the issues to life in a meaningful way for staff.

Appendix 2 ■ 205

5 EFFECTIVE SAFEGUARDING CULTURE
Safer recruitment

Non-compliance

Leaders encourage staff not to follow safe recruitment processes, often due to time pressures.

Roles are not consistently subject to open recruitment processes. People known to senior leaders are often recruited.

Safeguarding is not mentioned in the job advertisement, candidate information or at the interview stage.

Criminal records checks are only sought for a few roles.

References are not always taken up and only done briefly via email.

Induction does not occur or does not include a clear code of conduct.

An option in resolving staffing difficulties is to offer references in exchange for leaving quietly.

Minimal compliance

Safer recruitment principles exist and are documented within the organisation, although they may be only loosely applied.

There are significant differences in the processes of recruitment at the **senior leadership level** in comparison to other recruitment, for example at national levels.

Safeguarding is mentioned but not actively explored in in the application process or interview.

Criminal records checks are not followed up across all countries or roles.

References are requested but not to a standard format and are not verified.

Informal induction processes occur, but without specificity about expected behaviour.

Sometimes staff members are offered references in exchange for leaving quietly.

Effective safeguarding culture

All **staff**, from volunteers to board members and ambassadors, are recruited according to the same safer recruitment principles and standards.

Senior leaders actively **champion**, adhere to and model safer recruitment processes.

Organisational commitment to new initiatives that enhance screening of potential employees. All staff at all levels are asked carefully chosen safeguarding questions in interview.

No staff are allowed to be in post without completion and periodic review of criminal record checks.

References are requested in an agreed format and verified by recruiting managers.

Defined induction processes are provided for all new joiners and include a Code of Conduct.

Senior managers never authorise "deals", whereby staff members who have committed suspected safeguarding violations receive a reference in exchange for leaving quietly.

EFFECTIVE SAFEGUARDING CULTURE

6 Reporting

Non-compliance 	Minimal compliance 	Effective safeguarding culture
Staff do not report concerns and are unaware of a requirement to report. This is not addressed in policy and training.	Low number of reports from staff are received; may only relate to serious or "clear" cases of abuse.	Staff **routinely report** issues, including lower-level concerns.
Organisation does not receive reports from any **marginalised groups** (including children, women, people with disabilities, minority ethnic groups, LGBTQI, etc.) and does not explore the reasons for this.	Requirement to report is **not communicated** or encouraged. Reporting mechanisms are not accessible to some groups.	Staff report because it is the right thing to do and are **confident** about the response.
Staff are **discouraged** from reporting by overtly complex, unsafe or inaccessible reporting mechanisms.	Some staff feel **unsafe**, unsupported or unsure about reporting; they report feeling uncertain about how reports are handled.	There is **diversity** in reporting mechanisms, making it accessible to all groups.
Gossip and/or retaliation is unchecked, leaving staff feeling **unsafe** to discuss concerns.	Some reports from **community members** are shared but not from marginalised groups; organisation does not explore why.	Reports relate to incidents of possible abuse and to **concerns about behaviour**.
Staff overreact to reports leading to a fear that reporting will result in ill-considered excessive response to the alleged perpetrator.	No clear process to record or address gossip or retaliation.	Reports are actively encouraged and received from marginalised groups and the organisation routinely **reflects** on patterns, trends and how to improve.
	Senior leadership does not openly engage in discussion about **barriers** to reporting. No attempts are seen to find ways to overcome these barriers.	There are clear guidelines and processes to **prevent and address gossip and retaliation**.
	Reports are handled in a more appropriate manner, but there is a lack of clarity in process and role/authority of focal points and line managers.	Senior leaders are open to receiving feedback about all sorts of issues, never penalise those who ask difficult questions, but instead demonstrate accountability.
		Focal points and line managers are equipped to **respond to reports**.

○ bond

Bond is the UK network for organisations working in international development.

We unite and support a diverse network of over 400 civil society organisations to help eradicate global poverty, inequality and injustice.

Bond
Society Building,
8 All Saints Street,
London N1 9RL

+44 (0)20 7837 8344
bond.org.uk

Registered Charity No. 1068839
Company Registration No. 3395681 (England and Wales)

Index

abuse: awareness of abuse and exploitation by aid workers 80; definitions of 78–9; of power against local populations 136; risk of reporting 81; stigma associated with 80; *see also* sexual exploitation and abuse (SEA)
Academy to Innovate HR (AIHR) 92, 102
Ad Hoc Donor Technical Group on Safeguarding 168
#AidToo scandal (2018) 5, 136, 161, 164
Aid Worker Registration Scheme 11
aid workers 36; abuse and exploitation in West Africa 73; allegation of harassment 51; anxiety and depression 43; assessments and interventions related to mental health problem in 45–51; awareness of abuse and exploitation by 80; background 37; being the victims of harassment and abuse 16; engaged in capacity building in fragile countries 39; exploitative relationships with refugees 111; job stress 43; levels of mental health conditions found in 44; mental health problems 36; personal security systems 48; post-trauma support for 48; psychological screening and surveillance for high-risk roles 48; reports of sexual misconduct against 16; sexual exploitation and abuse committed against vulnerable populations 113; symptoms of Moral Injury 45
anti-racism and decolonisation 22, 34
anxiety and depression: among aid workers 43; symptoms of 47
Arabic language 76
assessments and interventions, into mental health problems in aid workers 45–51;

assessment 47–51; at government level 45–6; at individual level 49–51; at organisational level 46; at policy and system level 47
Australian Royal Commission 7
authority 39; organisational culture 100
Avenger 42

balance of power 50, 154
Beijing Platform for Action (BPFA) 138
biological disasters 38
body mapping and interactive games 171
Bosnian War (1992–1995) 127
breach of trust 113
Brunel University 61
bullying 76, 194–5
bureaucratic assessments 62

capacity building: aid workers engaged in 39; in fragile countries 39
capacity, notion of 39
caring organisational culture 101
Chair of the Trustees 7
Charity Commission for England and Wales 23, 26–7, 29, 162–3, 195; inquiry into allegations of harassment by senior staff at Save the Children UK 28, 164; inquiry into Oxfam 30; regulatory framework of 29
chemical, biological, radiological and nuclear (CRBN) contamination, risk of 38
child-headed households 115
Childlight Global Child Safety Institute 145, 146
child protection systems, importance of 15
child safe culture 6
child safeguarding systems 60, 174

209

child safe organisation, elements of 6
child sexual abuse material (CSAM) 146
child sexual exploitation and abuse: by aid workers and peacekeepers 12; boys reporting sexual abuse 12; community-level mechanism for reporting 13; experience of refugee children in Liberia, Guinea and Sierra Leone 15; in Kenya 187; levels of 13; prevalence of 12; tackling the root causes and drivers of 15; under-reporting of 12
child sexual exploitation and abuse (CSEA) 147
CHS Alliance 83, 105, 139–40, 153–6, 168
civil unrest 36
closed spaces 107, 113
code of conduct 7, 26, 28, 93, 102, 194
Cole, Teju 5
collaborative leadership 185
Commissioners of Refugees (COR) 109; sexual coercion by staff of 109
communal shame problem 80
community-based knowledge, on keeping people safe 183
community destruction and social control, use of rape as mechanism for 127
compensation, for the injuries and trauma 138
complaints/reporting mechanisms, creating effective and accessible 12–13
compliance, against a generic checklist of policies and procedures 59–60
Conaghan, Clare 24
confidential information, sharing of 9
confidentiality 8, 29, 62, 129, 131, 155, 168, 171, 175
conflict-related sexual violence (CRSV): challenges of accountability and response 129–31; consequences of 127; genital injuries 130; growing humanitarian impact of 130; importance of outreach and trust-building 131; innovation in documentation and access to justice 131; justice for survivors of 129; meaning of 125; medical consequences of 130; need for holistic responses against 129–30; obstetric fistulas 130; sexually transmitted infections 130; structural and legal barriers to justice 129; as tactic of terrorism 126; UN resolutions on 126; unwanted pregnancies 130; wartime rape 125; as weapon of war 126–8
Core Humanitarian Standard (CHS) 139, 168, 174
corruption, in the legal system 116
COVID-19 pandemic 22, 34, 147–9
crimes against humanity 127–9
criminal justice 187
cultural appropriation 5
cultural change, imposition of 38
culture: importance of 27; understanding of 25; of zero tolerance 150
customer relationship management (CRM) system 93

decision-making 24, 31, 34, 107, 109, 113, 185; fear of information being leaked and misrepresented 30; in Global North 75; HR Decision-Making Approach 92; survivor-centred 82; women's voices in 118
decolonisation of aid 74, 106
Dennis vs. Norwegian Refugee Council 138
Devex.com (global development journalism) 6
diplomatic immunity 147–8, 150
disclosure of abuse, consequences of 155
disease epidemics and pandemics 38
distribution of wealth and power, inequalities in 57
domestic violence 45
do no harm, principle of 80
donor advised funds 58
Drama Triangle 41–3
due diligence 11, 26, 59, 65
duty-of-care policies 136

East India Company 38
economic exploitation, use of rape as instrument of 128
economic self-reliance 118
Elizabeth I, Queen 38
empire-building 38
employment law 186
English language, use in international development 76
Ethics and Compliance initiative (ECI) 161
ethnic cleansing 36; use of rape as a tool of 127

Evans, Helen 162
Evans, Lord 31
eye movement desensitisation and reprocessing (EMDR) therapy 48

female-headed households 115
female refugees: economic opportunities for 112; engaging in transactional sex 114; gender roles and vulnerabilities of girls 112; instances of SEA involving NGO aid workers 111; sense of coercion and fear 112; vulnerability to SEA 112, 114–15; working as a community incentive volunteer for NGOs 112
forced displacement 127
forced marriages 45
forced pregnancy 117
funder-driven priorities 57
funder-grantee relationship, power inequalities in 59
Funder Safeguarding Collaborative (FSC) 58, 62, 64–5, 67; on key challenges faced by philanthropic funders 67
funders, definition of 58
funding for safeguarding 83

Gaventa's powercube 106–7, 117; for analysis of SEA in refugee camps 107–8; forms of power 106
GAVI 169
gender-based inequalities 106
gendered power imbalances 105, 117; causes of 139
gender equality, in program design 118
Geneva Conventions 137
Global Child Safety Research Institute 146
Global Fund 169
Global Majority countries 82
Global North 4, 77, 82, 84, 181, 183; decision-making power 75
global responses to exploitation, steps to improve 149–50
Global South 181
global standards of conduct 95–8
global systems and services, development of 13–14
government funders 58, 103
grantee organisations, provision for safeguarding in 68
grantee partners 58–9

grant-making organisations, global network of 58
Gross National Income (GNI) 180

Harris, Simon 187
Health and Safety Legislation 48
hidden power 106, 107, 111–14, 117
hierarchical organisations 27
high-risk organisations 43
Human Dignity Foundation 147
human-induced disasters 38
Humanitarian Accountability Partnership (HAP) 168
humanitarian crises 146; addressing the root causes of exploitation in 148–9; challenges of detection and response to 147; issue of exploitation in 146–7
humanitarian disasters, groups of 37–8
humanitarian organisations 47, 126; accountability and organisational duty of care 138–9; internal reforms 139–40; legal and jurisdictional efforts 140; policy responses and reforms 139–40; workplace culture and power dynamics 136–7
humanitarian security policies 138
human rights 15
Hunt-Matthes, Caroline 163

IDC Inquiry 81
Improving Child Safeguarding and Preventing Sexual Exploitation and Abuse in the Humanitarian Sector (2018) 13
incident management 93
Independent Review of Workplace Culture at Save the Children UK 7
indigenous heritage, loss of 38
inter-agency relationships 84
Inter-Agency Standing Committee (IASC) 139
International Aid and Development (IAD) 180; history of 37–8
international aid charities, challenges for domestic regulators 10
international aid organisations 38; Drama Triangle 41–3; prone to absorbing the trauma 41; role of 39; surveillance data 43
International Child Protection Certificate (ICPC) 149

International Committee of the Red Cross (ICRC) 140
International Criminal Court (ICC) 129
international criminal law 127
International Criminal Tribunal for the former Yugoslavia (ICTY) 127
international development 61
international development sector, decolonisation of 74
international donors 73, 80; policies and practices of 61
International Federation of Red Cross and Red Crescent Societies 139
international humanitarian law (IHL) 137
International Institute of Social Studies (the Netherlands) 14
international justice 126
international non-governmental organisations (INGOs) 25, 161
International Ombuds Association 168
International Ombuds for Humanitarian and Development Aid (IOHDA) 169
International Programme Leadership 193
INTERPOL, Project Soteria 11, 139, 146–7, 187
Into the Light report (Childlight, 2024) 147
invisible power 106–8
invited spaces 107
Islamic State (ISIS) 128

Joint Evaluation of Emergency Assistance to Rwanda (JEEAR, 1996) 168

Keeping Children Safe 78–9
Key Elements of Child Safe Organisations 7
key themes, in promoting safeguarding systems: donor influence and power dynamics 188–90; intersection of safeguarding, leadership, and culture 184–5; operational and ethical complexities 185–8; reflections and next steps on 190–2; reframing the starting point 182–4
Kids Company 29

labour laws 96, 186
law enforcement systems 186
leaders 24
leadership and culture 27; cross-sector 31; safeguarding of 32; values-based 29–30, 33; working group on 24–5, 32
learning organisational culture 100
legitimacy, notion of 39
LGBTQ+ groups 38
livelihood programs 118
Lucy Faithful Programme 51

"machismo" culture 137
mandatory reporting systems: consequences of disclosure of abuse 155; donor-driven accountability in 154; donor-driven policies and institutional priorities 154; donor-mandated reporting systems 155–6; implementation of 153; power asymmetries 155–6; risks and limitations of 155; in safeguarding 153–4; survivor-centred approach to 156; survivor-centric care 154
marginalised groups 38, 107, 180
May, Theresa 195
Médecins Sans Frontières (MSF) 105, 140
#MeToo movement 5, 18, 91, 93, 103
Midgley, James 74
misconduct by aid workers, reporting of 12
Misconduct Disclosure Scheme (MDS) 11
misuse of funds, controls for prevention of 59
Mordaunt, Penny 22, 195
mutual accountability, need for 66

natural disasters 38
Netherlands Ministry of Foreign Affairs 14
non-governmental organisations (NGOs) 4, 33, 61, 63, 155, 180, 183; accountability goals 111; accountability of 73; allegations of misconduct 73; calls for donors 118; case management guidelines 78; collaboration with law enforcement 150; ethical conduct and accountability 105; in Ethiopia 77; female refugee working as a community incentive volunteer for 112; impact of international standards to navigate complex risks 80–2; operational roles in refugee camps 111; organisational failings of 21;

public scrutiny of 102; safeguarding in organisational culture 118
non-profit organisations 58

ombudsperson (Ombuds) system for children: background of 168–70; Children's Representatives 172; National Ombuds 172; Ombuds Office for SOS Children's Villages 171–2; ombuds principles of independence 175; piloting and scaling up of 172; progress, impact, and challenges 173; Safeguarding Action Plan (2021) 169; Staff Representatives 172
online psychological surveillance programme 43
order organisational culture 100
organisational behaviour 6, 155
organisational culture 6–9, 98–101, 171, 184–5; appropriateness of 6; community reporting mechanisms 8; cultural commitments 7; healthy safeguarding of 30–3; identifiable range of 99–101; importance of 6; institution's governance structures 7; internalisation of safeguarding within 64; key elements of 98; key preparations 101–2; leadership modelling desired culture 7; processes to understand the experience of those involved 9; and reinventing the system 9–15; role of leadership in 6; safeguarding policies and procedures 8; sharing of confidential information 9; transparency of systems and processes 8–9; values and commitments 6
organisational leadership 183–4, 191
organisational ownership, safeguarding of 63–4; within grantee organisations 59
organisational values 32
organisations in crisis 38–41
Oversea Aid Assistance (ODA) 102–3, 180–1
Oxfam GB 12, 22–3, 26–7, 139; allegations against senior leadership of 193; behavioural code of conduct 194; Charity Commission inquiry into 30; Haiti programme 195; Haiti scandal (2018) 105; media coverage associated with 4; revelations of misconduct by 4; saviour mentality 4–6; sexual misconduct 194; significance of 10
Oxfam International Commission 13, 15

peacekeeping missions 105
peer-to-peer learning 64
Persecutor 42
philanthropic eco-system 58
philanthropic funders 57; role of 58; safeguarding of 58, 67
political repression and terrorism, use of rape as 127–8
post-traumatic stress disorder (PTSD) 41, 43, 46, 130
power imbalances 57, 63; accountability and recognition of 67; between donors and recipient organisations 188; sexual exploitation and abuse (SEA) and 105–6
power inequalities, in the funder-grantee relationship 59
prevention of sexual exploitation and abuse (PSEA/PSEAH) 60
professional imperialism 74
Project Soteria (INTERPOL) 11, 139–40, 146, 187; role of 147–8
Protection from Sexual Exploitation, Abuse and Harassment (PSEAH) Index 139
Protection from Sexual Exploitation and Abuse (PSEA) 139
Proteknôn Foundation 171
Proudlove, Sally 24
psychological screening and surveillance, for high-risk roles of aid workers 48
purpose culture 99–100

racial inequalities 106
racial justice 57
Ramalingam, B. 39
rape, as a weapon of war 125–6; as deliberate and organised strategy 126–8; forced impregnation 127; as form of torture 127; as instrument of economic exploitation 128; as mechanism for community destruction and social control 127; for sexual enslavement as crime against humanity 127; as tactic for political repression and terrorism 127–8; as a tool of ethnic cleansing 127; of Yazidi women 128
rape camps 127

refugee camps: aid workers and power 111–13; culture of impunity surrounding SEA in 116–17; decision-making processes within 110; gendered power dynamics of stakeholders and SEA at 109; in Guinea 110; host states' responsibility and abuse of power 109–10; NGOs operational roles in 111; power(lessness) of refugees in 113–14; prevalence of transactional sex in 114; rhetoric *vs.* practice discrepancies 111–13; Sex-for-Food scandal in West Africa Refugee Camps (2001) 161; in Sudan 108; Tunaybah Camp 111; Um Rakuba Camp (Sudan) 116; use of Gaventa's powercube to analyse SEA in 107–8

refugee children, sexual violence and exploitation of 15

refugees: abuse of visible and hidden power of NGO staff over 112; Commissioners of Refugees (COR) 109; exploitative relationships with aid workers 111; female refugees 112; power(lessness) of 113–14; protection of 109; UNHCR as first point of contact for 110; violations of rights in Kenya and Uganda 107

Rescuer 42

resources: allocation of 24, 109; availability of 61

responsible behaviours and conduct, importance of 26

result organisational culture 100

re-traumatisation, risk of 81

risk assessments 81, 85, 100

risk management 183, 186

Rome Statute (1998) 137

Royal British Legion 29

safeguarding 77; child safeguarding 60; commitments to raise standards on 57; commitment to 66; components of effective 25–30; concept of 61; concerns within the aid industry 36; as core to delivering a safe and proper service 57; defined 58, 60; due diligence 59; effectiveness of 61, 183; failure to implement 62; funder-driven 60; Funder Safeguarding Collaborative (FSC) 58; generic checklist of policies and procedures for 59; in grantee organisations 68; holistic approach to 34; implementation of 181; of inadequate resources 61–2; inconsistent expectations 60–1; in the international aid and development sector 181; lack of knowledge and understanding 62–3; in low resource settings 82–4; need for 'mutual accountability' in 66; organisational ownership of 59, 63–4; within philanthropy 58; pillars of effective 83; positive practices 63; quality of 61; of realistic resources 65–6; requirements of grantee partners 67; resourcing of 59; as responsibility of service delivery organisations 62; rise of mandatory reporting in 153–4; risk-informed 183; role of funders in raising standards of 57; scandal of 2018 105; standards-based approach to *see* standards-based approach, to safeguarding; survivor-centred 180; 'tick box' approach 59; trauma-informed 188; two-way communication 64–5; underlying challenges 59

safety organisational culture 100

Save the Children International 29, 105

Save the Children UK 12, 22, 29, 139, 195; Charity Commission inquiry into allegations of harassment by senior staff at 28

Savile, Jimmy 9

saviour mentality, notion of 4–6

saviour phenomena 102

sector crisis, responses to 23–4

Sex-for-Food scandal in West Africa Refugee Camps (2001) 161

sexual conversations 112

sexual enslavement 127–8

sexual exploitation, abuse, and harassment (SEAH) 140; allegations against WHO workers during the Ebola outbreak in the DRC 140; complexities of supporting survivors of 154; donor-driven reporting system 155–6; extraterritorial jurisdiction for cases on 140; fight against, within the aid sector 154; gendered nature of 156; within global aid delivery 153; against local populations 140; prevention of 153; UN zero-tolerance policy on

139; *see also* child sexual exploitation and abuse (CSEA)
sexual exploitation and abuse (SEA) 14, 47; approach to preventing 22; cash payments for sex 111; committed by aid workers against vulnerable populations 113; culture of impunity surrounding 116; drivers of vulnerability to 107; engaging communities to promote reporting 82; experience of refugee children in Liberia, Guinea and Sierra Leone 15; intersectionality of vulnerabilities for women and girls 115–16; power dynamics and 105–6; in refugee camps 107–8; Reports of 105; steps to improve global responses to 149–50; use of Gaventa's powercube for analysis of 107–8; verbal sexual abuse 111; victim blaming and insensitive handling of cases 81; victims and survivors of 15–17; vulnerabilities of female refugees to 114–15; vulnerability due to gender and socio-economic status 110; *see also* child sexual exploitation and abuse (CSEA)
sexual misconduct 11; allegations against Oxfam's then director of operations in Haiti 194; reports against aid workers 16
Sexual Offences Act 2003 (UK) 187
sexual violence 91; as act of genocide 126; committed against Bosnian women 127; committed in Syrian detention centres 128; as crime against humanity 126, 129; facilitative conditions of misconduct 136; in humanitarian aid 135; normalisation of 137; role in reinforcing war economies 128; as a strategic tool to achieve military, political, and economic objectives 126–8; to subjugate local communities 128; as a war crime 126; *see also* conflict-related sexual violence (CRSV)
shared learning, opportunity for 84
social good, promotion of 57
social harms, significance of 81
social justice, legal barriers to 137–8
social ostracisation 129–30
social welfare 83
soft law 73
SOS Children's Villages 168–70
sovereign immunity 138
Spanish language 76
speak-up culture 171
Sriskandarajah, Dhananjayan 27
standards-based approach, to safeguarding 74–6
Steering Committee for Humanitarian Response (SCHR) 11
stigma, associated with abuse 80
strategic planning 100
structural inequalities 57, 106–8, 114, 153
Sudanese refugee camps 105
surveillance data 43
survivors, of sexual abuse and exploitation 15–17, 82; access to justice 137; aid workers as victims 16; complexities of supporting 154; cost of accessing services for 83; decision-making centered on 82; harm inflicted on 15; importance of working with 81; justice for 129; long-term support and welfare of 81; risk of legal consequences 155; safeguarding of 23
Syrian detention centres, sexual violence committed in 128

Think, Empathise, Act (TEA) 92–3, 95
Times, The 194
Top Oxfam GB staff paid Haiti survivors for sex (2018) 4
Trades Union Congress (TUC) 91
transactional sex 117; prevalence of 114; within refugee camps 116
trauma drama: players in 42; playing of 41–3; roles within 42
trauma-informed leadership practices 185
trauma-informed practices, importance of 187
trauma symptoms and behaviours, found in traumatised organisations 41
trust-based philanthropy 67
trustees 7; defining and upholding of healthy organisational culture 29; role-modelling of values and conduct from the board of 30
two-way communication 64–5

UK Aid 10
UK Parliament 29; International Development Select Committee of 14
Ukraine conflict 146

UN Human Rights Council: International, Impartial, and Independent Mechanism for Syria (IIIM) of 127
United Kingdom (UK): aid and development sector in 25; charity sector in 29; commitment to align with the United Nations (UN) 180; Department for International Development (DfID) 9, 180, 195; Foreign, Commonwealth and Development Office (FCDO) 139–40, 147, 180; international aid and development community 23; International Aid and Development sectors 162; International Development Committee (IDC) 73; National Crime Agency (NCA) 187; Parliamentary Committee on Standards in Public Life (CSPL) 31; Parliamentary Inquiry 10; prosecution of UK nationals for sexual crimes overseas 140; Sexual Offences Act (2003) 140, 187
United Nations (UN): assessment of the number of people affected by long-term crises 37; internal justice system in court in Geneva 163; Sex-for-Food scandal in West Africa Refugee Camps (2001) 161; United Kingdom's commitment to align with 180; zero-tolerance policy on SEAH 139
United Nations Dispute Tribunal (UNDT) 163
United Nations High Commissioner for Refugees (UNHCR) 105, 107, 163; complaint mechanism to address sexual abuse 110; creation of camp management committees 113; decision-making processes 110; as first point of contact for refugees 110; quasi-state role 110–11; sexual exploitation and rape case involving staff members of 163
United States Agency for International Development (USAID) 180–1
University of Edinburgh 147
UN Peace Keepers: sexual abuse and exploitation of children in Congo 161

values-driven workplaces 34
verbal sexual abuse 117
Victim 42
victims and survivors of sexual abuse, vulnerability of 13
visible power 106–7
vocational training 118
vulnerabilities for women and girls, intersectionality of 115–16

wage stagnation 161
wartime rape 125
whistleblowers: identity of 162; role and experience in the aid sector 160
whistleblowing 136; meaning of 160–1; as sign of organisation failure 161–3
white saviour, concept of 5
White-Saviour Industrial Complex 5
white saviourism 74
white supremacy 57
Women's Refugee Commission 115
World Health Organisation (WHO) 37

Yazidi women: enslavement of 128; trafficking in Iraq 128
#YouToo movement 103

For Product Safety Concerns and Information please contact our EU
representative GPSR@taylorandfrancis.com
Taylor & Francis Verlag GmbH, Kaufingerstraße 24, 80331 München, Germany

www.ingramcontent.com/pod-product-compliance
Lightning Source LLC
Chambersburg PA
CBHW070315240426
43661CB00057B/2646